An Illustrated Hi
THE PORT C
AND ITS RAILWAYS

By Mike G Fell OBE

P&O North Sea Ferries *Pride of Hull* (59925gt) has just arrived at her berth on the River Humber on the daily sailing from Rotterdam. The ship was built by Fincantieri at the Marghera shipyard in Venice (Yard No.6066) and named by Cheri Blair at Hull on 30 November 2001. The *Pride of Hull* is still amongst the largest of European ferries afloat and carry 1,360 passengers, 250 cars and 400 freight vehicles. Hull's Rotterdam Terminal, seen to the right, was opened by the author's wife Darral Fell on 1 May 2001. [George Robinson]

Irwell Press Ltd.

Acknowledgements

George Robinson of Cottingham, my former deputy at Hull and latterly Port Manager at Goole, has been very supportive in the making of this book. He has checked over the text and used his wealth of knowledge of the British and foreign shipbuilding industries to assist in indentifying vessels mentioned in the text, which is much the richer for his involvement. My almost life-long pal, Allan C. Baker of High Halden, a professional railwayman, has also been most supportive and, at my request, has allowed his frequent visits to the National Archives at Kew to wander away from his own agendas towards matters appertaining to the Humber Estuary. David Rodgers, who, like me, lives in Elloughton, East Yorkshire has not only sourced several of the images but has assisted in enhancing them for publication and resolved untold computer problems along the way. Two local professional photographers, Ivor Innes of 11/13 The Square, Hessle and Tony Ward of Topcolor/Fotoworx, Hull have put their entire docklands collections at my disposal. I am most grateful to them all.

I would also like to acknowledge assistance received from the following individuals: Jocelyn Anderson-Wood, Collections Assistant, Hull Maritime Museum; Herbert Ballard, professional photographer, Hull; Andrew Brett formerly of Northern Cargo Services and ABP; Simon Brett, ABP Head of Projects, Humber; Tony Buckton, railway photographer, Hull; Paul Cox, Creative Director, Ivor Innes Photographers, Hessle; Chris J. Fell, my brother; John Fitzgerald, former ABP Port Director, Humber; Tom Goulder, Assistant Curator (Projects), Hull Museums; Simon Green, Hull Culture & Leisure Ltd; the late Charles A. Hill of Swinefleet; Patrick Hill of Hull; Douglas Hillas from Hull's timber industry; Charles Holehouse, Fernwood Group Limited; Matt Jukes, former ABP Port Director, Hull & Goole and now Chief Executive, Hull City Council; Jennifer Kutte (née Hudson) for permission to photograph her original portrait of George Hudson; Gerry Nichols, Stephenson Locomotive Society Librarian; Mick Nicholson, Network Rail signalman at Hull; Mick O'Rourke, Co. Clare, Ireland; Peter Robinson from Goole; David Woolliscroft from Wilmslow and Jack Wray, former ABP Port Engineer, Hull.

I have made extensive use of the British Library Newspaper Archive, the National Archive, the Archive of the Institution of Civil Engineers, Grace's Guide, records at the Hull History Centre and the Hull Maritime Museum. Similarly I have tapped digital formats of the *North Eastern Railway Magazine 1911-1926* published by the North Eastern Railway Association and of the *London & North Eastern Railway Magazine 1927-1947* published by the Great Eastern Railway Society. The unaccredited photographs are from my own collection. Any mistakes are, of course, entirely of my own making. I would welcome any comments by way of corrections or additional information via the publisher.

ABBREVIATIONS

ABP	Associated British Ports	HWOST	High water ordinary spring tides
ABPH	Associated British Ports Holdings plc	HWONT	High Water ordinary neap tides
AHL	Associated Humber Lines	ICE	Institution of Civil Engineers
BRB	British Railways Board	LMS	London Midland & Scottish Railway
BTC	British Transport Commission	LNER	London & North Eastern Railway
BTDB	British Transport Docks Board	LNWR	London & North Western Railway
DIWE	Docks & Inland Waterways Executive	LYR	Lancashire & Yorkshire Railway
EWS	English, Welsh & Scottish Railways	MLWST	Mean low water spring tides
EWL	Transport Division of Ellerman Lines Ltd	MSLR	Manchester, Sheffield & Lincolnshire Railway
GCR	Great Central Railway	NDLB	National Dock Labour Board
grt	Gross register tonnage	NER	North Eastern Railway
gt	Gross tonnage	Ro/Ro	Roll-on/Roll-off
GWR	Great Western Railway	SR	Southern Railway
HBR	Hull & Barnsley Railway	UBC	United Baltic Corporation
HDC	Hull Dock Company	YNMR	York & North Midland Railway
Hull & Humber	Hull & Humber Cargo Handling Co Ltd		

NB. Gross register tonnage (grt) was replaced by gross tonnage (gt) in 1994 under the International Convention on Tonnage Measurement of Ships 1969 and now applies to all ships built after July 1962. Gross tonnage (gt) is now regarded as a more straightforward and transparent method of calculating dues on ships levied by port and harbour authorities throughout the world.

DONATION

The author is donating the royalties derived from the sale of this book to a new charitable trust being established by Hull City Council to create awareness of Hull's rich nautical history and conserve the port's maritime heritage

First published in the United Kingdom in 2018
by Irwell Press Limited, 59A, High Street, Clophill,
Bedfordshire MK45 4BE
Printed by Akcent Media UK

Contents

DEDICATION

This book is dedicated to Kenneth Ernest Bantock (1926-1996) who in 1970 was responsible for starting my career in the ports industry. He was born in Goole and became the Penang Port Commission's Assistant General Manager. He joined the British Transport Docks Board in 1964 as Assistant Commercial Manager, subsequently becoming the Board's Secretary in 1967 and Port Director, Humber in 1972.

This amazing photograph of grain being discharged in King George Dock brings to life the quotation opposite. The bulk carrier *Silksworth* (16553grt) was built by J.L. Thompson & Sons Ltd at North Sands in 1964, Yard No.713 for British owners. With a cargo carrying capacity of some 24,000 tons, she well warrants the attention of three land based suction elevators and all four of the port's floating suction elevators. Of the latter, *Whitedale* (408grt) is in the foreground followed by *Ryehill* (408grt) and *Wansford* (403grt) – not necessarily in that order – and then *Carnaby* (391grt) which is furthest from the camera and easily distinguished by the taller tower. *Carnaby* had a greater pumping capacity than the other three. *Whitedale* and *Ryehill* were both built for the Ministry of Transport by the Goole Shipbuilding & Repairing Co Ltd in 1954 as *MoT Elevator No.5* and *MoT Elevator No.6*, Yard Nos.494 and 495, respectively; they were renamed in 1961. *Wansford* was not named until 1970 so is not carrying her name in this 1967 photograph. She was built by J. Samuel White & Co at East Cowes, Isle of Wight as *MoT Elevator No.3*, Yard No.451, but it is not known exactly when she came to Hull. *Carnaby* was actually built for the British Transport Commission by Richard Dunston at Hessle in 1962, Yard No.782. The floating suction elevators were equipped with diesel electric pumps but they were not self-propelled, so had to be winched into position or manoeuvred by tugs. They fell out of use when work started in 1977 to convert the silo to handle export grain. *Wansford* was broken up in March that year but the other three were laid up in William Wright Dock, remaining there until November 1989 when they were sold for breaking up at New Holland. The deep sea ship *Silksworth* was sold to Chinese owners in 1972 and was broken up in China in 1994 as *Hua Hai*. [Ivor Innes Photographers, Hessle]

4

Preface

The climax of my Hull dockland tour was a visit to the King George Dock, largest of all, and recipient of over six million pounds' worth of improvements and developments in recent years. Close by the huge 60,000-ton capacity grain silo, a big grain ship was being rapidly 'sucked dry' of its cargo by shore-based and floating pneumatic suction elevators, their long fingers thrust deep into her holds. From the shore elevators, grain was being conveyed under the quay into the silo, but the floating elevators were automatically weighing their share of the cargo and discharging it overside into barges. A small coaster had just loaded grain from the silo for a Scottish port, while on the quay, lorries were receiving bulk loads delivered down chutes from the huge bins, and 'bagged' grain was being delivered to rail wagons. Then a walk along the impressive North Quay, a 3700-ft stretch of new concrete, every berth occupied by big cargo boats. Above, lofty cranes danced their dockland ballet, bobbing and weaving and turning this way and that. Huge new transit sheds loomed behind, enclosing piles of neat cargoes, and busy little fork-lift trucks darted in and out through their wide doorways fetching and carrying a nation's lifeblood. **British Transport Docks Magazine, January 1964**.

This work follows on from my previous books about the Ports of King's Lynn and Goole and their railways, published by Irwell Press in 2012 and 2016, so completing a trilogy. I spent more time working in Hull than in either of the other two ports: I was employed by the Hull & Humber Cargo Handling Company as a Stevedoring Operations Manager from 1977 to 1979 and had total responsibility for the port as Port Manager/Director from 1987 to 2003. Like my other works, this is not intended to be a definitive history but an informative and well illustrated portrayal of Hull's docks and riverside installations with the railways that connected them to the national network, drawing on my own experience. I hope it will be a catalyst for others to undertake further more detailed research not only of Hull's railways and its maritime past but also of the people involved to whom I have drawn attention. Hull used to be tagged 'Britain's Third Port', after London and then Liverpool. Although originally intended as a compliment, the description has become something of a millstone around its neck as in modern times it is wrongly perceived as not being as important as it used to be. Not so! The term *Third Port* was not based on the size of the port, cargo throughput or the tonnage or number of vessels accommodated but the actual value of cargo handled. It is not a measurement commonly used today. Moreover, the role of the Port of Hull is often misunderstood as, almost to the exclusion of everything else, it has become synonymous with fish which some readers might be surprised to learn is no longer landed there. The bobbers have gone. Hull's fame and success was built upon its ability to handle increasingly larger and deeper draughted ships that could trade throughout the world. More importantly, its growth in the late 19th and early 20th centuries was largely founded on the export of coal, primarily from the South Yorkshire coalfield; that, like fish, is no longer on the menu! Yet the Port of Hull has survived and continues to thrive. It has an annual throughput of over 10 million tonnes of cargo and handles one million passengers a year on P&O Ferries' nightly sailings to Rotterdam and Zeebrugge. Moreover, in 2017, Hull witnessed the completion of one of the UK's largest port developments in the form of the £310 million *Green Port Hull* project, jointly funded with Siemens. This comprises a new offshore wind turbine manufacturing and export facility based on the port's Alexandra Dock which reopened for business in July 1991 after a decade of disuse. What a revival!

Dressed to the nines and boasting English, Welsh & Scottish Railways livery, Class 56 Co-Co diesel-electric 56087 *ABP Port of Hull* leaves the Hull Steel Terminal following the opening ceremony on 2 October 1997. [Tony Buckton]

This view was taken from the extreme east end of the Victoria Dock and looks west. No. 1 Coal Hoist is to the left and two belt conveyors are located at the end of the jetty jutting out into the dock. No. 2 Belt is to the left and No. 3 Belt to the right; both are in use loading coal which was their primary purpose. Each belt could cope with 55 wagons per hour as opposed to only 20 wagons per hour at the hoist. The wagons were tipped by hydraulic rams and their contents released through end doors. One can be seen in the tipping position near to No. 2 Belt. The four loaded wagons to the left of the picture appear to contain grain which might soon be loaded into Rank's Barge No. 3 waiting alongside. Joseph Rank (1854-1943) was a leading Hull flour miller, corn merchant and seed crusher. His business was registered as a limited company on 12 May 1899. Note the enormous stack of loose timber planks to the right and the mixture of gas and electric lighting. [Courtesy, Nick Deacon]

Introduction

The first enclosed dock to be built in Hull was Queen's Dock which was formally opened on 22 September 1778, although it did not acquire that name until 1854. It was built by the Hull Dock Company which had been incorporated by The Kingston-upon-Hull Dock Act 1774, to become the first statutory dock company in Great Britain. The Hull Dock Company was also responsible for Humber Dock (1809), Prince's Dock (1829), Railway Dock (1846), Victoria Dock (1850), Albert Dock (1869), William Wright Dock (1880) and St. Andrew's Dock (1883). By the time St Andrew's Dock was opened there had been a major happening. On 26 August 1880, the Hull, Barnsley and West Riding Junction Railway and Dock Act received the royal assent. This Act not only sanctioned the construction of Alexandra Dock and broke the monopoly hitherto held by the Hull Dock Company over Hull's maritime trade but introduced a new railway company into Hull which broke the stranglehold over Hull's railways held by the powerful North Eastern Railway Company. By 1893 cut-throat competition between the dock and railway interests resulted in the North Eastern Railway Company acquiring the Hull Dock Company. It was time to call a truce and allow co-operation and compromise to overcome foolhardy competition. The North Eastern Railway entered into an agreement in principle with the Hull & Barnsley Railway to construct a jointly owned dock to the east of Alexandra Dock, but it took until 9 August 1899 for that to be sanctioned by parliament in the form of Hull Joint Dock which was formally opened by King George V on 26 June 1914 and named King George Dock.

On 1 January 1923, by virtue of the Transport Act 1921, all the docks and railways at Hull, together with those on the opposite bank of the River Humber at Grimsby and Immingham, became part of the London & North Eastern Railway Company, bringing unified control to the major ports on the Humber estuary and the railways which served them. That remained the situation until the nationalisation of the railway and port industries took place with effect from 1 January 1948, under the Transport Act 1947, with the British Transport Commission taking overall control through a Railway Executive and a Docks & Inland Waterways Executive, which added the Port of Goole to the trio of enclosed dock systems on the Humber Estuary. Hitherto Goole had been part of the Aire & Calder Navigation. The Commission was not a success; its organisation proved to be too unwieldy and ineffective, such that it was abolished under the Transport Act 1962. In its stead separate boards were established to control the railways and docks with the ownership of Hull's docks and those at Grimsby, Immingham and Goole passing to the British Transport Docks Board (BTDB).

The BTDB became the first UK nationalised industry to be privatised under the Thatcher Government when, by virtue of the Transport Act 1982, the ports under its control were vested in Associated British Ports, a wholly-owned subsidiary of the newly created Associated British Ports Holdings plc (ABPH) which was floated on the London stock exchange in February 1983. In August 2006, ABPH was acquired by a consortium of private investors and its shares de-listed from the stock exchange.

In summary, since 1778, the enclosed docks and most of the other riverside installations at Hull have been owned wholly or partly by the Hull Dock Company, the Hull & Barnsley Railway Company, the North Eastern Railway Company, the London & North Eastern Railway Company, the British Transport Commission, the British Transport Docks Board and Associated British Ports which currently owns the Ports of Hull, Grimsby, Immingham and Goole. The Humber ports have passed from private ownership through nationalisation back into the private sector where they continue to thrive. In total the Humber ports handle more than 65 million tonnes of cargo annually which equates to some 13% of total UK seaborne trade. The Humber Estuary is extremely important to the UK economy and the Port of Hull continues to have a major role to play.

'Jack-up' ship *Sea Challenger* (15934gt) gets underway from one of the new river berths at Alexandra Dock with the first shipment of wind turbine components from the new Siemens factory, 5 January 2017. They are destined for the Dudgeon Offshore Wind Farm, off the Norfolk coast. The blades are stowed athwartships thereby significantly increasing its beam and requiring a special passage plan to the North Sea. The specially designed ship was completed in March 2014 by COSCO Shipyard, Nantong, China. [Sean Spencer, Hull News & Pictures/Siemens Gamesa]

An oil on canvas painting by Hull marine artist John Ward (1798-1849) depicting the Hull waterfront circa 1837. The vessel in the centre of the picture is the Hull Trinity House yacht *Zephyr* which played a prominent part in the opening of Junction Dock (later named Prince's Dock) in 1829. The tower of Holy Trinity Church can be seen above the vessel's bow. To the extreme left is the steam packet *Pelham* which was launched from the Gainsborough shipyard of Smith & Co in February 1828 for the Grimsby & Hull Steam Packet Company. At the bottom right is a raft of timber baulks that have been discharged directly from a ship into the river, collected together and floated into the river to be received by a Hull timber merchant. [Ferens Art Gallery, Hull]

1. Early Dock Development

Old Harbour

The City of Kingston-upon-Hull is located on the north bank of the River Humber some 24 miles from the North Sea at Spurn Point. The lowest major tributary to the large Humber estuary is the River Hull whose confluence with the River Humber is at Hull, so providing a naturally attractive site for a harbour which served Hull for some eight centuries. It is still known as the Old Harbour. Goods loaded and unloaded there to and from sea going ships could be transhipped from and to smaller vessels which used the Rivers Hull, Trent, Ouse, Don and Aire to access inland towns and cities. All the berths fronting the River Hull dried out at low tide leaving the vessels aground until the next high water time. As sea going sailing vessels grew larger and the Old Harbour became more congested, a solution was found in the form of a wet dock where vessels could remain afloat at all states of the tide. There was also another impetus driving the quest for a wet dock. Unlike other English ports, Hull did not possess a legal quay where dutiable goods could be inspected by HM Customs Officers. Legal quays were established at all the significant ports in England during the reign of Queen Elizabeth I, excepting, for some obscure reason, the Port of Hull. At Hull such inspections were carried out on board the berthed vessels which rendered inspection more difficult, especially when clambering from one ship to another. Smuggling was rife.

Town Docks

The first four docks to be described in this chapter, Queen's Dock (1778), Humber Dock (1809), Prince's Dock (1829) and Railway Dock (1846), became known collectively as the Town Docks. They became a focal point in Hull city centre and were there for all to see. It was inevitable that they should become the first docks to close as their small size did not permit access to increasingly larger ships that were accommodated in newer docks built to the west and east of Hull along the River Humber. During my tenure in Hull, I never experienced these docks in operational use and so I have found their history particularly fascinating and can draw parallels with their early construction and maintenance problems and the more modern port installations with which I became very familiar. In the case of the first three of the Town Docks I have drawn heavily upon *An Account of the Harbour and Docks at Kingston-upon-Hull* from the Transactions of the Institution of Civil Engineers published in 1836. The account was presented by John Timperley (1796-1856) who was resident engineer to the Hull Dock Company (HDC) responsible for the construction of Prince's Dock, originally known as Junction Dock (see below). He subsequently became involved in the construction of the Hull & Selby Railway, the first railway to enter Hull which was opened in 1840 and is covered in Chapter Two. The Institution awarded its first Telford Gold Medal to Timperley for the presentation of his account (Note 1). Much more recently, on 10 October 1973, M.W. Baldwin read a paper entitled *The Engineering History of Hull's Earliest Docks* at the Science Museum in London and I have also found the content of that document most useful in understanding the problems associated with early dock construction and maintenance.

Queen's Dock

The first enclosed dock at Hull can be attributed to civil engineer, John Grundy Jr. (1719-1783). He was well known in the locality for drainage works in Holderness and at Adlingfleet, south of the junction of the Rivers Ouse and Trent. Moreover, his work in connection with the Louth, Driffield and Weighton Navigations was well known. He reported unfavourably on building a

Another painting by John Ward showing a Humber keel laden with timber and another raft of timber baulks secured with staples and ropes. [Ferens Art Gallery, Hull]

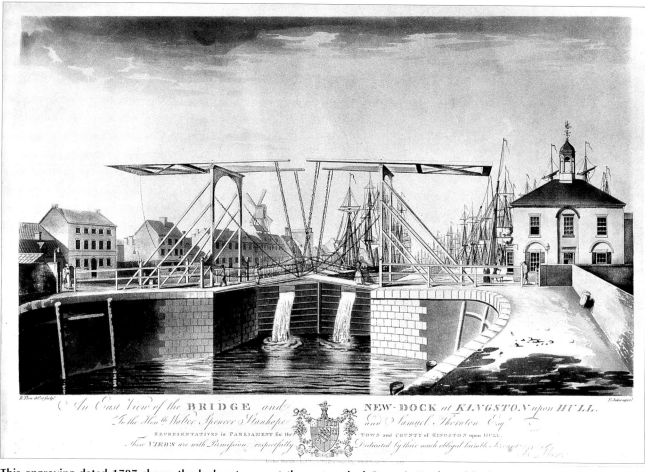

This engraving dated 1787 shows the lock entrance at the east end of Queen's Dock and looks west. It was undertaken by Robert Thew (1758-1802) who was born in Partrington, Holderness and was dedicated by him to Walter Spencer Stanhope (1749-1822) and Samuel Thornton (1754-1838), Members of Parliament for the Town and County of Kingston upon Hull. The original prints were by John Harris (1740-1811) of 3 Sweetings Alley and 8 Broad Street, London. [Hull Maritime Museum]

A contemporary engraving showing Queen's Dock from the opposite direction. [Hull Maritime Museum]

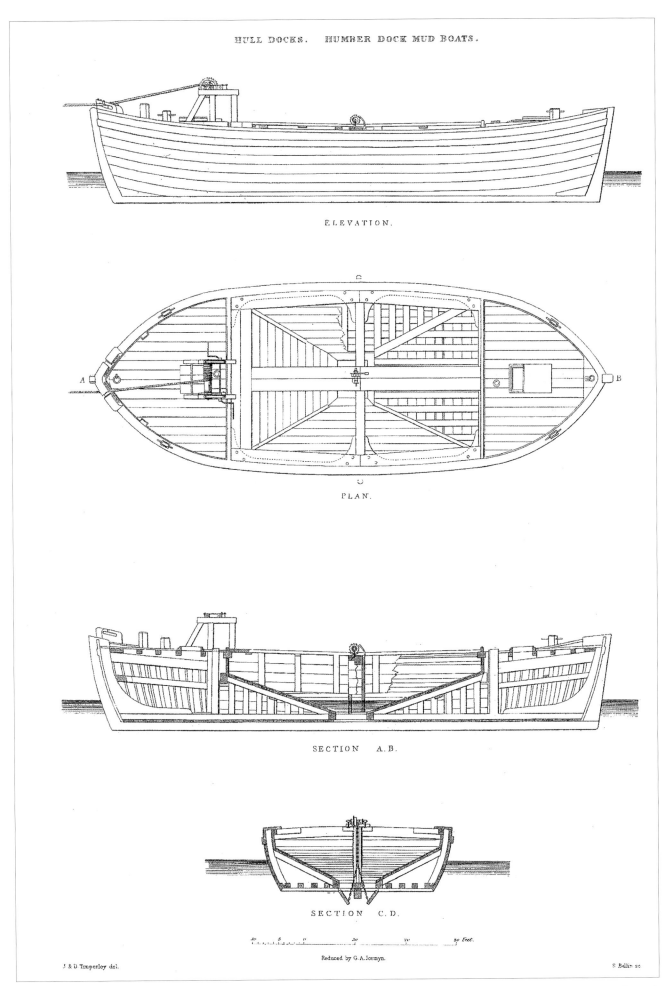

HULL DOCKS.   HUMBER DOCK MUD BOATS.

ELEVATION.

PLAN.

SECTION A.B.

SECTION C.D.

J.& D. Timperley del.

Reduced by G.A. Jormyn.

S. Bellin sc

A drawing of the Humber Dock mud boats as described by John Timperley (1796-1856), Resident Engineer to the Hull Dock Company. The boats were used to dump dredgings from the dock in the River Humber. [Institution of Civil Engineers]

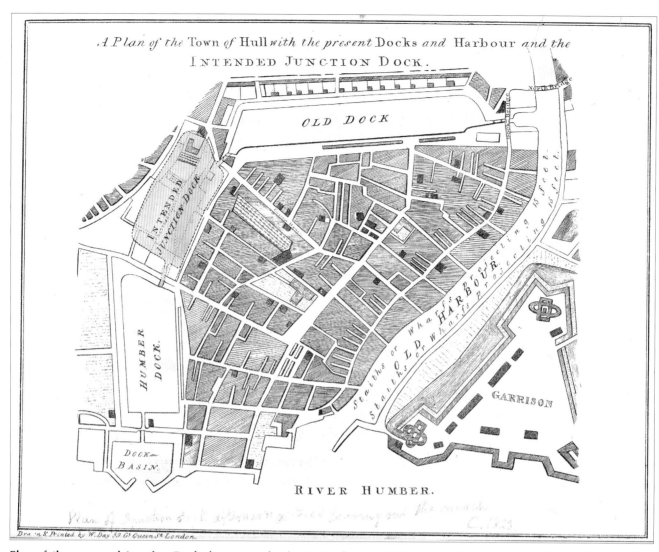

Plan of the proposed Junction Dock (later named Prince's Dock) on which construction commenced in October 1826. It opened on 1 June 1829 and connected Humber Dock with Queen's Dock, here shown as Old Dock. [Hull Maritime Museum]

legal quay in the Old Harbour as, with a width of 40ft, it would have provided too great an obstruction to flood waters in the River Hull. However, he deduced that a flood water relief channel could be provided by enlarging the old moat around the town with the great advantage that the northern part of it would provide a suitable site for a large wet dock with lock gates so enabling the water level to be maintained after each high tide. Ships would remain afloat at all times and greatly relieve pressure on the berthing space in the harbour. The new dock would also possess a legal quay. This idea was adopted to the satisfaction of all interested parties and led to the promotion of a Bill in Parliament incorporating the HDC, with powers to construct Hull's first enclosed dock. The Bill was successful and the Kingston-upon-Hull Dock Act 1774 received the royal assent on 20 May that year (Note 2). The HDC was the first statutory dock company in Great Britain and the new dock was the second largest wet dock in the country, second only to the Howland Great Wet Dock at Rotherhithe on the South Bank of the River Thames in London.

The design and costing for the dock is attributed to Grundy. No plans seem to have survived, nor do the earliest minute books in which his commission might have been recorded but the HDC made a significant payment of £300 to him in November 1774 no doubt in connection with the proposed new dock. Construction began in March 1775 with Luke Holt (c1723-1804) and George Miller as resident engineers and Henry Berry (1719-1812), the Liverpool dock engineer, as consultant. Berry recommended that the dock should be made wider by 17ft and this was adopted. He was an infrequent attendee at Hull which drew criticism; his main contact seems to have been by occasional correspondence with Holt who, in effect, had full responsibility for the dock's construction.

The foundation stone for the lock was laid by Joseph Outram, Mayor of Hull and wine merchant on 19 October 1775. A copper plate was fixed to the stone bearing the following inscription:

'For the improvement of commerce by the enlargement of the port of Kingston-upon-Hull, his most gracious majesty King George the Third, did, with consent of his parliament, appropriate the military works surrounding the town, with a further aid of royal and parliamentary munificence. In gratitude to their gracious sovereign, and to transmit a dutiful remembrance thereof to the latest posterity, the dock company have caused this to be transcribed on the first stone, which was laid by Joseph Outram, Esq. Mayor, October 19, 1775.'

That day was ushered in with the ringing of bells. The company's commissioners, and their four principal officers, met at the dock-office at twelve o'clock, and proceeded from thence with colours flying to the mayor's house, where being elegantly regaled with cake, wine, etc, they proceeded from thence with the mayor, preceded by a large band of music, constables and flags, to the lock pit, where his worship laid the first stone, in the presence, and with the loud acclamations of some thousands of people. The mayor then gave the workmen fifteen guineas to drink, five on his own account, and ten on account of the company, after which there was a discharge of nine cannon, placed at the entrance of the lock, and then the procession proceeded to Mr. Baker's, The Cross Keys, in the market-place, where an elegant dinner was provided. After dinner the healths of the king, queen, and royal family, with many

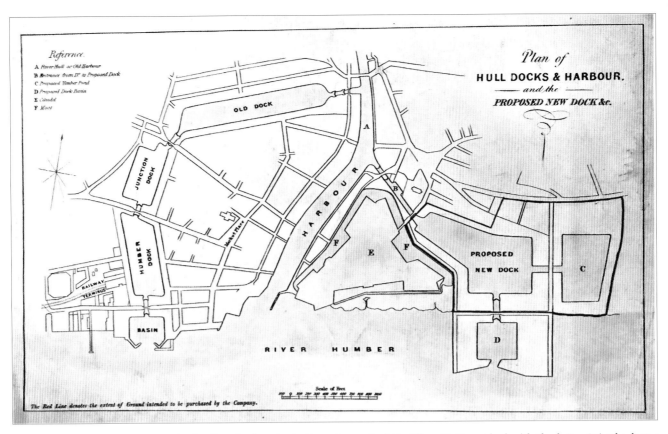

The proposed new Victoria Dock, the first dock to be built to the east of the River Hull, marked with the letter 'A'. The letter 'B' indicates the position of what became known as Drypool Basin, 'C' indicates the first of two timber ponds and 'D' the position of the Victoria Dock Basin. Strangely the plan does not show Railway Dock which was authorised by the same Act of Parliament and was constructed to the west of Humber Dock. Railway Dock opened on 10 December 1846; Victoria Dock was much larger and took nearly five years to build, opening on 3 July 1850. [Hull History Centre]

Hull Dock Company plan of 1859, of Railway Dock and Victoria Dock as completed, including also a proposed westward extension of Victoria Dock which was not built. [Hull Maritime Museum]

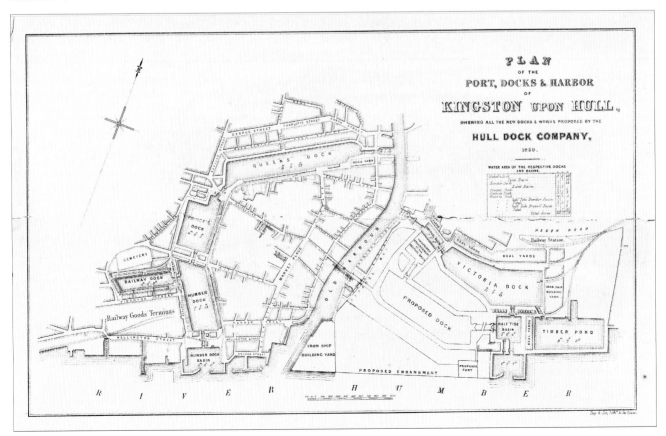

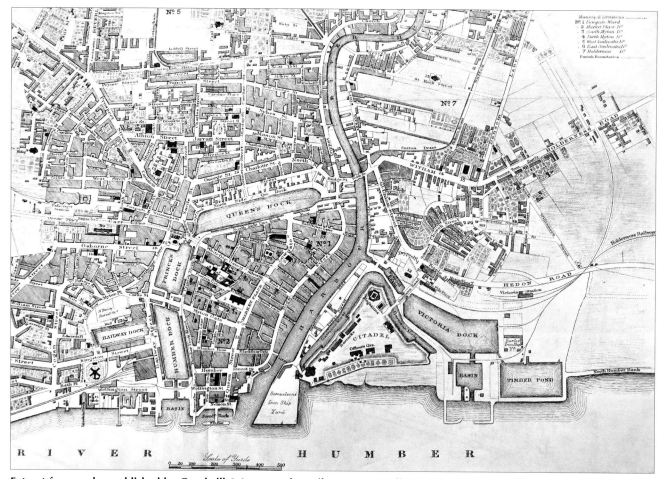

Extract from a plan published by Goodwill & Lawson of 22 Silver Street, Hull in 1859. It illustrates the completed Town Docks system with its connections to the Rivers Humber and Hull and shows how Victoria Dock was similarly connected. The Victoria Dock Branch railway crossing Hedon Road towards the bottom right was opened in 1853. [Hull History Centre]

other loyal and constitutional toasts were drank, and the whole was concluded with the greatest unanimity and good order (Note 3).

The dock was 1,703ft long and 254ft wide and was capable of accommodating no less than 100 square rigged sailing vessels. The walls were carried on three rows of timber piles 10ft long joined by a timber platform. Piles of 7ft 6in in length supported counterforts at 42ft centres but as the timber platform was at the same level as the dock floor, there was very little resistance to the forward movement of the walls which were constructed of brick with a stone coping. John Smeaton (1724-1792) of lighthouse fame was consulted on what type of mortar to use and he recommended pozzolana – volcanic ash which when mixed with lime and water formed hydraulic cement ideal for structures submerged in water. Berry was ignorant about its use and had to seek advice on its composition and application. The foundations for the walls proved to be inadequate and in 1776 before the dock had been completed bulging had occurred on the north side necessitating extra piles being driven in at the toe of the wall on the bulged sections. The maximum deflection was as much as three feet, the tendency of the wall to move being aggravated by its poor design. The lock, which originally had

a wooden drawbridge at its east end, was more solidly built with its walls faced in stone set in pozzolana mortar. The walls were carried on a timber platform similar to that under the dock walls and the floor of the lock was timbered. Although of stouter construction, the lock walls were more severely loaded than the dock walls such that similar faults had to be rectified before the lock was put into service. The approach to the lock from the River Hull was via a basin 212ft long by 80ft wide with brick walls similar to the dock walls but the wall on the north side, due to some defect in the foundation, gave way before it was finished and it was never raised to the intended height until it was rebuilt in 1815.

Although the inaugural Act allowed seven years for construction, the work proceeded well enough for water to be let into the dock in August 1778 and its formal opening with 'great rejoicings' took place on 22 September that year. The first vessel to enter was a Hull whaling ship returning from Greenland named *Manchester*, followed by *Favourite*, 'a ship of 1,000 tons burthen' (Note 4). Troops from the local garrison fired a *feu de joie* and officials from the HDC breakfasted aboard the *Manchester* before continuing the celebrations at the Guildhall. The new dock was an immediate commercial success leading to a dramatic growth in trade but the

dock's maintenance proved very costly. The amount of dredging required had not been anticipated. There was only one small sluice in each lock gate which when opened did not create sufficient power to cleanse the lock and basin, necessitating the use of a small lighter and drag to loosen and remove the mud while scouring. More seriously, large quantities of silt entered the dock at each locking-in operation necessitating the removal of an average of 20,000 tons of mud annually, all of which was removed by means of horse power and dumped in the River Humber using mud boats. Timperley described the horse dredging machine as follows: *The machine was contained in a square and flat bottomed vessel 61 feet 6 inches long, 22 feet 6 inches wide, and drawing 4 feet of water: it at first had only eleven buckets, calculated to work in 14 feet of water, in which state it remained till 1814, when two buckets were added so as to work in 17 feet of water, and in 1827 a further addition of four buckets was made giving seventeen altogether, which enabled it to work in the highest spring tides. The machine was attended by three men, and worked by two horses, which did it at first with ease, but since the addition of the last four buckets, the work has been exceedingly hard.* Poor horses! Timperley went on to explain that the mud engine was employed for six or eight months in each year with the dredged material being discharged

14

into six mud boats. These had bottom opening doors and when loaded were taken down the Old Harbour and discharged in the Humber. The greatest quantity of silt entered the dock on spring tides and particularly in dry seasons when there was not much fresh water coming down the River Hull. There was much less egress on neap tides.

The condition of the original lock chamber deteriorated to such an extent that in 1780 orders were given to maintain a minimum depth of 12ft of water in the lock between each high water cycle. The south wall of the lock was rebuilt in 1785 and the opposite wall the following year and so the lock survived in its original state for less than a decade. On the advice of John Rennie the elder (1761-1821) work started in May 1814 on rebuilding the lock and basin between it and the River Hull. The lock was rebuilt with a brick invert and the basin walls were rebuilt with heavier foundations with brick struts across the basin at 10ft centres to prevent the walls sliding forward. The reconstruction work took about eighteen months to complete during which time the dock was closed to shipping; Humber Dock, opened in 1809, provided alternative accommodation during the stoppage. The new lock and basin were opened on 13 November 1815, the first vessel to enter being *Kingston* under the command of Captain Collinson on the afternoon's tide. A cold collation was served on board the vessel to mark the occasion (Note 5). A new cast iron bascule bridge with two leaves was erected over the rebuilt lock to replace the original wooden bridge. It was cast and erected by Ayden and Etwall of the Shelf Iron Works, near Bradford, weighed about 80 tons and was balanced such that two men could raise or lower each leaf in 30 seconds. The bridge was 81ft long and 15ft wide with a carriageway of 7ft 6in and two footways, each being 3ft 6in in width.

The dock walls stood better than those of the lock and basin but were by no means trouble-free. When Rennie was planning the rebuilding of the lock, he decided not to drain the dock itself for fear the walls might collapse. By 1836, the worst deflection was nearly four feet and several sections had been rebuilt or buttressed with clay deposited in the dock. The area of quays on the north and south sides of the dock amounted to about 29,000 square yards and they were paved with pebbles collected from Spurn Point at the mouth of the Humber. Two sheds were provided on the legal quay and there was a range of warehouses, each with three floors and cellars. The dock had six cranes constructed of timber – four on the south side and two on the north. Timperley said the latter were 'well' cranes, very lofty, fixed about six feet from the side of the quay and calculated to lift four or five tons. The others were of lighter construction with the jibs closer to the dock, one of which was worked by a tread-wheel.

Initially Hull's first dock was simply known as 'The Dock', subsequently becoming coined 'The Old Dock' after the opening of Humber Dock. However, after the royal visit by Queen Victoria and Prince Albert, which took place on 14 October 1854, it became known as Queen's Dock. Her Majesty actually sailed through the dock on board the royal steam yacht *Fairy* which had been built by Ditchburn and Mare at Leamouth on the River Thames in 1844 and commissioned the following year. An Ordnance Survey map based on an 1853 survey and published on 21 November 1856 shows that the north side of Queen's Dock was entirely taken up with timber yards whilst the south side accommodated general warehouses and a bonding warehouse. Much the same situation is depicted on maps published in 1890, 1908 and 1928.

After over 150 years in use, Queen's Dock was closed in 1930. It was

This wonderful view of Prince's Dock looks north towards the entrance to Queen's Dock, the Wilberforce monument and the Dock Office. The steamship *Winifred* (289grt) to the extreme right was built by J.P. Rennoldson & Sons of South Shields in 1894 for E. & H.W. Packard of Ipswich. The steamship just visible to the extreme left of the sailing ship registered at Malmo, Sweden, has the distinctive so-called 'tombstone' funnel of Hull shipowner Bailey & Leetham which merged with the Wilson Line on 15 July 1903, so the photograph was definitely taken between 1894 and 1903. Further study reveals that the bridge over the entrance to Queen's Dock is almost certainly the original lift bridge which was widened in 1899 to accommodate the new electric tramway which narrows the date of the image to between 1894 and 1899. [Courtesy, Tony Ward, Topcolor Fotoworx, Hull]

The widened Monument Bridge looking west towards Carr Lane and Anlaby Road after the introduction of the electric trams on 5 July 1899. A tram bearing the letter A signifies that it is working the Anlaby Road route. The horse drawn van in the centre of the picture belongs to the Great Central Railway. The workmen in the foreground seem to be involved with putting some final adjustments to the railings on the new bridge. It was demolished in 1932 following the closure of Queen's Dock. St. John's Church can be seen behind the OXO sign and there is no sign of Monument Buildings which were constructed by the NER between 1902 and 1908. [Courtesy, Tony Ward, Topcolor Fotoworx, Hull]

purchased by Hull City Council at a cost of £118,000 to become the present day Queen's Gardens. The in-filling of the dock commenced on 14 August 1930 using foundry waste, dredgings and other materials, a task which was not completed until 1934.

Humber Dock

The outstanding commercial success of the first dock led to much pressure to build a second but it was not until 22 June 1802 that the royal assent was granted to the Act of Parliament authorising its construction (Note 6). Half the cost was contributed by the HDC, the remainder being borne equally by the Corporation and Hull Trinity House. The latter organisation received its official title as the *Guild or Fraternity of Masters and Pilots, Seamen of the Trinity House of Kingston-upon-Hull* in 1581 by the charter of Queen Elizabeth I. One of its main concerns was the safety of navigation on the River Humber and in order to achieve this aim it provided a pilotage service and established navigational aids. Nowadays these functions are carried out by Associated British Ports, present day owners of the Humber ports of Grimsby, Immingham, Hull and Goole.

Reverting to the 1802 Act it also defined, with great foresight, when and

where a third dock should be built and stipulated that it should be financed in the same manner as the second. The second dock was the first of Hull's enclosed docks to be accessed from the River Humber. The HDC chose John Rennie the Elder as its engineer and employed William Chapman (1749-1832) to work with him. Chapman was well known in the area having been involved with the Beverley and Barmston drainage works. Chapman oversaw the planning while Rennie concentrated on the structural design. John Harrap (1769-1812) was appointed resident engineer; he was assisted by George Miller. Harrap had been employed by the HDC since February 1779 and it was he who had the responsibility of rebuilding the walls of the entrance lock to the old dock in 1784-1785.

Humber Dock, which had a water area of seven and a half acres with a length of 914ft and a width of 342ft, could accommodate 70 square-rigged sailing vessels. It was approached from the Humber via a basin and a lock. Work began early in 1803 and one of the first tasks was to construct a coffer dam at a site to the south of the lock to keep out the tidal waters. A six-horse power stationary steam engine was erected to the east side of the lock which worked two 11in pumps to assist in keeping the

works free of water and two 7cwt rams for driving the piles for the coffer dam. A strongly flowing fresh water spring found during the excavation of the lockpit proved difficult and costly to stop-up. The lock had an inverted brick arch on a timber piled foundation. It was 42ft wide at the top with a length of 158ft between the gates which were made of English oak; each gate had two cast iron sluices. The lock walls were faced with masonry and each wall was backed with six counterforts. A cast iron swivel bridge constructed by Ayden and Etwell was erected over the centre of the lock. It was 81ft 9in in length and 12ft 3in wide composed of two parts which met in the middle to form a segment of a circle. As with the bascule bridge in the old dock, one man could shut or open either part of the swivel bridge with ease in half a minute.

The excavation of the dock, which had an average depth of 24ft, was mainly in alluvial soil but the upper part contained a 5ft layer of good clay which was used for brick making. The quays were again paved with pebbles from Spurn and along the legal quay on the east side there was a range of sheds constructed of timber and roofed with slates. There were doors on the east side of the sheds but the west sides were open to the quays, excepting the bale

Reputed to be taken from an airship, this photograph is said to date from 1920. There was a Royal Naval Air Service station at Howden from 1916 to 1921. Prince's Dock is to the left with Queen's Dock to the right separated by the widened Monument Bridge. Monument Buildings erected by the NER as offices between 1902 and 1908 can be seen just to the left of the Wilberforce monument. The nearby St. John's Church, later demolished to make way for the Feren's Art Gallery which opened in 1926, is still intact. The top left of the picture features the Royal Station Hotel and Paragon Station. [Courtesy, Tony Ward, Topcolor Fotoworx, Hull]

This aerial view, also from the 1920s, shows Humber Dock to the right, Railway Dock to the left, Prince's Dock in the centre and the still operational Queen's Dock to the top right above the Guildhall. St. John's Church has been demolished. The massive Kingston Street goods station at the bottom of the picture occupies part of the site used as the original passenger terminus for the Hull & Selby Railway and the nearby array of warehouses occupies the south side of Railway Dock. The one at the end near the junction with Humber Dock still survives as Warehouse 13. The ship berthed at the north east corner of Railway Dock is almost certainly the steamer *Harrogate* (1029grt) built in 1925 by Ramage & Ferguson Ltd of Leith, Yard No.260, for Wilsons & North Eastern Railway Co Ltd – see Appendix One for her subsequent history. [Hull Maritime Museum]

Aerial view of Queen's Dock still in use with its extensive timber yards along the north side. The Guildhall is again prominent and the Dock Office can be seen at the head of the dock with the Wilberforce Monument nearby. Queen's Dock was closed in 1930 and is now the site of Queen's Gardens. [Courtesy, Tony Ward, Topcolor Fotoworx, Hull]

shed at the south end which was all enclosed. Some of the mooring posts comprised twelve pounder cannons! The breech or lower end of the cannons were let into stone blocks below quay level and secured with wrought iron straps and bolts. They were then surrounded with brickwork built up to quay level. Seven cranes of cast iron construction were provided, four on the east side and two on the west. The one at the north-west corner was a 'well' crane capable of lifting ten tons; the remaining six were pillar cranes with lifting capacities of three tons. Additionally there were four cranes located on the basin walls used principally for the steam packets, possibly to lighten them before entering the dock. These varied in lifting capacity from two to four tons.

The foundation stone of the south east hollow quoin of the lock was laid by the chairman of the HDC, Colonel Henry Maister (1730-1812) on 13 April 1807. He was Colonel of the East Yorkshire Militia and before laying the stone deposited some current gold, silver and copper coins of the realm, together with medals featuring amongst others William Pitt, Charles James Fox and Lord Nelson. A brass plate was fixed to the stone which was engraved with the following words.

THIS STONE
Was laid in the Foundation of the South East
corner of the Lock of the HUMBER DOCK,
on the 13th day of APRIL, anno domini 1807
By HENRY MAISTER, Esquire, Chairman of the Dock Company
At Kingston-upon-Hull.

THE HUMBER DOCK
Was made in pursuance of an Act of Parliament
passed in the 42nd year of the reign of
His Majesty King George the Third for the
Benefit of the Commerce and Shipping
of the
PORT of KINGSTON-UPON-HULL
And for the Admission of his Majesty's
SHIPS of WAR of FIFTY GUNS

Water was let into the dock for the first time on 3 December 1808 and it was formally opened for business on 30 June 1809. The *Hull Packet* reported on the occasion as follows (Note 7). *The morning was ushered in with a merry peal from the bells of the churches, flags were hoisted upon the steeples; and the different ships in the Roads, the Old Dock, and the Harbour, were gaily decorated with colours. At half past six o'clock, the Members of the Corporation, the Trinity-House, and Dock Company, assembled at the Dock-Office, and at seven, set out in procession.* The newspaper went on to say that the procession paraded from the dock office via the east side of the new dock to the entrance basin where the ship *Effort* was waiting armed with cannon and decorated overall. The vessel was owned by Harry Brown, one of the Elder Brethren of the Hull Trinity House, and her yards were manned by the scholars of the Trinity House Marine School in their naval uniforms. *At eight o'clock, the Effort entered the dock, amidst the acclamations of an immense concourse of spectators, and immediately fired a royal salute, which was returned by another from twenty-one pieces of cannon, placed in front of the Entrance Basin; the music playing "Rule Britannia", and closing with "God save the King".* Humber Dock was open for business. Breakfast was served at the Neptune Inn and in the evening the *Effort* was moored in the middle of the dock and illuminated with 180 lamps, representing the number of available shares in the HDC. The total cost of the works at £233,000 greatly exceeded the original estimate of £84,000, such that another Act of Parliament had to be

The AHL-managed steamship *Bury* (1634grt) in Humber Dock. She was built by Earle's of Hull, Yard No.596, in 1911 for the Great Central Railway, subsequently passing to the BTC. The vessel was broken up at Nieuw-Lekkerland, Holland in July 1958. The coaling hoist behind the ship's mast had a lifting capacity of 20 tons and was capable of lifting 28 railway wagons per hour. [Charles A. Hill]

The Panama-registered steamship *Sur* (707grt) berthed head west in Railway Dock on 26 June 1958. She was built as *Laura* by Kjobenhavns Dockyard, Copenhagen, Yard No.76, in 1908 and carried no less than five other names before becoming *Sur* in 1956 when ownership passed to Dabaco & Co, Panama. She was broken up in Santander, Spain in July 1965. [Charles A. Hill]

On 17 September 1952 the steamship *Arild* (518grt) is berthed at the extreme west end of Railway Dock on the south side loading barley which is arriving in bags on lorries owned by the nationalised British Road Services. Some of the uncovered bags still bear the legend *London & North Eastern Railway*. They were probably ripped on deck and their contents tipped into the ship's holds to form a bulk cargo. The ship was built at Wallsend by Swan, Hunter & Wigham Richardson Ltd for H. Harrison (Shipping) London in November 1920, Yard No.1149. She was renamed three times and had three different owners before being sold to Risted & Nerdrum, London and renamed *Arild* in 1952. In 1955 she was sold to Greek interests and again renamed *Aspasia*. Four years later she was converted to a motor vessel and changed Greek owners in 1961 who gave her the final name *Marilena*. She was broken up in Greece in 1971. [Ivor Innes Photographers, Hessle]

obtained in 1805 to raise the additional capital (Note 8). However, these two costs are not strictly comparable as the dock was built during a period of rapid inflation.

Amazingly the new dock was not dredged for three and a half years after opening, such that during this time mud had accumulated to a height of 12ft at the south end of the dock and 3ft at the north. The situation was so bad that on neap tides deeply laden vessels could neither enter nor leave. A bucket ladder dredger was introduced to deal with the problem. The flat bottomed vessel was 80ft long with a beam of 20ft and a draught of 5ft. A 6hp steam engine drove an endless chain on the ladder which accommodated 29 wrought iron buckets; it also provided power to a roller around which revolved a cable used to position the dredger. The other end of the cable was attached to the various mooring posts around the dock as required. The ladder with its buckets was raised or lowered through an opening in the middle of the vessel. Four men, including the engine-keeper, were required to work the dredger which under normal circumstances could lift

about 45 tons of mud per hour, filling twelve mud boats with a total of some 500 tons in a working day of between twelve to 15 hours.

The following is Timperley's description of the mud boats. *The mud boats are flat bottomed and sharp at each end, and draw, when fully laden, about 4 feet water. Six of them, which were formerly used exclusively for the Old dock, are 48 feet long at top, 17 feet 6 inches wide in midships, by 5 feet 6 inches deep, and carry 40 tons on an average; the six Humber dock boats are rather larger, carrying 48 tons each. They are ceiled inside in a sloping direction like a hopper, with two trap doors in the bottom, through which the mud is discharged, the water rising in the boat to the same level as on the outside, but the cavity between the ceiling and the bottom preserving the buoyancy. When laden, these boats are linked together in pairs, six usually forming a set, which require ten or twelve men to work them; they generally go out of dock when the gates are all opened, a little before high water, and are warped 100 or 150 fathoms from the pier-head, where the mud is discharged; the empty boats then return to the dock, the time occupied being usually from two to three hours, according*

to the rapidity of the tide, and as the passage is more or less clear of shipping. After the introduction of the dredger the quantity of mud removed from Humber Dock was about 36,000 tons a year.

There was also a problem with mud accumulating in the tidal basin between the lock and the river. Cast iron water pipes leading from the dock and lock were laid within the basin walls with the intention of using the head of dock water to flush the basin. However, these proved to be too flimsy and many fractured before the dock was opened and had to be replaced. It was not until a more substantial flushing arrangement had been introduced in 1831 that the problem of cleansing the basin was alleviated.

Prince's Dock
Prince's Dock, the third to be built at Hull, was originally known as Junction Dock as it literally joined Humber Dock with Queen's Dock to create a through waterway link between the River Hull and the Humber. It was named Prince's Dock on 14 October 1854 at the same time as the old dock was named Queen's Dock in recognition of the visit by

Queen Victoria and Albert, Prince Consort. As previously mentioned, the Act authorising the construction of Humber Dock also defined when and where a third dock should be built and stipulated that it should be financed in the same manner as that used to finance Humber Dock, i.e. half the cost to be funded equally by the Corporation and Hull Trinity House and the remainder by the HDC. The trigger for the construction of the third dock was when the shipping frequenting the port reached a certain tonnage. However the formula, which was spelt out in section 58 of the 1802 Act, was complicated. It was based on the average tonnage of vessels visiting the port and paying dues to the HDC during the years 1791-1793 which, of course, related to the original dock. Once that average figure applied to vessels visiting the new Humber Dock, the HDC was required to make a third dock joining the two 'to contain Sixty Sail of Ships or square rigged vessels' based on the average tonnage (i.e. size) of vessels then visiting the port.

The recovery of trade after the Napoleonic Wars led to continuing demands for the construction of the third dock as the port became increasingly congested. A Parliamentary Committee in 1825 revealed that: *Many instances have lately occurred of ships having performed their voyages from St. Petersburg and other ports in the Baltic to the port of Hull, in less time than ships of late have been able to pass from the River Humber to the Old Dock* (Note 9). A Bill was put before Parliament in that same year but petitioners, no doubt with vested

interests, argued that the HDC's controversial right to levy dock dues on shipping in the Old Harbour should be withdrawn. Rather than make this sacrifice, the HDC withdrew its Bill and decided to finance the third dock solely at its own expense as evidenced by this short report which appeared in the *Cambridge Chronicle and Journal* for 7 October 1825: *New Dock at Hull – At a meeting of the members of the Dock Company, last week, it was unanimously resolved to make a Junction Dock at the expense of the Company, to contain, we understand, sixty sail of ships.* A substantial Government loan was made available to the company to finance the capital expenditure for construction which amounted to £180,000.

Work on the third dock commenced in October 1826 and the engineer responsible for its construction was James Walker (1781-1862) assisted by resident engineer Thomas Thornton as superintendent of the works. An opportune visit to Hull by Telford early in 1826 enabled the HDC to receive his assurance of the suitability of Walker's plans. In July 1827 Thornton was succeeded by John Timperley whose account of the construction and maintenance of Hull's first three docks has provided much of the information for the early part of this chapter. The new dock had a water area of six acres and, as stipulated in the 1802 Act, was capable of accommodating 60 square rigged vessels with room for passing to and from the other two docks with which it inter-connected. The initial preparatory works involved the construction of two coffer dams constructed of timber. The

south dam, next to Humber Dock, was the largest having a 220ft span; the north dam located at the west end of Old Dock had a span of 115ft. The construction of the dock was generally straightforward. Walker's respect for the variable nature of the ground was well-developed. He kept pile driving records to enable softer areas to be identified with the foundation design being adjusted accordingly. There were two locks with inverted arches with the quoins well tied back to a stone slab laid on edge in the ground behind. The slab was further tied back to piles driven 50ft from the locks. The lock located at the north end of Humber Dock was known at Myton Gate Lock and that at the west end of the Old Dock was known as Whitefriar Gate Lock. The first stone of the Myton Gate Lock was laid on 10 December 1827 by the chairman of the HDC who used an inscribed silver trowel to complete the task. The stone had a cavity in which was placed an example of every piece of currency then in circulation. The cavity was then covered and secured by a brass plate bearing the following inscription: *This stone was laid in the foundation of the South Lock Pit of the Junction Dock, on the Tenth Day of December, An. Dom. 1827 by John Cowham Parker, Esquire, Chairman of the Dock Company, at Kingston-upon-Hull. The Junction Dock was made at the Sole Expense of the Dock Company* (Note 10). The plate was covered with a piece of flannel saturated with tallow. Each of the two new locks was 120ft long between the gates with a width at the top of 36ft 6in and a depth of 25ft. There was a lift bridge over both locks constructed by

The livestock carrier *Inger Clausen* (299grt) berthed head south in Humber Dock on 17 November 1962. She was built for C. Clausen D/S A/S, Graasten, Denmark at the Titovo Shipyard, Kraljevica, Croatia, Yard No.356, in 1958. When photographed here, she was no doubt working to the abattoir at the head of Railway Dock – note the fodder stowed on deck ahead of the bridge. By 1979 she was under the Chilean flag and named *Corcovada*; she sank on 9 March 1983 on passage from San Antonio for Valdivia. [Charles A. Hill]

The mv *Indunaval Primero* (653grt) was built by the Indunaval Shipyard, Bilbao, Spain in 1958 for Transportes Fruteros de Mediterraneo, Bilbao. Seen here on the east side of Humber Dock, her cargo may well have been discharged for sale on the Hull fruit market. In 1968 she was renamed *Garbi* by the same owners but met with a sad end on 23 August 1976 when she exploded and sank while at anchor at 27.05N – 13.30W off the west coast of Africa. [Charles A. Hill]

Hunter and English, millwrights of Bow, London who also made the wooden lock gates. The associated ironwork was cast by the Butterley Company at its ironworks near Alfreton in Derbyshire. The northern bridge became known as Monument Bridge after the 102ft high Wilberforce Monument was completed nearby in Queen Victoria Square on 12 November 1835 (Note 11).

A significant problem manifested itself during the morning of 21 March 1829 when a leak appeared under the northern coffer dam. Remedial action was taken immediately to reduce the pressure on the dam by lowering the water levels but the breach became so extensive that it undermined a 60ft section of the Old Dock wall which collapsed. This was an unfortunate setback occurring so close to completion of the works. However, the Old Dock wall was quickly rebuilt and the new Junction Dock was opened on 1 June 1829 having been completed in just over two and a half years.

The *Hull Packet* in its issue published the following day reported extensively on the event and the following extracts taken from the newspaper convey very well the festive atmosphere of the occasion. *The morning was gloomy, and a slight shower or two had fallen; the inauspicious appearance of the weather, however, did not seem to have the slightest effect in keeping back visitors from the interesting spectacle. Previous to the commencement of the ceremony, the bells of the several churches were heard pealing a merry strain in honour of the day. Flags were displayed from many of the public buildings, from many private establishments in the vicinity of the docks, and from most*

of the vessels at their moorings. The whole of the steamers in port paid the compliments of hoisting flags, &c. with a single exception – the 'Eagle' of Goole. The Trinity House yacht, which was to perform a prominent part in the formalities, was observed in the north east corner of the Humber Dock, near Myton-gate bridge, gaily decorated with the colours of all nations, floating in the breeze from her yards and rigging. The boys of the Trinity House Marine-School, in their uniforms, were already aboard. The Junction Dock, which preparatory to the opening had been cleared of all the floating timber, presented a fair and open expanse of water, and all obstructions had been removed from the surrounding quays. The 'Kingston' recently built for towing vessels by steam from this port to Selby, lay in the Mytongate lock-pit, with her bow projecting into the Junction Dock, ready to bring in the yacht.

A platform covered by an awning having been provided for the accommodation of company, on the Humber Dock-side of the lock at Mytongate end, a number of ladies and gentlemen assembled in it, some time before nine o'clock. Everything being ready for the opening of the dock, the towing ropes were adjusted, and the Trinity-house boys ascended the rattlings and manned the top-sail yard. Shortly after this J.C. Parker, Esq., chairman of the Dock Company, attended by a number of gentlemen connected with that establishment, arrived on the spot. The chairman then addressed those present stressing the benefits of the new facility to the welfare of Hull and thanking all those responsible for the new dock's construction. *At the close of his address, which was received with acclamations, Mr. Parker intimated that the time had now arrived to open the dock. Mr. Dewear, the Humber Dock master, immediately, with his*

speaking trumpet, gave the word to "open the gates and clear the bridge". These operations were performed with extraordinary facility, notwithstanding the dense throng of people that crowded every part where standing room was to be found. The paddles of the steamer were put in motion the instant the gates were fully opened and the bridge elevated to its height, and the two vessels glided gently into the open expanse of the newly completed dock. As the yacht passed through the bridge, the lads on the yard and booms, and the company on board the steam tug, gave three animating cheers, which were answered by the immense throngs on the quays. Fire arms of small calibre were heard popping off in every direction, and were answered by the heavy booming of some large pieces of artillery, placed on the quays of the Old Dock. Swivel guns and musketry were also discharged from many of the vessels in the Old and Humber Docks. A band of music stationed on board the yacht, enlivened the scene by its martial and animating strains. The yacht on entering the Junction Dock, with its flowing streamers, and gay little crew, presented a most striking and picturesque object to the eye of the spectator, and a number of smart gigs and row boats, that followed in her wake and spread themselves rapidly over the surface of the dock, gave to the scene the animating experience of a regatta. After entering the dock the yacht was towed by the steamer once round, amidst the occasional cheers of the populace, and the discharge, at intervals, of fire-arms, from some of the spectators and from the windows of houses on the walls. Both vessels then proceeded through the Whitefriargate lock-pit and bridge into the Old Dock, and came to moorings near the bonding yard, at the east end of the Old

22

Dock. On conclusion of the ceremony the gentlemen connected with the Dock Company, we understand, adjourned to the Kingston Hotel, where they took of a handsome déjeuné.

There was now a through connection between the Humber Dock entered from the River Humber and the Old Dock with its lock onto the River Hull, in effect creating an island between the three docks and the Old Harbour. As part of the opening ceremony, it was intended that the Trinity House yacht should complete the circuit of the island but the state of the tide prevented this from happening in the morning. However, the circumnavigation was completed on the afternoon tide with further pomp and ceremony. The Trinity House yacht would have been the *Zephyr* which was acquired when lying at Rochester on 4 June 1823 for £1,000. She was about 55ft in length, cutter-rigged with a mainsail and two jibs. The vessel was subsequently fitted up as a buoy yacht serving in that capacity until November 1844 when she was sold for £205.

The earlier reference to the *Eagle* of Goole not being dressed for the occasion is interesting. The HDC did not take kindly to the opening of the Port of Goole in 1826 and got further agitated when Goole was formally constituted as a Customs Port in 1828, thereby attracting foreign trade. The acrimony reached fever pitch in 1831 when the HDC claimed that dues should be levied on ships passing Hull by on their way up to Goole, so depriving the larger port of its foreign trade. The matter was heard by the Court of the King's Bench and dismissed causing the Aire and Calder Navigation, owners of the Port of Goole, to issue this statement in March 1831: *The Court of the King's Bench, after mature deliberation, by an unanimous decision, relieved the Port of Goole from the attempt made by the Dock Company of Kingston-upon-Hull, to strangle it in its infancy, the Undertakers of the Aire and Calder Navigation feel it a duty to themselves to announce to the Public, THAT GOOLE IS DECLARED EXEMPT FROM ANY DUES TO THE SAID DOCK COMPANY AT KINGSTON-UPON-HULL.* No love lost here!

The opening of the Junction Dock not only attracted still more trade but also substantially reduced dredging costs. The cleaner water of the River Hull now largely supplied the whole system and although the siltation in the Old Dock increased as more water entered it, this was more than offset by the reduction of siltation in the Humber Dock. The direct passage from the River Hull to the River Humber via Junction Dock enabled the steam dredger to work in all three docks and so the old horse dredger was scrapped. In 1846 gas lighting was installed on the western quays of this dock and Humber Dock.

Railway Dock
All three of the original Town Docks were connected by an internal railway. It is not known of what gauge and whether the system was worked by horse or manpower but it greatly facilitated the movement of cargo between the three docks. Hull's first public railway, the Hull & Selby Railway, was opened formally on 1 July 1840 with passenger and parcels traffic commencing the following day. Arrangements for carrying goods, cattle and sheep followed shortly afterwards. The railway created a new dimension for the port. Hitherto almost all exports and imports were carried to the port and away from the port for inland

The three most prominent vessels seen here in 1953 in Prince's Dock were all built at the Cook, Welton & Gemmell yard at Beverley. They are in Prince's Dock for fitting out. The trawler nearest to Monument Buildings on the right is *Ella Hewett* LO.47 (595grt), Yard No.871. She was built for the Heward Fishing Company, Fleetwood, launched on 4 December 1952 and completed on 19 March the following year. Unfortunately she sank on 3 November 1962 after running over the wreck of HMS *Drake* off Rathlin Island, Antrim. The trawler next to her is *St. Bartholomew* GY.178 (635grt) built for the North Cape Fishing Co Ltd, Grimsby, Yard No.865. She was launched on 20 November 1952 and completed on 16 April 1953. In 1954 she was sold to Ostend owners as *Van der Weyden* but was wrecked on the south east coast of Iceland on 30 March 1957. The vessel on the left is a 'Ton' class minesweeper which must be HMS *Brinton* (M.1114), Yard No.853, launched on 8 August 1952 but not completed until 4 March 1954. She was sold in 1997 and broken up the following year. [Ivor Innes Photographers, Hessle]

This view of Victoria Dock probably dates from the mid-1930s. The Finland Line vessel *Polaris* (1543grt) was so named in 1933. She was originally built in 1912 as *Prinzessin Sophie Charlotte* by Stettiner Oderwerke, Yard No.632 and between 1922 and 1933 was named *Preussen*. In 1945 she was further renamed *Sestroretsk* and handed to Russia as war compensation to be operated by Baltic and Murmansk Shipping, surviving until January 1972 when she was broken up at Split, Croatia. The dumb craft in the foreground was one of the fleet of former North Eastern Railway lighters operating at Hull. *NER 16* was built in 1889. [Hull Maritime Museum]

distribution by the network of navigable rivers and canals but now there was competition from a new form of transport which revolutionised the movement of goods. The railway was also well patronised by the public to the great detriment of the passenger river steamers which plied between Hull, Goole, Selby and York. The railway's Hull terminus was in Railway Street, west of Humber Dock. The original building was replaced by a substantial goods station in 1858, some ten years after the passenger business had been diverted to Hull's Paragon station which opened on 8 May 1848.

The coming of the railway attracted still more shipping to Hull and so intensified the need for still more dock accommodation. An Act for the construction of Railway Dock received the royal assent on 6 August 1844 (Note 12). It comprised a branch dock with a water area of some two acres to the west of Humber Dock to the north of the new railway terminus. The length of the dock was 700ft with a breadth of 180ft; the north, west and south quays were provided with transit sheds and on the north and south quays there were cranes capable of lifting 20 tons. The engineer responsible for its construction was John Bernard Hartley (1814-1872) with Edward Welsh (b.1821 Ireland) as the resident engineer; the

contractors were Messrs Bowers and Murray. The foundation stone for the dock, which cost £106,000, was laid by William Henry Huffam (1805-1881), secretary of the HDC, on 28 May 1845 and it was formally opened on 10 December 1846. The formal opening appears to have been a low key affair with the *Yorkshire Gazette* in its issue for 12 December reporting as follows: *The Railway Dock at Hull was opened for the reception of shipping on Thursday last, but will only be used chiefly as a laying up berth until the spring. The ship 'Russia' of this port, 336 tons measurement, and 500 to 600 burthen, was the first ship to enter, which she did at ten o'clock, in flying colours, and was followed by 'Tanjore', of 306 tons per register, the steam ship 'Yorkshireman', and a number of the Dock Company's useful vessels.* The 1844 Act (section 186) gave the HDC power to make railways or tramroads and turntables on the quays but not to use a locomotive engine on such railways or tramroads. The powers were duly exercised with standard gauge lines crossing Kingston Street to gain access to the south and north sides of Railway Dock and the west side of Prince's Dock. Moreover the bridge across the Humber Dock lock (Note 13) was renewed in 1847 to carry railway lines so enabling the east sides of that dock and Prince's Dock to be rail served as well as the south side of Queen's

Dock. Horse power was used to move the wagons.

Victoria Dock
The opening of Railway Dock completed the Town Docks system but the 1844 Act also authorised the construction of another dock, Victoria Dock. This was very different as it was the first dock to be constructed to the east of the River Hull. It was originally intended to build Victoria Dock with access only from the River Humber but that proposal met with opposition and it was subsequently determined to have an additional entrance off the River Hull. This configuration was authorised by the 1844 Act, together with a half tide basin which acted as a holding area for vessels entering or leaving the dock at the River Humber entrance, prior to high water. As with Railway Dock, the engineer was John Bernard Hartley and the resident engineer was again Edward Welsh (Note 14). Excavation commenced in September 1845 and the foundation stone was laid on 5 November 1846 by HDC chairman John Beadle, 1787-1869 (Note 15) who succeeded John Cowham Parker, the previous holder of the post. The ceremony was a private one involving only the engineer, the secretary to the HDC, the contractor and those immediately employed on the works.

When first opened the dock had a water area of 12½ acres necessitating the removal of 937,000 cubic yards of earth. The following materials were used in its construction: 2,376,000 cubic ft of stone, 850,000 cubic ft of timber, 21,000 cubic yards of mortar and 80 tons of iron. In contrast to the opening of Railway Dock it was inaugurated with considerable pomp and ceremony on 3 July 1850 by Thomas Firbank (1777-1866) who had followed John Beadle as HDC chairman. The occasion was accompanied by a strong south-westerly wind which would have been of some concern to those master mariners under whose command vessels were entering the new dock for the first time. The *Hull Packet* for 5 July 1850 reported extensively on the occasion which lasted all day and what follows is largely taken from that source. At the suggestion of the mayor, Thomas William Palmer, the day was generally regarded as a public holiday. The shops were closed and the principal streets were crowded by *persons of all classes clad in their best attire*. Church bells pealed and banners and flags were

waving from every conspicuous position. Just before 10am the HDC directors assembled at the Dock Office to receive the company's shareholders and others who would form part of a procession to the new dock.

The procession left at precisely 10.30am; those participating included the mayor, the acting master warden and elder brethren from Hull Trinity House, merchants, ship owners and representatives of the HDC. The procession, accompanied by a military band, was routed over the River Hull at North Bridge, down Great Union Street and Drypool to gain access along the south quay of the new dock. It halted at the east side at the new basin where a platform had been erected on the quay at the northern side of the lock entrance. It was estimated that between 30,000 and 40,000 people were present. At 11am the lock gates were opened and the HDC's colours hoisted at the flag staff at the Humber entrance of the dock. The guns of the citadel then fired a royal salute as a signal for the Trinity House yacht *Ariel* to approach (Note 16).

Thomas Firbank then announced that it was the pleasing duty of the HDC *to throw open to the trade and commerce of the world the 'Victoria Dock' – called after our beloved and gracious Queen.* The Rev John Healey Bromby (1770-1868), Vicar of Hull, then blessed the new undertaking and just after the crowd had joined him in saying Amen, the *Ariel* came into the basin amid enthusiastic cheering. The vessel was adorned from the deck to her topmast with flags of all nations and although the wind was blowing very strongly, the yacht passed smoothly through the entrance into the dock. She was followed by the steam tug *Lioness* which was laden with passengers. Other vessels entering the dock were the yacht *Phoebe*, a railway steamer, the yacht *Leda* and the steamer *Lion* owned and built by Brownlow and Pearson. She was carrying some 1,500 passengers and encountered some difficulty in passing through the lock gates. After the vessels had entered it was the mayor's turn for speech making which ended with him calling on all those present to give three cheers for the

Victoria Dock in 1950, illustrating to good effect loose timber being discharged to rail wagons. The operation was clearly very labour intensive. Note the temporary stages erected between the ship and the wagons, the shunting tractor to the right of the loaded wagon and the capstans also used to move the wagons along the quayside. *Hesnes* (1170grt) was so named in 1946 when she was acquired by Jorgensens Rederi, Grimstad, Norway. She was originally built by Stettiner Oderwerke as *Paul L-M. Russ*, Yard No.705 and was subsequently renamed on five occasions before being broken up as *Alkmini* at Split in October 1973. [Ivor Innes Photographers, Hessle]

Victoria Dock in 1964, with at least three timber carriers with the cargo still stowed as loose planks. *Weser* (833grt) was built by Claus Luhring, Brake, Yard No.5802, in 1958 for P/R Weser, Bremen. Subsequently she carried several names but is still sailing as *Pola1* under the Panama flag. The two ships ahead of her are the Greek registered vessel *Stelianos* (1923grt) next to the quay with the Finnish registered *Airisto* (1840grt) alongside. The Greek vessel was built in 1944 by Deutshe Werft of Hamburg, Yard No.425 and had several changes of name and owners before being broken up as *Euripides* in Hong Kong in July 1969. *Airisto* was completed by Fredriksstad M/V in 1915 and started out life as *Silkeborg* changing to *Airisto* when acquired by Shipping Lines Ltd, Naantali, Finland in 1947. She was broken up in Finland in November 1966. [Ivor Innes Photographers, Hessle]

HDC. Afterwards a 'sumptuous' lunch was provided for the VIPS at the Dock Office. Not content with this, a dinner was provided in the evening at the public rooms in Jarratt Street when upwards of 200 gentlemen sat down to eat and listen to still more speeches. The company present was said to have been one of the most influential that ever assembled in the town. During the day 75 masters and boys of Hull Trinity House were entertained at dinner with roast beef and plum pudding at the expense of the Corporation.

As previously mentioned Queen Victoria and Prince Albert paid a visit to Hull in October 1854. The royal party arrived by train from Edinburgh during the afternoon of 13 October and the following day participated in a tour of the docks on board the royal steam yacht *Fairy*. The vessel, built by Ditchburn & Mare, Leamouth, London in 1845, was actually tender to the larger royal yacht *Victoria and Albert* and was able to cruise in shallow waters (Note 17). The waterborne tour commenced at the Corporation Pier on the River Humber and then proceeded through Humber Dock, Junction Dock and the Old Dock into the Old Harbour before accessing Victoria Dock from the River Hull. From there the *Fairy* passed once more into the River Humber back to the Corporation Pier, so completing a circumnavigation of all Hull's Docks. It was after this visit that Old Dock became known as Queen's Dock and Junction Dock was renamed Prince's Dock.

The Victoria Dock had become the largest dock in Hull and it continued to expand. During 1862-1864 it was extended to the east and at the same time a new timber pond was added and an existing timber pond extended. A 12hp wrought iron steam crane built by James Taylor & Company, Britannia Works, Birkenhead, was installed in 1864 capable of lifting 20 tons. The timber industry was and still is very important to Hull with softwood being imported in large quantities from the Baltic and Russia. Victoria Dock became a centre of importance for the timber trade and the ponds were used to receive timber discharged from ships overside directly into the dock water after which it was floated into the timber ponds for storage and re-delivery. This would be anathema to modern day timber merchants who require wood to be as dry as possible and kept under cover but in the days when timber was delivered as loose baulks there was a considerable saving in labour, wharfage charges and transport costs by simply floating it into the ponds for storage. When giving evidence at Hull Sheriff's Court on 26 July 1847, Frederick Allitt (1809-1884), a raft yard foreman in the employ of Hull timber merchants Messrs Harrison & Co, stated that: *The timber was not the least injured by being kept in water, and it kept better there than on dry land.* He had *repeatedly seen timber in open yards rotten. The amount of saving in labour by having a pond, would be from 1s 6d to 1s 8d per load* compared to storage in a yard (Note 18). The loose baulks floating in the docks were formed into rafts held together by ropes and large staples.

An interesting account of how timber was handled in the early days at Victoria Dock was given by the North Eastern Railway's Chief Timber Foreman, Robert Henry Pawson (1860-1928), who retired at the end of March 1925 (Note 19). Referring to the year 1875 or thereabouts he said: *In those days deals and timber were brought to Victoria Dock in sailing ships and one could walk the length of the dock on rafts of floating timber. The winter in those days was severe and we had to employ men to saw the ice in the Pond Channels and push the blocks into the dock. Some of the ice blocks were six inches thick and six feet wide. The sailing ships were all berthed end on to the quay and the deals were discharged through port holes on to a stage and then landed on the quay and the vessels, no matter how large, were only allowed their own width for quay space. The merchants had to employ men to load trucks and cart as much away as possible during the discharge of the vessel.*

The following is a description of Victoria Dock at its fullest extent as presented in a paper to the Institution of Civil Engineers on 23 March 1875 by Sir William Wright (1812-1884) who was Chairman of the HDC from 1866 to 1878. *The Victoria Dock covers upwards of 20 acres of water space; there are besides three basins which comprise upwards of 6 acres more. Its length is 2,000 feet, and breadth 378 feet. The depth of water on the sills at neap tides is 22 feet, and at spring tides 27 feet 6 inches. It has two entrances – one into the Humber and one into the Old Harbour. The width of the former is 60 feet, and of the latter 45 feet. The quays of this dock are provided with lines of railway, behind which are extensive yards, the property of the Company, let to various firms engaged in the timber trade, to which trade this dock is chiefly devoted. At its east end, and also to the south, are two extensive timber-ponds, the former upwards of 11 acres, and the latter 14 acres in extent; both of which are almost fully occupied. In the immediate vicinity of this dock are two patent slips, the property of the Company, for hauling up and repairing vessels. They are capable of accommodating ships of 2,000 tons burden and upwards. On the quays are several cranes, capable of lifting from 10 tons to 60 tons each.*

Although timber was the predominant cargo handled in Victoria Dock it also became important for the shipment of coal and was the first dock to have a coal shipping appliance on the belt-conveying principle. The *North Eastern Railway Magazine* for June 1914 (Vol. 4, No.42) recorded that there were two such conveyors and contained an interesting description of their operation as follows: *it is decidedly interesting to watch wagon after wagon pass over the hoppers, which are sunk in the ground below rail level, and to see those that are end-doored tipped at one end or other by a hydraulic ram so that their contents are quickly unloaded. Each hopper feeds an inclined endless belt which, travelling at a speed of maybe 400ft per minute, conveys the coal upward to be delivered into the hold of a ship. There is a continuous procession of wagons over the hoppers, the capacity of each belt being 650 tons per hour.* Victoria Dock also sported a coal hoist with a lifting capacity of 20 tons capable of tipping 20 wagons per hour and a 40 ton capacity coaling crane capable of dealing with 10 wagons per hour. Each of the conveyors could cope with 55 wagons per hour, almost one per minute! The dock was also home to the Finland Line for which the famous firm of John Good & Sons were agents. Amazingly this Hull business still thrives today having been founded in 1833 and acquiring limited company status on 10 January 1908.

HULL AND SELBY, OR HULL AND LEEDS JUNCTION, RAILWAY.
OPENING OF THE LINE
FOR PASSENGERS AND PARCELS ONLY,
ON THURSDAY, JULY THE 2nd, 1840

THE Public are respectfully informed that this RAILWAY will be OPENED THROUGH-OUT from HULL to the JUNCTION with the LEEDS and SELBY RAILWAY., at Selby, on WEDNESDAY, the First Day of July next, and that PASSENGERS and PARCELS only will be conveyed on THURSDAY, July 2nd ; thus presenting a direct Railway Conveyance from Hull to Selby, Leeds, and York without change of Carriage.

TRAINS WITH PASSENGERS WILL START FROM HULL AS UNDER

AT SEVEN O'CLOCK, A.M   AT THREE O'CLOCK, P.M.

AT TEN O'CLOCK, A.M.   AT SIX O'CLOCK, P.M.

ON SUNDAYS, AT SEVEN O'CLOCK, A.M., AND SIX O'CLOCK, P.M.

The Trains from LEEDS and YORK, for HULL, will depart from those Places at the same Hours; and Passengers and Parcels may be Booked through at the Leeds, York, and Hull Stations. Arrangements are also in progress for Booking Passengers to Sheffield, Derby, Birmingham, and London.

THE FARES TO BE CHARGED ARE AS UNDER :

	First Class.	Second Class.	Third Class.
Hull to Selby	4s. 6d.	4s. 0d.	2s. 6d.
Hull to York	8s. 0d.	6s. 6d.	4s. 6d.
Hull to Leeds	8s. 0d.	6s. 6d.	4s. 6d.

No Fees are allowed to be taken by the Guards, Porters, or any other Servants of the Company.

The Trains, both up and down, will call at the Stations on the Line, viz. :—Hessle, Ferriby, Brough, Staddlethorpe, Eastrington, Howden, and Cliff.

Arrangements for carrying Goods, Cattle, Sheep, &c., will be completed in a short time, of which due Notice will be given.

By Order,

GEORGE LOCKING, Secretary.

Railway Office, Hull, June 24th, 1840.

A Hull & Selby Railway advertisement announcing the opening of the line on 2 July 1840 for passengers and parcels only. It was officially opened the previous day.

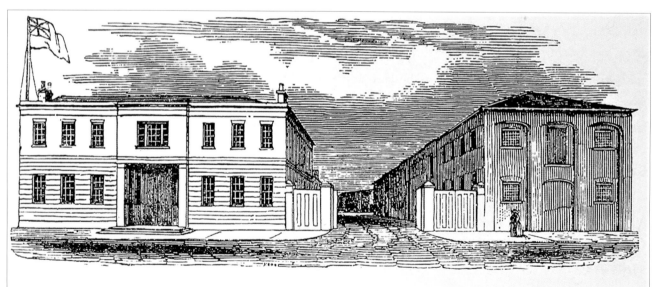

Woodcut in Hull Packet, *July 3, 1840.*

FIRST RAILWAY STATION AT HULL (FROM THE HUMBER DOCK SIDE).

A woodcut of Hull's first station looking west from Humber Dock. The passenger station is on the left with the goods warehouse to the right.

2. The Coming of the Railway

Early Proposals

Hull was a little tardy in joining the national railway network. The west coast port of Liverpool was connected with Manchester in 1830 and both of those cities had direct rail access to London via Birmingham by 1838. There was a force at work against early railway proposals to link Hull to Leeds, via Selby and on to Manchester. The reluctance was generated by the vested interests of ship owners whose vessels plied the rivers Humber and Ouse between Hull, Selby and York with both passengers and merchandise. The Leeds and Selby Railway opened on 22 September 1834, possibly with the hope of reviving Selby as a major port but hopes in that direction had already been dashed by the opening of the port of Goole in 1826 and its continuing success both as a port for coastwise traffic and, more importantly, foreign trade.

Hull & Selby Railway

The formal opening of Hull's first public railway, the Hull & Selby Railway, took place on 1 July 1840 with public traffic beginning the following day. The Act of Parliament authorising the construction of the railway with a capital of £533,333, to be raised by shares or by loan, had received the royal assent on 21 June 1836 (Note 20). The first

company chairman was Henry Broadley (1793-1851) who held the office until 1843. He was from the Hull family of merchants, bankers and landowners and was Member of Parliament representing the East Riding from 1837-1851. The length of this double-tracked pioneering line was 30¾ miles with stations at Hull, Hessle (4¾ miles), Ferriby (7½ miles), Brough (10½ miles), Broomfleet (14¼ miles), Staddlethorpe (17 miles), Eastrington (19¼ miles), Howden (22¼ miles) Wressle (25 miles), Cliffe (28 miles) and Selby (30¾ miles). Remarkably with the exception of Cliffe, which was re-named Hemingbrough on 1 September 1874 and closed on 6 November 1967, all the original stations are still open. Brough was re-sited in 1904 slightly to the east but some of the original buildings still exist and Staddlethorpe was re-named Gilberdyke but not until 7 January 1974.

Construction began in 1838, several contractors being engaged on particular sections of the route. The resident engineer was John Timperley, formerly of the HDC; the principal engineers were James Walker (1781-1862) and Alfred Burges (1797-1886) acting in partnership. Walker was responsible for the original survey. The contract for the section of line out of Hull along the Humber foreshore was awarded to

Charles Faviell (1796-1852) of Harrogate but was cancelled in July 1838 due to unsatisfactory progress and awarded to Townshend and Harker. At the general meeting of the company held on 1 February 1839, it was reported that 700 yards at the west end of the foreshore stretch had been completed with 200 yards at the east end nearly ready to receive the stoning. Another 200 yards was in progress leaving a middle section of 600 yards not yet begun. The section from the Humber bank to Melton was also let to Townshend and Harker. Spoil from the cutting at Hessle, the deepest on the line, was used to form the embankments with excavated rock and gravel being used as ballast. It was hoped that the whole of the construction works throughout the line would be completed in time for an opening in the spring of 1840. As things turned that ambition was not fulfilled but only by a couple of months.

The Hull terminus was to the west of Humber Dock with its frontage on Railway Street. The passenger station consisted of a stone fronted building (100ft x 70ft) and the ground floor had a booking office, parcels office and waiting rooms; the company's offices occupied the first floor. The station had a train shed covering four lines of rails and two platforms. It was 170ft in length and 72ft wide and was supported by 22 cast iron columns. A broad passage 30ft long, gave access to the trains from the entrance hall. On the north side of the passenger station, separated by a road by which passengers gained access to and from the station, there was a goods warehouse 270 ft in length and 45ft wide with lines on each side of it and running through it to reach Humber Dock. The railway workshops, occupying an area of 5,000 sq yards, had a frontage on Kingston Street. At Limekiln Creek, just outside the station yard, the company also had a wharf covering about 4,000 sq yards.

The opening of Hull's first railway was dampened by the weather. The *Yorkshire Gazette* for 4 July 1840 reported as follows. *At about six o'clock in the morning the rain began to fall very heavily, and from the appearance of the clouds, which were mingled in one great mass, the likelihood of the day turning out fine was highly improbable.. However, the merry bells of the Holy Trinity Church attempted to enliven the scene by their occasional sweet peals: the whole of the ships in the Humber, too, hoisted their colours and from the different public buildings there were also flags flying. But the watery element proved conqueror, and from the continued rain and now dirty state of the street, it was determined that the idea of a procession should be relinquished. As soon as this became pretty generally known, the holders*

The design of the Hull & Selby Railway's seal clearly demonstrates that the railway company was expecting to benefit from the Port of Hull's expansion and growing trade.

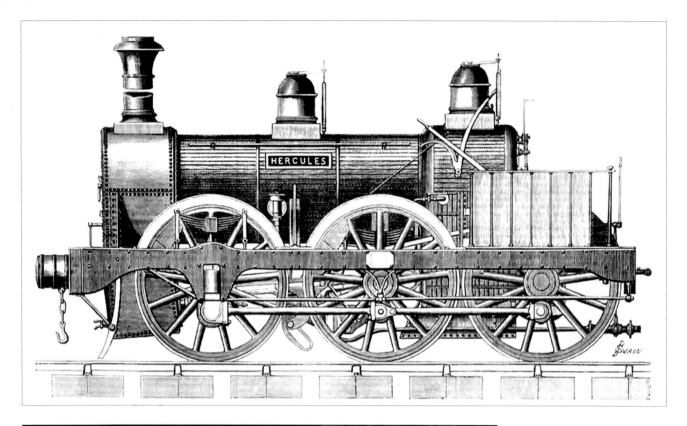

Above. This engraving appeared in *The Engineer* for 16 January 1880. It purports to be the Hull & Selby Railway's 0-6-0 tender engine *Hercules* built circa 1842 by Shepherd & Todd of Leeds for the York & North Midland Railway which leased the Hull & Selby line from 1 July 1845. The locomotive had coupled wheels of 5ft 6in diameter and 16in x 24in inside cylinders. The engraver, John Swain (1829-1898), seems to have exercised a little artistic licence as you cannot have the leading axle with outside frames and the other two with inside and then couple them all together with side rods!

Left. George Hudson (1800-1871), known as *The Railway King*, once controlled a third of Britain's railway network. Thrice Mayor of York and Chairman of the York & North Midland Railway, he was responsible for the building of Paragon Station and its hotel. The original painting is in the possession of Jennifer Kutte, née Hudson. *The Railway King* was her great, great, great uncle. [Courtesy, Jennifer Kutte]

of the tickets for the trip who felt anxious to go with the trains to Selby and back, began to hurry onto the terminus to secure their places, and the sight of the variety of Mackintosh coats, cloaks, capes, and umbrellas was most amusing. On our arrival at the station about eleven o'clock, we found one of the trains, consisting of seven or eight carriages, well filled; the first class by a number of highly respectable females, and the other by some of the most influential gentlemen connected with the town of Hull.

No less than five trains left Hull in quick succession on the opening day. The first left at 12.15pm hauled by the locomotive *Kingston* with eleven carriages, the second was headed by *Exley* with nine carriages, third was *Selby* with seven, fourth *Prince* with twelve and last *Andrew Marvell* with eight. *Exley* was named after John Exley, a Customs Officer at Hull, whose letter published in the *Hull Rockingham* on 28 December 1833 started the agitation for a railway between Hull and Selby which eventually led to the formation of the railway company. The locomotive hauling the fifth train was named after Andrew Marvell (1621-1678) the famous metaphysical poet, satirist and politician who was born at Winestead in East Yorkshire and educated at Hull grammar school. With the exception of *Prince*, all the locomotives were built in 1840 by Fenton, Murray & Jackson of Leeds: *Kingston* in April, *Exley* and *Selby* in May and *Andrew Marvell* in June. They were all 2-2-2 tender engines with 12 x 18in inside cylinders and 5ft 6in diameter driving wheels. *Prince*, loaned from the

Leeds & Selby Railway, was a 2-2-0 tender engine built by Kirtley & Co of the Dallam Foundry, Warrington in 1839 and was probably of the 'Bury' type with bar frames.

During its independent existence the Hull & Selby Railway possessed a total of 19 locomotives: seven 2-2-2 tender engines built by Shepherd & Todd, Railway Foundry, Leeds; six of the same wheel arrangement from Fenton, Murray & Jackson and six 0-6-0 tender engines for goods traffic. Four of the latter were also built by Shepherd & Todd but the remaining two 0-6-0s were apparently built in Hull in 1844 at the company's own workshops. The locomotive superintendent was John Gray (1810-1854) who patented an expansion valve gear known as the 'horse-leg' motion (Note 21). This gear was fitted to the two locomotives built at Hull. Very interestingly some of the carriages were also built in Hull by Hurstwick & Bean of Carr Lane. Hitherto, the firm had specialised in producing horse drawn road coaches. They produced ten first class carriages, twenty second class and six third class. Other rolling stock was borrowed from the Leeds & Selby and York & North Midland Railway companies. Hurstwick & Bean also built two horse-drawn omnibuses for the conveyance of passengers to and from the station.

The inaugural trains were blessed with better weather on the way to Selby where a cold collation was served to invited guests at the George Hotel. The trains started to return to Hull at 4.30pm taking about an hour to reach

the terminus where another cold collation had been prepared in the upper part of the company's warehouse. Some 500 people attended; they were entertained by a band, participated in toasts and listened to several speeches, as was the custom on such grand occasions. Hull was now accessible by railway but it was not until 19 August 1840 that the company was in a position to receive goods traffic. The final link in the Manchester & Leeds Railway was not completed until 1 March 1841 but from that date there was a strategic east-west railway route from Hull to Liverpool.

The line from the west of Brough to the crossing of the River Ouse at Selby is absolutely straight and level for a distance of 18 miles, the longest such section on any British railway. One of the most interesting features of Hull's first railway was its permanent way as it was probably the first main line in the country to be built throughout using wooden sleepers, as opposed to stone blocks or a mixture of both. About 17 miles of the line were laid with longitudinal sleepers and the remainder with transverse sleepers. Flat-bottom rail weighing 55lb per yard was used for the longitudinal sleeper sections while rail of 63lb per yard was utilised for the transverse sleepers. The gauge was set at 4ft 9in, the variation of an increased half an inch from the standard gauge being made to give more play to the flanges of the wheels. The longitudinal sleepers had disappeared by 1860 and the track was adjusted to standard gauge.

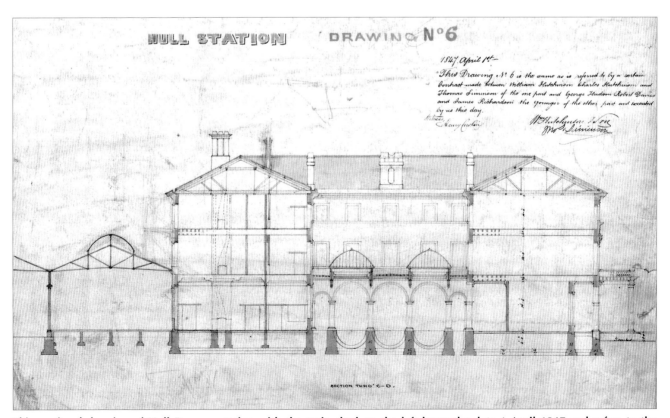

This sectional drawing of Hull Paragon station with the train shed on the left bears the date 1 April 1847 and refers to the contract between contractors William Hutchinson & Son and Thomas Siminson of Hull and George Hudson, Robert Davies and James Richardson of the York & North Midland Railway. [Network Rail]

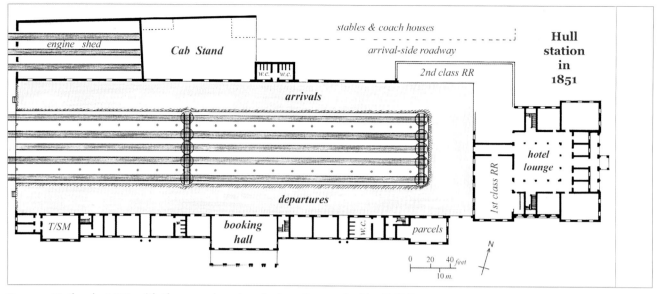

Paragon Station in 1851 with three-road engine shed on the north side. [Bill Fawcett]

The Hull terminus station, originally known as Manor House Street, closed to passengers on 8 May 1848 when the passenger trains were diverted to the new station at Hull Paragon. However, the station was again opened for local passenger traffic between 1 June 1853 and 1 June 1864 in connection with a service to Victoria Dock station (see below). After that it was developed solely for goods traffic.

York & North Midland Railway

The Hull & Selby Railway was leased to the York & North Midland Railway (YNMR) with effect from 1 July 1845. The YNMR, which had absorbed the Leeds & Selby Railway in 1844, had as its chairman George Hudson (1800-1871) the famous or infamous, depending on your viewpoint, *Railway King*. That title was bestowed upon him as a result of his energy, vision and success in developing the country's railways. He was born in the Yorkshire village of Howsham and had a lowly start in life but by 1848 he had become a millionaire controlling a third of Britain's railway network. He was thrice Mayor of York (in 1836, 1837 and 1846), a long serving Member of Parliament for Sunderland and was present at the opening of the Hull & Selby Railway. However, his power and influence did not last. His meteoric rise to success also nurtured opposition amongst those who were jealous of his fame and in 1849 his enemies gleefully claimed that he had been buying railway shares for his personal account and then selling them at huge profits to the companies of which he was chairman. His fall from fame was spectacular. On 17 May 1849 he resigned from his position as chairmen of the YNMR and shortly afterwards, following several court rulings against him, was reduced to living in miserable penury, in exile in France away from the public glare.

At the time the YNMR leased the Hull & Selby Railway, the latter company had just gained statutory powers to build a branch line from Hull to Bridlington which was to leave the main line on its approach to Hull at Dairycoates Junction and head north through Cottingham, Beverley and Driffield. The Act authorising construction was the Hull & Selby Railway (Bridlington Branch) Act which received the royal assent on 30 June 1845 (Note 22); the line was opened with much ceremony on 7 October 1846. The inaugural train consisted of no less than 66 carriages drawn by three YNMR locomotives named *Hudson*, *Antelope* and *Ariel*. The appropriately named leading locomotive was a 0-6-0 tender engine built by Robert Stephenson & Co in 1844 with 15in x 24in cylinders and 4ft 6in diameter coupled wheels. *Antelope* and *Ariel* were 2-2-2 tender locomotives built by Shepherd & Todd in 1840 and fitted with Gray expansion gear; they had 13in x 24in cylinders, 6ft 0in diameter driving wheels and 3ft 6in diameter leading and trailing wheels. The huge train left Hull at 11.10am in pouring rain and *en route* to Bridlington called at Cottingham, Beverley and Driffield as if to pay its respects to the inhabitants of those towns. The *Hull Packet* for 9 October carried a full and enthusiastic report. In referring to the *spacious and handsome* station at Beverley the newspaper said that the *inhabitants are very greatly indebted to Mr. Hudson and his colleagues for their liberality in erecting an edifice so complete and so well calculated amply to provide for the present and future requirements of the town*. Hudson was still riding high. At Driffield *the band bade us 'fierce welcome' and many of the inhabitants looked on our conveyance with such unequivocal amazement and contemplated the puffing and snorting engines with such 'fear and trembling', as made it evident they were unaccustomed to such fearful visitants*. The party lunched at Bridlington, returning to Hull by train at 3.35pm in readiness for dinner that same evening in the Jarratt Street Rooms. Hudson, who

featured prominently throughout the proceedings, had clearly seen the YNMR lease of the Hull & Selby Railway as a strategic means of facilitating not only an east-west cross country route but also as a means of linking the YNMR's proposed line to Bridlington from its Scarborough to York line at Seamer Junction. That link was completed via Filey on 20 October 1847 when trains began running from Hull to Scarborough.

Paragon Station

The route north from Hull to Scarborough never carried much dock traffic but it did stimulate the construction of a new station and hotel in the centre of the town, both built on a grand scale, thanks largely to the vision of Hudson who clearly saw the potential for Hull's continued growth as a major port city. The original station designed to handle passengers and freight soon became congested and so the YNMR obtained powers to build a new station and hotel, together with 4½ miles of new railway to connect the new station to the Hull & Selby line, via Hessle and Hessle Road Junctions, and the newly opened Bridlington line via Cottingham Junction. The new lines and station opened without any undue ceremony on 8 May 1848. The station and hotel were designed by George Townsend Andrews (1804-1855), an Exeter born architect who had already designed many of the stations for the YNMR and on other lines within the Hudson empire. The contractors were a local partnership comprising William Hutchinson (b.1781) and his son Charles (1817-1875) and Thomas Siminson (1804-1860). They had built the original Hull & Selby station at Hull and the line from Hull to Bridlington (see above). The hotel opened on 6 November 1851 after Hudson's downfall. For a while the new buildings were condemned as *Hudson's Folly*, being regarded as over extravagant. However, the station and

The Anlaby Road entrance to Paragon Station in North Eastern Railway days with the Royal Station Hotel to the right. [Mick Nicholson collection]

Plan of Paragon Station in the LNER era.

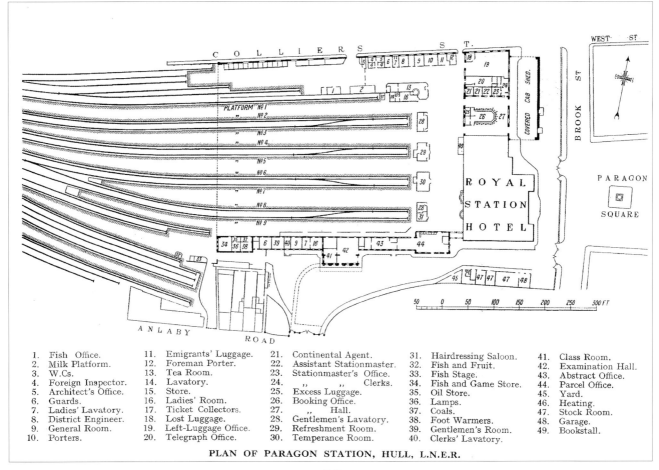

1. Fish Office.	11. Emigrants' Luggage.	21. Continental Agent.	31. Hairdressing Saloon.	41. Class Room.
2. Milk Platform.	12. Foreman Porter.	22. Assistant Stationmaster.	32. Fish and Fruit.	42. Examination Hall.
3. W.Cs.	13. Tea Room.	23. Stationmaster's Office.	33. Fish Stage.	43. Abstract Office.
4. Foreign Inspector.	14. Lavatory.	24. ,, ,, Clerks.	34. Fish and Game Store.	44. Parcel Office.
5. Architect's Office.	15. Store.	25. Excess Luggage.	35. Oil Store.	45. Yard.
6. Guards.	16. Ladies' Room.	26. Booking Office.	36. Lamps.	46. Heating.
7. Ladies' Lavatory.	17. Ticket Collectors.	27. ,, Hall.	37. Coals.	47. Stock Room.
8. District Engineer.	18. Lost Luggage.	28. Gentlemen's Lavatory.	38. Foot Warmers.	48. Garage.
9. General Room.	19. Left-Luggage Office.	29. Refreshment Room.	39. Gentlemen's Room.	49. Bookstall.
10. Porters.	20. Telegraph Office.	30. Temperance Room.	40. Clerks' Lavatory.	

PLAN OF PARAGON STATION, HULL, L.N.E.R.

Paragon station in July 1967 looking south towards the River Humber; St. Stephens Street is in the foreground. Ridsdale & Walker's coal yard with two hopper wagons placed above the coal cells or drops is on the left. Two loading gauges placed side by side can just be seen next to the nearest part of the trainshed roof. They served two lines used for goods traffic which was loaded and unloaded within the station. There is a Class 03 diesel-mechanical shunter to the right centre of the picture. The cranes on the skyline are in the western docks. [Ivor Innes Photographers, Hessle]

hotel soon justified their size, well able to accommodate further growth in traffic and remain as George Hudson's chief memorial in Hull. The hotel was re-named the Royal Station Hotel after Queen Victoria's stay there in 1854.

The station, built in Italianate style, covered an area of almost two and a half acres. The main buildings were aligned east-west, south of the tracks, facing onto Anlaby Road. They included a parcels office and the station master's house. The trainshed originally contained five tracks and two platforms within a three-span roof. In the 1870s further growth in traffic caused the North Eastern Railway (NER) to increase the accommodation by adding a third middle platform within the train shed, the existing platforms were lengthened beyond the shed roof and short bay platforms added on either side. The concourse was widened at the expense of the length of the platforms. In 1871 an emigrant waiting room was constructed alongside Anlaby Road. Built of yellow brick with ashlar dressings and a hipped slate roof, it was designed by NER architect Thomas Prosser (1817-1888); it was doubled in size in 1881 under the supervision of William Bell.

In 1953 it was converted to a social club but in recognition of its historical importance, it became a listed structure in 1994 and is now the Tigers Lair Public House.

In 1887 a canopy was added over the section of the south side departure platforms that protruded beyond the train shed. In 1902 work began on enlarging the station on its north side to the designs of NER architect, William Bell (1844-1919), who was also responsible for several major improvements to the other facilities which were carried out as part the overall scheme. The works included a completely new roof consisting of five glazed arches over all the platforms and two similar arches over the concourse. Ironwork work was provided by the Cleveland Bridge & Engineering Company of Darlington with cast iron columns supporting wrought iron ribs and lattice girders. The offices were re-sited to the east end of the station facing the concourse adjacent to the hotel. A new entrance hall was created facing Paragon Square leading to the booking hall which had a mosaic floor, an elaborate glazed brick and faience decoration, arcaded round-arched

windows and a coved matchboard roof with sky lights. A central wooden ticket office was provided in the same style. The booking hall and the ticket office still exist and are now listed structures but sadly are no longer used for their original purpose. The new track layout and other facilities in connection with the enlarged part of station were brought into use on 12 December 1904. It was not until then that work began on replacing the old station roof. A large portion of the old roof had been taken down when on Saturday, 7 January 1905 a large section of the remainder at the west end collapsed. Eight men employed by Sheffield contractors, Longden & Son, were working on the roof at the time and they were all injured, some seriously and one of the men died soon afterwards. The final part of the improvement scheme was a new signalling arrangement using the Westinghouse electro-pneumatic system, but that did not become fully operational until 3 July 1905. Two new signal boxes were installed: *Paragon Station* box with 143 levers and *Park Street* box, located 714ft to the west of the station, with 179 levers. On 5 March 1916, during a Zeppelin air raid on Hull which killed 17 people, a bomb blast blew out the glass in the overhead canopies at Hull Paragon. On a happier note part of the station was used in 1919 to warehouse loose bags of imported soya beans in order to relieve congestion at the docks. A total of 16,100 bags, amounting to 1,350 tons, were stacked in huge piles under the station roof using battery operated electric appliances (Note 23). During the Hull blitz of 1941 the station received direct hits on the night of 27 May, with many incendiary bombs hitting the trainshed roof.

The hotel and the station happily survive as Grade II listed structures. The hotel was further extended c.1936 and restored in 1990-1992 after serious fire damage on 7 October 1990. The trainshed, booking hall and many of the associated original buildings are now protected. In 1962 the main entrance canopy to the station was replaced by an ugly office building known as Paragon House. In 2006 for the first time in over 40 years, the original Victorian frontage was revealed following the demolition of Paragon House. This took place as part of a £12m regeneration programme which included the creation of the Hull Paragon Interchange which enables rail and bus services to come together in one place. The new facility was officially opened by the Queen and the Duke of Edinburgh when they unveiled a plaque on 5 March 2009 to commemorate the occasion, after arriving at the station by Royal Train. Since then the Anlaby Road side entrance to the railway station has been painstakingly restored and the station is currently undergoing yet another £1.5m facelift. It is currently served by four train operating companies: Hull Trains, Northern Rail, Transpennine and Virgin Trains.

Victoria Dock Branch

The opening of Victoria Dock gave the YNMR an opportunity to gain additional traffic and so, with the full co-operation of the HDC, powers were obtained to link the new dock with the growing railway network. The branch of 3¼ miles started at Anlaby Road Junction on the new line into Paragon station, crossed the Bridlington line on the flat and then ran around the outskirts of the city via new stations located at Cemetery, Stepney, Sculcoates, Southcoates and Victoria Dock. The branch crossed the River Hull at Southcoates by means of a swing bridge. Thomas Cabry (1801-1873) was responsible for the erection of the bridge with ironwork provided by Beecroft Butler & Co of Kirkstall, Leeds. Cabry was the YNMR's engineer and was later to become the engineer for the North Eastern Railway's southern division. The line was opened for goods traffic on 16 May 1853 and 1 June for passengers.

The passenger trains ran from the original Hull & Selby Railway station at Manor House Street which was reopened to passengers for the new branch line service. However, the passenger initiative was not a success; the service was diverted to Paragon station in 1854 but was withdrawn completely from 1 November that year. It was, of course, a completely different story with regard to goods traffic much to the annoyance of road users who were frequently stopped by the closing of the level crossing gates over Hedon Road, Holderness Road, Stoneferry Road (now Cleveland Street) and Beverley Road. By 1864 the Victoria Dock branch had been doubled in order to cope with the traffic, especially the increasing amounts of imported Scandinavian and Baltic timber. The timber was tripped from the dock to the Outwards Goods Yard to the west of Hull at Dairycoates where the wagons could be attached to the main line goods trains.

When the line was doubled the two tracks were interlaced over the River Hull swing bridge in order to avoid the cost of renewing the bridge. However, by the turn of the century with the onset of still more traffic and increased axle loadings, the old bridge was becoming a bottleneck and so it was decided to replace it with a new double-tracked skew bridge immediately to the north

The Victoria Dock Branch Hedon Road level crossing looking west circa 1900, so Victoria Dock is to the left of the NER Class E1 0-6-0 tank engine and van. The building immediately behind the locomotive is a railway-owned cottage and beyond that the rooftops of the houses to the left before the telegraph pole are in Seward Street. The tall chimney just discernible in the right background beyond the distinctive footbridge is that of a sawmill in Bellamy Street. The horse drawn coal merchant's cart has no doubt just been loaded in Alexandra Dock. [Mick Nicholson collection]

Circa 1900 photograph of the Hedon Road crossing but this time the view looks in the opposite direction with the footbridge hidden from view on the left and the entrance to Victoria Dock on the right. The standard gauge tracks in the roadway were used by steam trams introduced by the Drypool and Marfleet Steam Tramways Company, which commenced operations on 21 May 1889. The level crossing was replaced in 1903 by two substantial bridges. [Mick Nicholson collection]

of the original one. At Hull Corporation's cost the new bridge was also designed to carry a footpath on its north side. The bridge was designed by John Triffitt (1863-1941), assistant engineer for the NER's Southern Division with Walter McDougall Malt, 1867-1937, (Note 24), resident engineer for the works, assisted by Harold John Lexow Bruff, 1873-1946 (Note 25). The principal contractors were the Hull engineering firm of Harman & Langton with whom a contract was signed on 29 October 1905; the subcontractor for the steelwork was John Butler & Co Limited of Staningley, near Leeds. The task was quite a challenge as rail and river traffic had to continue with the minimum of disruption during the construction works. The bridge was pivoted from its centre which required a caisson to be sunk into the river bed. This was completed quickly and was well in hand by July 1906; by 7 September the centre bearing casting had been put in place. The new bridge itself, including the machinery, was constructed on a temporary foundation on the east bank of the river. Once completed the bridge was moved into position by means of a wire cable attached to a locomotive via several pulley blocks. The bridge travelled along a specially constructed path consisting of a double row of piles with waybeams and a double line of rails under each girder. The bridge was carried into position on eight six-

wheeled bogies, each designed to carry a load of 90 tons. The total weight of the bridge was 490 tons. A special train ran over the bridge for the first time on 5 May 1907 and it was brought into regular use on 10 May.

The bridge was powered by electricity supplied by Hull Corporation. The bridge control room, which contained two duplicate Siemens 30hp motors, was mounted atop of the structure over the centre of the bridge which gave it an unusual appearance akin to a NER signal box. However, the swing bridge was not a block post, the bridge foreman's duty being restricted to opening and closing the bridge to allow the passage of shipping in conjunction with the signalman at Sculcoates Junction. It took 56 seconds to open the bridge and exactly the same time to close it. In 1907 the bridge foreman was M.A. Burdon who was assisted by two steersmen; the bridge was then operated about six times per day.

The Victoria Dock branch closed in 1968 but Wilmington swing bridge, now owned by Hull City Council, remains in operational use to provide a footpath/cycleway and is a listed structure.

Hull & Holderness Railway
The founder of this railway was Anthony Bannister (1817-1878), a businessman and a notable figure in mid-Victorian Hull. He was Sheriff of Hull for the years

1849 and 1850 and Mayor of Hull for 1851 and 1855. The prospectus for the railway issued in 1852 included the following statement: *The object of this undertaking is to provide for the extensive district of Holderness, in the East Riding of the County of York, the great advantages of Railway Communication; and for the inhabitants of Hull, Beverley, surrounding country, and the large and populous towns in the West Riding of Yorkshire, an easy access to the German Ocean.* With a capital of £150,000 in 7,500 shares of £20 each the Act authorising the construction of the railway received the royal assent on 8 July 1853. The engineer for the line was Thomas Cabry; the contractors were Messrs Jackson, Bean and Gow. Bannister had his eye on not only opening up the wealthy agricultural area of Holderness but also developing a seaside resort. The line passed through flat countryside and was relatively easy to construct, opening on the public on 27 June 1854, after the customary festivities held the previous day. The Hull terminus was at Victoria Dock station which was designed by Cabry and built at the joint expense of the YNMR and the Hull & Holderness Railway. The other stations were at Marfleet (2¼ miles), Hedon (5¼ miles), Rye Hill & Burstwick (7¾ miles - Note 26), Keyingham (9½ miles), Ottringham (10¾ miles), Winestead (13½ miles - Note 27), Patrington (14 miles) and Withernsea (18 Miles). The mileages

1925 aerial view of the replacement bridges over Hedon Road with what is probably a LNER Class J72 (NER Class E1) 0-6-0 tank engine and its short train about to cross over the furthermost bridge. The Cleveland Bridge & Engineering Company of Darlington was responsible for the steel work with the masonry being undertaken by J & H Bentley of Bradford. Part of a Victoria Dock timber pond can be seen at the bottom right and Drypool goods station is to the left with its generous covered accommodation. The topmost line of the triangular railway junction is the line to Withernsea. It can be seen passing first under Craven Street road bridge, then under the Hull & Barnsley line to Alexandra Dock and finally under the high level line to King George Dock, on which there is a very long train heading towards the dock. The sidings towards the top right were known as Sweet Dews Sidings, so named after a nearby farm. The rail connected industrial premises with the tall chimney in the centre of the image is the timber yard and sawmills of Hollis Bros & Co Ltd. [© Historic England]

This view on the Victoria Dock Branch on 15 April 1907 shows the original swing bridge over the River Hull. The view looks west and immediately beyond the Wincolmlee level crossing gates is the solitary platform of Sculcoates station. The initial passenger service inaugurated on 1 June 1853 was not a success and ceased in November the following year but goods traffic to and from Victoria Dock blossomed and by 1864 the branch had been doubled. However to save costs the up and down lines were interlaced across the swing bridge as can be seen here. Traffic continued to grow and the NER decided to renew the bridge with a new double-tracked span which took place during 1906/1907. The new bridge was erected on the east bank of the river, north of the existing railway. It can just be glimpsed here on the right before it was finally rolled into position. Sculcoates station was reopened in 1865 but closed again on 9 June 1912. The bowstring girder bridge in the far distance is carrying the HBR main line into Cannon Street station. [Mick Nicholson collection]

37

On 25 October 1906 the new bridge is nearing completion on the east bank of the river. [Mick Nicholson collection]

shown are from Victoria Dock station. Although the Hull & Holderness Railway was very much an independent line, it negotiated an arrangement with the YNMR for working the line on the principle of a fixed sum for the net mileage of trains run. This avoided the need to purchase and maintain its own locomotives and rolling stock.

North Eastern Railway

1854 was a very significant year in the history of Hull's railways for in that year the North Eastern Railway (NER) was incorporated by an Act of Parliament which received the royal assent on 31 July. The NER was formed by the union of three established railway companies: the York, Newcastle & Berwick, the Leeds Northern and the YNMR. The lease of the Hull & Selby Railway to the YNMR was assigned to the NER as a part of the new arrangement which overall made the NER the largest single railway undertaking in the country with 703 route miles of line.

The NER must have inherited the arrangement entered into with the YNMR for working the Hull & Holderness Railway but a fundamental change took place in 1860. On 16 February that year the Hull & Holderness shareholders were informed that their company had entered into a provisional agreement with the NER for the sale of the undertaking, *the line forthwith to be worked by the North Eastern Railway*. At this point the NER must have

taken over the complete management of the line rather than just provide locomotives and rolling stock under a hiring arrangement. Parliamentary powers for a complete amalgamation were granted on 7 July 1862. The following year the NER arranged for the Withernsea trains to run into Paragon station via a new curve, appropriately known as the Paragon Curve. It was intended that the new service should start on 1 July 1863 but the Board of Trade inspector refused to sanction the use of the curve because of a serious signalling problem, such that the diverted service did not commence until 1 June 1864 when Victoria Dock station was closed to passenger traffic. As part of the new arrangement the old station at Southcoates was re-sited and brought back into use as was Stepney which closed when the Victoria Dock passenger service ceased. The other closed stations on that line were also reopened: Sculcoates by August 1865 and Cemetery, renamed Cemetery Gates, by September 1866 (Note 28). The new service to Withernsea offered four trains each way on weekdays and three each way on Sundays, although one of them only ran from and to Southcoates. When the Withernsea line was opened it was single track throughout but it was doubled in the early 1900s, excepting the sections between Hedon and Rye Hill and Ottringham and Winestead.

Earlier in 1864, on 28 March, the NER had commenced operating another new

service to the east coast resort of Hornsea. This was another independent line but unlike the Hull & Holderness Railway was worked from the outset by the NER. The key promoter of the Hull & Hornsea Railway was Joseph Armytage Wade (1817-1896), a Hornsea resident and a Hull timber merchant. He and his colleagues were convinced of the *superior residential amenities* which Hornsea had to offer compared with Withernsea. An Act authorising the line received the royal assent on 30 June 1862 and on 8 October that year Wade using an elegant wheelbarrow of Italian walnut and a polished electro-plated steel shovel *turned the first sod and filled his barrow in a truly workmanlike manner amidst prolonged and vociferous cheering*. The initial enthusiasm was somewhat dampened as, although the terrain was basically flat, the construction of the line was beset with difficulties. These included the boggy nature of the ground at Hornsea and the unsuitability of the excavated clay soil for embankments, plus a personal attack on Wade by some of the shareholders over land and material allegedly purchased by him and sold to the railway company at a profit – shades of Hudson! These problems raised the estimated cost from £68,000 to £122,000. Moreover, during the official inspection of the completed works Inspecting Officer, Captain Frederick Henry Rich (1824-1904) fell into Sutton Drain to the scarcely suppressed amusement of the

Here the new bridge has been rolled into position complete with its control cabin and the eastern section of the old bridge has been rolled back prior to scrapping. The next job would be to demolish the old swivel bearing and its caisson so allowing the new bridge to be swung. [Mick Nicholson collection]

View inside the control cabin on 6 May 1907 just four days prior to the crossing of the first train. The swing bridge was not a block post and so unlike a signal box, the bridge man did not accept trains. Two of the levers in the McKenzie & Holland locking frame were spare, the other three were marked: No.1 Release; No.2 Disengagers; No.3 Latches. Note the early use of electric lighting and the telephone (then referred to as a *Speaking Instrument*) which would give the bridge man direct communication with the Sculcoates signalman. Shipping movements had priority. [Mick Nicholson collection]

accompanying officials! He was not happy with the junction arrangements in Hull with the Victoria Dock branch, or the arrangements made at Marton and other level crossings.

The Hornsea line, length 13 miles, commenced at a new station called Wilmington located in the 'V' of the junction with the Victoria Dock branch. Stations *en route* to Hornsea were located at Sutton, Swine, Skirlaugh, Marton, Whitedale, Hatfield, Goxhill, Hornsea Bridge and Hornsea (Note 29). On 15 June 1864 the Hornsea trains began running from Hull Paragon and on 16 July 1866 the Hull & Hornsea Railway was formally taken over by the NER (Note 30). The railway was constructed as a single line but was upgraded to double track early in the 20th century. Goxhill, re-named Wassand on 1 October 1904, was unusual in that it was only open on Tuesdays which was Market day. One train called in each direction until the station closed on 21 September 1953. On 9 June 1912 a new station at Wilmington was brought into use 300 yards to the west of the original station which was then closed. From that date onwards it was used by most advertised passenger trains bound to and from Hornsea and Withernsea.

The Withernsea and Hornsea branches carried very little dock traffic but a significant NER development in 1869 had a major impact on traffic bound to and from Hull and its docks. This was the opening of the line from Staddlethorpe on the Hull & Selby line via Goole to Thorne where it joined the Manchester, Sheffield & Lincolnshire Railway (later Great Central Railway) over which the NER obtained running powers to Doncaster. The new line was authorised on 23 July 1863 and opened on 2 August 1869. It was quickly established as part of the shortest route from Hull to London via Doncaster for passenger, fish and freight traffic and the NER put it to good use. Shortly after this development the NER directors considered that the time was opportune for completing the purchase of the Hull & Selby Railway which, as recorded above, still retained its position as a leased line and so on 1 September 1871 the requisite six months' notice was given to the Hull & Selby Company. The exchange of Hull & Selby shares for cash or NER preference stock began almost immediately and so as at 1 March 1872 the NER obtained complete control of all the railways leading to Hull. Those carrying the bulk of the dock traffic were the pioneer line from Hull to Selby, the new line to Doncaster via Goole and, of course, the Victoria Dock branch.

Right. **This modern view shows the bridge opened to allow the passage of the Hull registered vegetable oil tank barge *Swinderby* which is heading down river and is about to pass a petroleum depot owned by J. R. Rix and Sons Ltd. The railway lines have been removed from the bridge decking but the bridge, now owned by Hull City Council, carries a public right of way which was a condition stipulated at the time of its authorisation. The barge was originally built at New Holland in 1974 as a workboat for Lincoln & Hull Marine Contractors Limited and converted to a tank barge in 2000 with the name *Selby Paradigm*, reverting to *Swinderby* in 2005.**

Bottom right. **Wilmington swing bridge became a Grade II listed structure on 21 January 1994 and now carries this plaque fixed in 2001.**

The lady waits patiently at Wincolmlee level crossing on 20 July 1967 as two Class 14 0-6-0 diesel-hydraulic locomotives double head a chalk train from Hessle Quarry to Earle's cement works at Wilmington just to the east of the River Hull. The control cabin proudly displays the name of the swing bridge which by this time had been in use for 60 years. The former GWR works at Swindon produced 56 of these 650hp locomotives in 1964/1965. They were designed for local trip workings and short distance freight trains and became known as *Teddy Bears*. The identity of the leading locomotive is unknown but the second engine is D9547 which Swindon turned out on 20 July 1965. It was withdrawn 1 April 1968 and sold to the British Steel Corporation for use at Corby steelworks where it remained until scrapped in August 1982. [Rev. David Benson/Mick Nicholson collection]

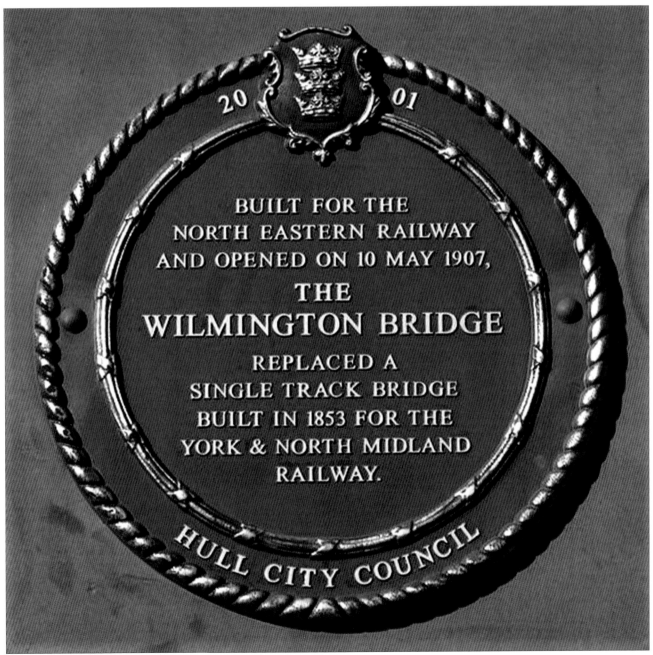

BUILT FOR THE
NORTH EASTERN RAILWAY
AND OPENED ON 10 MAY 1907,

THE

WILMINGTON BRIDGE

REPLACED A
SINGLE TRACK BRIDGE
BUILT IN 1853 FOR THE
YORK & NORTH MIDLAND
RAILWAY.

HULL CITY COUNCIL

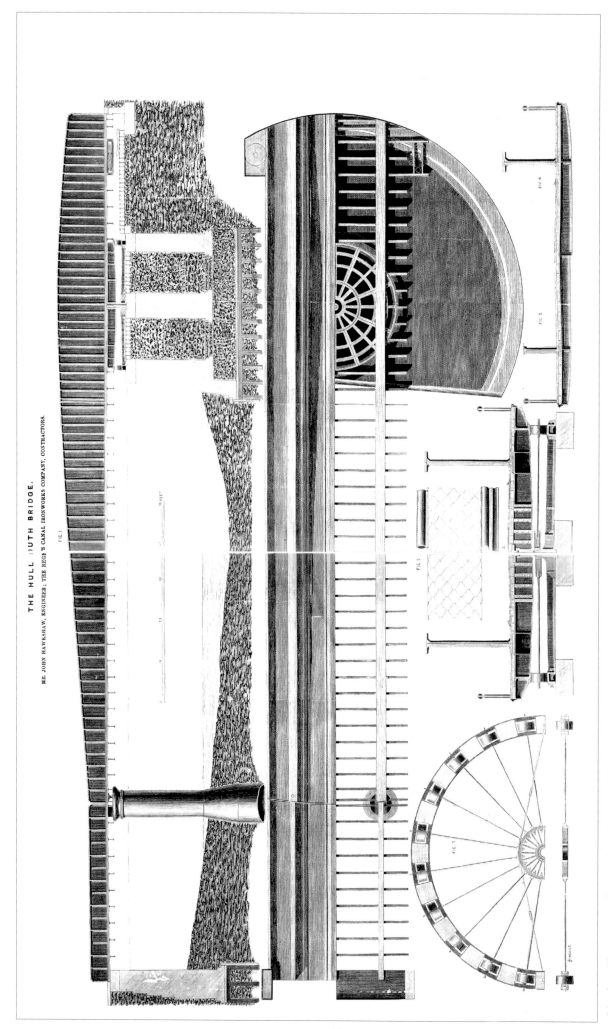

THE HULL SOUTH BRIDGE.

MR. JOHN HAWKSHAW, ENGINEER; THE REGN'S CANAL IRONWORKS COMPANY, CONTRACTORS.

This plate illustrates Hull's South Bridge over the River Hull – the *Ha'Penny Bridge* – opened on 16 October 1867 and which ultimately became the responsibility of the LNER. The illustration is taken from *Modern Examples of Road and Railway Bridges* by William Henry Maw (1838-1924) and James Dredge (1840-1906), published in 1872. The bridge was closed on 31 December 1934 but not demolished until 1944.

42

3. The Western Docks

Sir John Hawkshaw 1811-1891

Following the opening of Victoria Dock in 1850 and its subsequent extensions, the HDC turned its attention once more to the area west of the River Hull for further development of what became known as the Western Docks with direct access from the River Humber. First on the scene was Albert Dock for which statutory powers were obtained in 1861 (Note 31). In 1862 the HDC appointed Sir John Hawkshaw (1811-1891) as its consulting engineer in which capacity he was retained until his retirement in 1888.

Hawkshaw had been responsible for the enlargements to Victoria Dock and its timber ponds previously mentioned, also for the South Bridge over the River Hull which connected Blackfriargate with South Bridge Road. The bridge consisted of two parts: a swinging span on the eastern side which, when opened, gave a waterway clearance of 100ft and a fixed span on the opposite side with a clear span of 40ft. The support for the swing bridge, which weighed 800 tons, was a brick pier resting upon timber piles driven to a depth of about 60ft below high water spring tides. The west end of the swinging portion rested on two cast iron caissons filled with concrete, also sunk to a depth of 60ft. These caissons also supported the span of the fixed bridge at its eastern extremity. There were two walkways and a roadway for horse drawn traffic and the bridge could also accommodate horse drawn railway wagons, although quite why the latter facility was warranted is unclear as the bridge was not opened until 16 October 1867, some 14 years after the opening of the Victoria Dock Branch. Perhaps there was limited rail traffic to the Humber Iron Works and adjacent shipyards on the north bank of the Humber between the River Hull

and Victoria Dock. A report in the *Hull Packet* for 28 February 1868 refers to traffic by railway wagons forming a considerable source of revenue as *soon as the tramway approaches to the bridge are complete* but I have been unable to prove that the approach tracks were actually laid. An 1890 Ordnance Survey does not show any line of railway across the bridge but does show a railway along South Bridge Road which is connected to the Victoria Dock rail network. The construction of the bridge was executed by Henry Grissell (1817-1883) of the Regent's Canal Ironworks. The moveable portion was originally worked by hand but the hand-operated mechanism was soon replaced by hydraulic machinery. The bridge replaced a ferry and its prime purpose was to make it easier for workers to reach Victoria Dock. It was promoted by the Hull South Bridge Company, whose shareholders included the HDC and the NER. Tolls were levied for its use and it quickly became known as the Ha'penny Bridge with reference to the toll originally charged for pedestrians. The demise of the bridge is covered in Chapter Seven.

Albert Dock

Construction of Albert Dock, first referred to as the Western Dock, began in October 1862 and the first stone of the north dock wall was laid on 21 May 1864 by William Wright (1812-1884), deputy chairman of the HDC. There was a serious incident during the ceremony when a block of stone slipped narrowly missing the deputy chairman who fortunately escaped injury (Note 32). William Wright was appointed chairman in 1866 and served in that capacity until his resignation in 1878. He was knighted in 1869 and lived at Sigglesthorne Hall at Hornsea, no doubt journeying to and from Hull by train.

Sir John Hawkshaw appointed his son John Clarke Hawkshaw (1841-1921) as the resident engineer. He was assisted by Henry Marc Brunel (1842-1903) and John George Gamble (1842-1889). Establishing sound foundations for the dock and lock proved to be very troublesome. The strata included two beds of boulder clay separated by a bed of sand. The top bed of clay and the sand had to be removed. The bottom bed of clay was separated from the chalk strata by another bed of sand some 16ft thick. Considering the great depth of this bed of sand, 80ft below quay level, it did not appear likely to affect the foundations but in the event it caused much delay in carrying out the works. On 17 September 1866 a breach occurred in the river bank letting water into the lockpit which was then under construction. It took nearly four weeks

Sir John Hawkshaw 1811-1891. He was the Hull Dock Company's consulting engineer from 1862 to 1888. He was knighted in 1873.

Albert Dock, the first of Hull's Western Docks was opened on 22 July 1869 by Albert Edward, Prince of Wales, later to become King Edward VII. This scene, from *The Illustrated London News* depicts HMS *Vivid*, a paddle steamer of 1848 vintage, moored in the lock and about to commence a tour of the dock with the royal party on board. The view looks west.

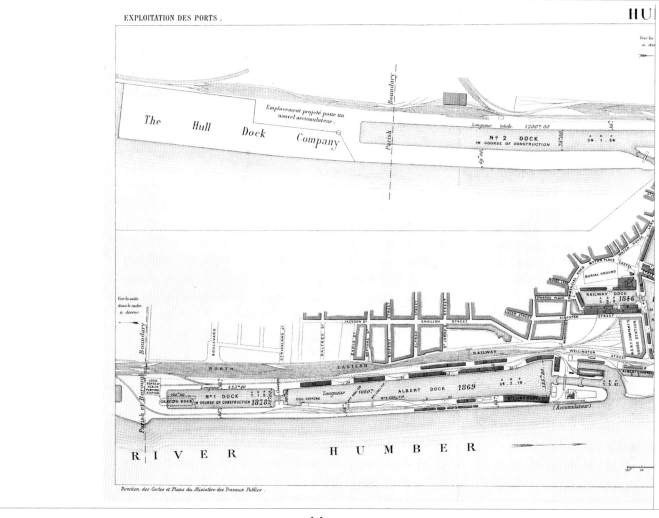

Thanks to the presence of the steam paddle tug *Toby* (73grt), this amazing view of Hull's busy waterfront can be dated between 1883 and 1898 as that is when the tug was registered at Hull. It was built at Greenwich in 1856 and entered on the London register. From 1862 the tug was operated by three Jersey owners but was purchased by a French owner in 1879 and named *Pere X*. The vessel's name reverted to *Toby* in 1882 when acquired by London owners who sold the tug to Thomas Gray (b.1834) of Hull in February 1883. He died on the following 16 April and from then until October 1898 *Toby's* ownership switched between the Hull tug owning families of Gray, Newton and Tulley. Its last Hull owner was William Henry Tulley (1864-1911) who sold it to Woodman Hill, London; its end came in 1904 when it was sold for demolition. The waterfront picture looks west with the River Humber to the left. Victoria Pier is nearest the camera, *Toby's* bow is by the East Pier, which is followed by the West Pier and beyond that is the entrance to Albert Dock. All part of Hull's rich maritime history. [Hull Maritime Museum]

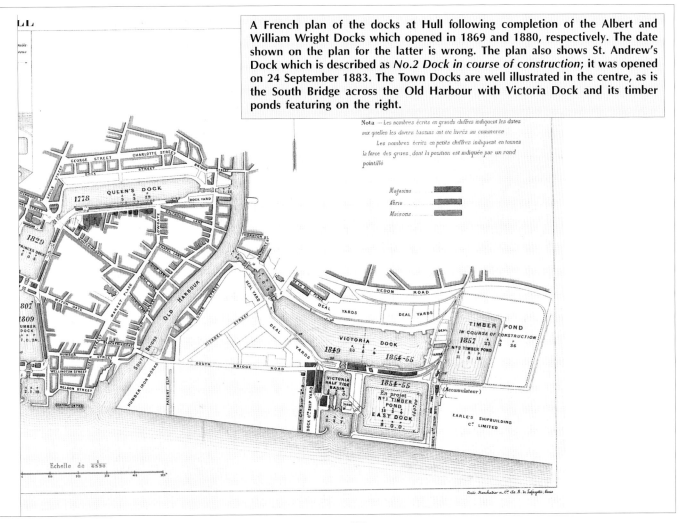

A French plan of the docks at Hull following completion of the Albert and William Wright Docks which opened in 1869 and 1880, respectively. The date shown on the plan for the latter is wrong. The plan also shows St. Andrew's Dock which is described as *No.2 Dock in course of construction*; it was opened on 24 September 1883. The Town Docks are well illustrated in the centre, as is the South Bridge across the Old Harbour with Victoria Dock and its timber ponds featuring on the right.

This is a 1952 view of Albert Dock looking west with the River Humber to the left. The accumulator house for the hydraulic mains was very much a distinctive feature. The nearest vessel is Argo Line's *Drossel* (999grt) trading to and from Hamburg and Bremen. She was built as *Horneck* in 1924 for DG Horn AG of Lübeck and was transferred to Norddeutscher Lloyd with the DG Horn fleet in 1926 and renamed *Drossel*. The ship was transferred to Argo Reederei AG in 1937; she was sold in 1956 and had two further owners before being scrapped in 1965. The other vessel on the far side of the dock is the DFDS vessel *Bergenhus* (1398grt) trading to Copenhagen and other Danish ports. She was built in 1922 and scrapped in 1961. [Ivor Innes Photographers, Hessle]

to repair the breach but the damage was such that work on the lock could not recommence for another three months. On 3 March 1867 a boil appeared not far from the centre line of the lock, near the site of the east sill and a deposit of sand about five feet in diameter rose to the surface. A boil is an unexpected release of water at great pressure from an underground source. A pile of 25ft in length was driven into the centre of the boil and disappeared after only a few hammerings. More boils appeared soon afterwards at regular intervals and it was not until 20 November 1867 that all was made good and the flow of unwanted water reduced to an insignificant quantity. It was proved that the problem had arisen through previous bore holes, nothing whatsoever to do with the construction of the new dock, penetrating the lower bed of boulder clay and piercing the chalk strata below thus destabilising the clay. The total cost of the works for the dock construction was £559,479.

The dock was officially opened on 22 July 1869 and named Albert Dock by Albert Edward, Prince of Wales, later to become King Edward VII. The Prince, his wife and entourage travelled by special train from Manchester to a well decorated Brough station on 21 July arriving at 5.25pm to stay overnight at Brantingham Thorpe Hall, which was then owned by Christopher Sykes, MP (1831-1898), a noted friend of the Prince and a conservative politician. The next day they returned to Brough station to

complete their journey to Hull, departing some 25 minutes late at 12.55 pm for a reception at the Royal Station Hotel. Three balconies, erected at Paragon station, provided standing room for 2,500 spectators and additional balconies had been erected in the station yard to accommodate 5,000 school children and their teachers. After the reception at the hotel, the royal party passed through the entrance to the new dock at 1.45pm to the accompaniment of a royal salute fired by the guard of honour and also by HMS *Dauntless*, which was moored nearby in the Humber. After speeches on behalf of Hull's Danish Residents, the Chamber of Commerce and Hull Trinity House, the Prince named the dock Albert Dock after which a signal was passed to superintendent dock master, Captain Dale Brown (1809-1879), to open the lock gates so that HMS *Vivid*, a paddle steamer of 1848 vintage, could enter the dock. The royal party then boarded the vessel for a tour round the dock prior to returning to the Royal Station Hotel for lunch and more speeches. They departed from Hull Paragon at 3.50pm.

The following description of the dock was given in a paper presented to the Institution of Civil Engineers on 23 March 1875 by Sir William Wright (see Bibliography). *The Albert Dock contains upwards of 24 acres of water space. It is 3,400 feet long, with an average width of 300 feet. The depth of water on the sill at neap tides is 23 feet and at spring tides 28 feet 6 inches. The length of the entrance*

lock is 300 feet and the width 80 feet. This dock is surrounded by lines of railway and has warehouses along its northern quay. The ground-floor of the warehouses is left open, with doors that can be closed if required, so that it can be used for the storage of goods or as sheds [for goods in transit]. *On the north quay there are several ordinary cranes, capable of lifting from 15 tons to 30 tons each, besides hydraulic cranes attached to the warehouses, both in front and behind the buildings. At the east end, on the quays of a creek specially constructed for the purpose, the North Eastern and the Manchester, Sheffield and Lincolnshire Railway Companies have shipping places, with cranes and other conveniences.* The dock was equipped with its own power supply consisting of three boilers supplying steam to a 40hp steam engine which powered the hydraulically operated machinery. This included the warehouse cranes, capstans, the lock gates and a swing bridge over the lockpit designed to carry both road and rail traffic. All of this equipment was manufactured by Sir W.G. Armstrong & Co, Elswick Engine Works, Newcastle-upon-Tyne. The lock gates were made of wrought iron with heel posts, mitre posts and sill pieces of greenheart timber. Part of the route of the old Hull & Selby railway had to be diverted to accommodate the new dock which was connected to the NER system at its western extremity. The creek referred to by Sir William had to be constructed to replace the old railway wharf in Limekiln Creek which had been

Left. A close up of the accumulator house with its clock tower and two of its four clock faces. The North Eastern Railway invited tenders for its construction in 1907 and it was completed the following year. NER chief architect William Bell (1844-1919) was responsible for its design. It survived the Second World War but was demolished as part of the scheme to reconstruct the south side of Albert Dock and Riverside Quay on which work commenced in 1955. The ship to the right is the *Audacia* (499grt) registered and built at Overschie, near Rotterdam in 1951; she was sold for the first time in 1963 and renamed *Pioneer* and then had no less than six further owners before being broken up in Lebanon as *Hassan* in 1998. [Ivor Innes Photographers, Hessle]

Below. This creek at the east end of Albert Dock was specially constructed for the Manchester, Sheffield and Lincolnshire Railway to replace the old railway wharf in Limekiln Creek when the area occupied by that was required by the Hull Dock Company for the construction of the new dock. It is seen here circa 1913 in Great Central Railway days, as evidenced by the GCR lighter which was built in 1903.

The loading of this Ruston & Hornsby 165DS class 0-4-0 diesel-mechanical locomotive is taking place on the north side of Albert Dock in 1951 using a 40 ton capacity hydraulic crane. The locomotive is probably Maker's No.310083 which went to Oslo in September in 1951. The vessel receiving the locomotive is the steamship *Tejo* (1125grt) which was built in 1948 by James Lamont & Co Ltd at the Castle Yard, Port Glasgow, Yard No.365, for Norwegian owner E.B. Aaby's Rederi A/S, Oslo. The accumulator house with its clock tower is prominent in the background. [Ivor Innes Photographers, Hessle]

Albert Dock in 1969, looking east with the refurbished south quay and its bank of semi-portal electric travelling cranes to the right, contrasting very markedly with the surviving hydraulic crane on the north quay. The hydraulic power for the Western and Town Docks was generated at Albert Street Pumping Station and No.2 Pumping Station near St. Andrew's Dock. [Ivor Innes Photographers, Hessle]

acquired by the NER and was used by the Manchester, Sheffield & Lincolnshire Railway (MSLR) for a lighterage service giving access to all the Hull docks. The new creek was known as Railway Creek. The MSLR, later known as the Great Central Railway, had running powers over the NER from Thorne Junction to Hull for all traffic, except coal and had a substantial goods depot adjacent to Kingston Street. Other railways having running powers to Hull over the NER included the Lancashire & Yorkshire Railway (LYR) from Goole for passenger and merchandise traffic and the London & North Western Railway (LNWR) from Leeds for all traffic. Hull's first coal hoist was installed in Albert Dock and by 1913 there were three others all used for shipping coal from railway wagons and bunkering steam ships.

William Wright Dock

In 1866, while construction of Albert Dock was continuing apace, the HDC obtained statutory powers to extend it to the west (Note 33). Construction of the extension began in 1873 with John Hawkshaw as consulting engineer. The contract for the excavation was let to John Bayliss & Son but the whole of the masonry work was undertaken by the HDC using direct labour under the superintendence of the company's engineer, Robert Aspland Marillier (1825-1903). The foundation stone was formally laid on 19 April 1876 by Sir William Wright, after whom the dock has always been known. The extension had a water area of 8½ acres and was 1,390ft long and 220ft wide; the entrance from Albert Dock being 50ft wide. Its opening on 24 May 1880 was a very low key affair. The ceremony was performed by Lt. Col. Joseph Walker Pease (1820-1882) who had replaced Sir William as chairman of the HDC in 1879. Shortly after 1.30pm on the opening day Pease and his fellow directors embarked on the company's tug *Active* which was moored on the north side of the Albert Dock lockpit. The *Active* followed by HDC tug *Lively* then steamed swiftly to

the west end of the dock were the directors were landed. There was then some delay while the screw steamer *Essex* in the ownership of Bailey & Leetham was towed towards the new dock by the Hull registered tug *True Briton* which was owned by Thomas Gray (1834-1883). The chairman then pulled on a lever which opened the bridge spanning the passageway between the two docks; the party then re-embarked on the *Active* which entered the new dock, followed by the *Lively* and the *Essex*. The *Essex* (1184grt) was built by Humphrey & Pearson of Hull (Yard No.7) in 1869 and along with other ships in the ownership of Bailey & Leetham, became part of the Wilson Line fleet when Bailey & Leetham was acquired by Thos Wilson Sons & Co Ltd on 29 July 1903. She was sold in May 1909 for breaking up at Dunkirk, France.

St. Andrew's Dock

St. Andrew's Dock, named after the patron saint of fishermen, was opened on 24 September 1883 and was the last

William Wright Dock, an extension of Albert Dock, was opened on 24 May 1880. This 1930s view shows two steam trawlers undergoing an annual survey in the dry dock located at the west end of William Wright Dock. They were both built at the Grovehill shipyard of Cook, Welton and Gemmell of Beverley: H290 *Tourmaline*, Yard No.282, in 1926 and H115 *Orsino*, Yard No.529, in 1929. *Tourmaline* was owned by Kingston Steam Trawlers Limited until sold in 1939 to Belgian owners at Ostend as *Van Oost*. In May 1940 she fled to Milford Haven and was requisitioned into the Royal Navy as an anti-submarine vessel, returning to the owners in November 1945. In 1948 she was sold to the Polish Government as *Merkury* surviving until broken up in 1962. *Orsino* was managed by Hellyer Bros until sold in 1938 to Dutch owners at Ijmuiden and named *Walrus*. She was requisitioned into the Kriegsmarine in 1940 and sunk on 14 September 1943 by Royal Navy motor torpedo boats west of Scheveningen. [Hull Maritime Museum]

St. Andrew's Dock, named after the patron saint for fishermen, opened on 24 September 1883. This 1954 aerial view looks north and shows the west end of the dock where, on the left under the swing bridge, it joined the St. Andrew's Dock Extension opened in July 1897. The River Humber is in the foreground. The lengthy footbridge spanning the rail tracks to the left of the picture was removed on Sunday, 26 April 1964. [Ivor Innes Photographers, Hessle]

This 1930s view looking east shows a cluster of trawlers at the entrance to St. Andrew's Dock. The one most readily identifiable is H518 *Lorenzo* built by Cook, Welton & Gemmell at Beverley, Yard No.579, in 1933 and managed by Hellyer Bros. She joined the Grimsby fleet in 1939, saw Second World War service with the Admiralty as an anti-submarine trawler and then went back to Hull before joining the Fleetwood fishing fleet. She was broken up at Bruges in 1959. [Hull Maritime Museum]

Loading fish to both road and rail on the north side of St. Andrew's Dock in 1930. The view looks west and the dock is behind the sheds to the left. Note the ex North Eastern Railway 0-4-0 tank engine carefully shunted so that its chimney is just outside the shed entrance. The motor lorry in the foreground with the registration number BJ5208 belonged to George William Lamb (1862-1930) of The Fold, Hessle High Road, Hull. [Hull Maritime Museum]

dock to be constructed by the HDC. It was built with powers obtained under the Hull Docks Act 1867 (Note 34) as a further extension of the western docks system with a separate entrance from the Humber to the west of Albert and William Wright Docks. The dock was constructed under the same arrangement as applied to the William Wright Dock with John Hawkshaw as the consulting engineer and Marillier as the resident engineer using direct labour employed by the HDC Company to execute the masonry works. The dock had a water area of ten acres and was 1,901ft long and 250ft wide. The lock was 250 in length with a width of 50ft; the depth of water on the sill at average spring tides being 28ft 6in reducing to 23ft 6in on neaps, similar to the situation at Albert Dock. The lock gates and sluices and a road/rail swing bridge over the lock were all worked by hydraulic power (Note 35). The dock, which cost £414,707 to build, was dedicated to the

fishing industry which hitherto had been based in Albert Dock.

In spite of inclement weather with 'incessant and unusually heavy' rain, the opening was a grand affair. Between 11am and 12 noon the HDC directors and their guests boarded the Hull Trinity House steam yacht *Duke of Edinburgh* and the paddle steamer *Isle of Axholme* at the East Pier in the Humber Dock basin. The chairman, John Raspin Ringrose (1822-1905) – successor to Pease – boarded the *Duke of Edinburgh* which was dressed overall and flew the HDC's flag (Note 36). He was accompanied by the master warden and elder brethren of Hull Trinity House and a number of boys from the navigation school. The deputy chairman, Edward Philip Maxsted (1828-1903), with the other directors and their guests boarded the *Isle of Axholme* which was owned by the Gainsborough United Steam Packet Company and normally plied between Hull and Gainsborough. She too was

dressed overall and was followed by four fishing sailing smacks and a steam cutter under tow of the company's tugs. The dignitaries were landed at the new lock entrance where chairman Ringrose was invited to open the dock. After the ceremony the swing bridge across the lock was swung open and the *Duke of Edinburgh* and the *Isle of Axholme* entered the dock followed by the tug *Active* towing fishing smacks *Beaconsfield* and *Sir Stafford Northcoate*. Having made a circuit of the dock, the Trinity House yacht and the paddle steamer returned to the East Pier. The directors and guests then proceeded to the HDC's office where luncheon was served to about 120 people. When the dock was opened the Hull fishing fleet numbered about 420 smacks of 70-75ft in length. Hull's first steam trawler, the *Magenta*, was built in Hull at Cook, Welton & Gemmell's yard in 1885 for F&T Ross. By 1903 the Hull fishing fleet consisted entirely of steam trawlers.

Dock Offices

The HDC's most lasting legacy to Hull must be its magnificent Dock Office which forms the centre piece of the city and very appropriately now forms the Hull Maritime Museum. On 8 December 1865 the *Hull Packet* carried the following advertisement which had probably also occurred in earlier issues:

TO ARCHITECTS

The Directors of the Dock Company, at Kingston-upon-Hull, are prepared to receive Designs for a **NEW DOCK OFFICE**, proposed to be erected in Junction-street, in the said Borough, for which they will award the following premiums, viz.: £100 to the design they may consider to stand first in order of merit, and £50 to the second-best design.
A Plan of the site, and full particulars may be obtained at the Dock Office, Hull, on and after the 20th of November, 1865. Designs to be sent in not later than the 20th day of January, 1866.
By Order,
W.H. HUFFAM,
Secretary
Dock Office, Hull,
10th November 1865.

The winning candidate was Christopher George Wray (1828-1913) who was born in Cleasby, North Yorkshire. He was a Fellow of the Royal Institute of British Architects and became Civil Architect to the Government of Bombay. He was present at the laying of the foundation stone which took place on 20 April 1868 when he ceremoniously submitted the drawings and plans of the building to the chairman of the HDC, William Wright. The chairman then set about laying the foundation stone using a golden trowel, the handle of which was embellished with precious stones. The trowel bore on the upper side of its blade the following inscription: *Presented* to Wm. Wright, Esq., chairman of the Dock Company at Kingston-upon-Hull, on the occasion of his laying the first stone of the Dock Offices, and in acknowledgement of his great exertions on behalf of the company. 20ᵗʰ April, 1868. After the stone had been laid the chairman was also presented with a mallet, adorned with a suitably inscribed silver plate, with which he set the stone in its place. A parchment previously placed in a bottle underneath the stone recorded the names of all of those present. The proceedings were of a quiet character bearing in mind that the company would shortly incur expenditure on the formal opening of Albert Dock.

The building was opened 'with as little pomp or ostentation as possible' on 5 October 1871. Even so it aroused great interest. The building, in an Italianate style, occupies a triangular plot in the centre of the city which, at the time of its construction, was the epicentre of the dock complex. Indeed its eastern frontage looked out upon Hull's very first dock, Queen's Dock, now Queen's Gardens. The building, now listed, boasts three very distinctive cupolas with ribbed lead domes, topped with domed lanterns and finials. The south cupola has a clock at its base which was supplied by Barnard Cooke (1813-1887), Hull clock maker and optician, of Savile Street. The building is faced with Ancaster ashlar stone whilst the basement is of Bramley Fall stone with the sculptures executed in Portland stone. John Underwood (1820-1915) of London was responsible for the principal sculptures and Thomas Frith (1839-1915) of Hull carved the exterior capitals, friezes and decorative panels. The building was acquired by the City Council in 1968 and converted for use as the Town Docks Museum in 1975, more recently becoming known as Hull Maritime Museum.

Happily the previous dock office also survives. It was located next to the lockpit in Queen's Dock and bears a blue plaque stating that it was built in 1820, although it may have been built sooner. The building and a later extension have two hipped slate roofs, the walls are of red brick with painted ashlar dressings and there is a distinctive wooden cupola with a lead dome, finial and weather vane.

A congested St. Andrew's Dock looking west in 1949; the lock entrance is to the left. Prominent amongst the trawlers is *Kingston Peridot* built by Cook, Welton & Gemmell at Beverley, Yard No.797, in 1948. Sadly she was one of three Hull trawlers all lost in quick succession during January and February 1948. She went missing overnight on 26/27 January and was later found to have sunk off Kopasker, Iceland with the loss of all twenty crew. The trawler to the right of *Kingston Peridot* on the north *market* side of the dock is H572 *Cordella* owned by J. Marr & Son Ltd. She was built by John Lewis & Sons Ltd at the Torry Yard in Aberdeen, Yard No.202, in 1948 and survived until 1965 when she was sold for breaking up at Antwerp. [Ivor Innes Photographers, Hessle]

Kits of fish being loaded to rail vans and road transport in St. Andrew's dock in 1952. Note that a solitary horse and cart patiently waits attention amongst the plethora of motor vehicles. [Ivor Innes Photographers, Hessle]

Assisted by steam tug *Gilder*, the stern trawler *Lord Nelson* is returning to St. Andrew's Dock in 1961 after her maiden voyage to the Barents Sea and Bear Island which commenced on 19 July that year with Skipper Walter Lewis in command. The vessel was built by Rickmer Werft, Bremerhaven for the West Dock Steam Fishing Co (Associated Fisheries) and survived in the Hull fleet until laid up by British United Trawlers in 1980. She was scrapped in October 1981 by Drapers of Hull. The tug was one of five ex TID tugs which worked the fish dock; they were owned by the Hull Steam Trawlers Mutual Insurance & Protection Co Ltd. In 1943 the Ministry of War Transport decided to introduce a new class of tug using a new technique of pre-fabricated sections for their construction that were welded together, rather than riveted. They became known as TID (technical and industrial development) tugs and a total of 182 were built. *Gilder*, originally TID 87 was completed by Richard Dunston at Thorne in 1944, Yard No.496, acquiring her name in 1946 and surviving until broken up at New Holland in 1963. [Ivor Innes Photographers, Hessle]

Above. This image from an original painting by Adrian Thompson is dominated by the Dock Office built for the Hull Dock Company and opened on 5 October 1871. The view circa 1910 looks down King Edward Street towards Monument Bridge with the William Wilberforce monument on its original site to the left. The tram displaying the Route B sign ran via Beverley Road and the one with the Route S sign ran via Spring Bank.

The Hull Dock Office bedecked for the Coronation of Queen Elizabeth II which took place on 2 June 1953. The building is now the Hull Maritime Museum. [Ivor Innes Photographers, Hull]

This quintessentially Hull scene was taken from the deck of a ship entering Hull's Humber Dock which was opened in 1809 and closed to commercial traffic in 1967. Pedestrian traffic is held up as the ship passes through the lockpit with the swing bridge swung to permit access for the ship. The Dock Master's house is prominent in the centre of the picture. The vessel with the yellow funnel immediately behind the house is the pilot cutter *J.H. Fisher* (461grt) built by Earle's of Hull in 1931. She had probably entered the dock to take on bunker coal and was waiting to sail. The cutter sank off Spurn Head on 12 January 1963 after the tanker *Esso Glasgow* (10297grt) ran into her. The classic steamer berthed at the north east end of the dock with the buff funnel with a red band and a black top is Associated Humber Lines vessel *Bury* (1634grt) operating between Hull and Rotterdam. She was also built by Earle's (Yard No. 569) but much earlier for the Great Central Railway, being launched by Winifred May, daughter of General Manager, Sam Fay, on 10 November 1910. The ship was taken out of service in 1958. Humber Dock now forms part of the Hull Marina. [Courtesy, Tony Ward, Topcolor Fotoworx, Hull]

The original Hull Dock Company offices in Dock Office Row, now a Grade II listed building.

Charles Henry Wilson (1833-1907) as he appeared in *Vanity Fair* on 21 February 1885. The caricaturist was Carlo Pellegrini (1839-1889) known by the pseudonym *Ape*.

4. Prelude to Change

Unease and discontent

Great as was the work accomplished by the Hull Dock Company, its efforts had not, in the opinion of many people, kept pace with the demands of the growing commerce of the port. On the one hand, the Dock Company were charged with not moving with the requisite celerity, and on the other, the North Eastern Railway Company, which alone had direct communication with the port, was charged with favouring Hartlepool and the Tyne ports, to the detriment of Hull. Those words can be found in *Bulmer's Gazetteer* published in 1892. They refer to a period of unease that began in the early 1860s and festered for some 25 years. The main protagonists for the discontent were Hull Corporation and Hull based ship-owners who perceived the NER and the HDC as having monopolies prejudicial to the trade of Hull and advantageous to rival ports.

Readers wishing to know more about this conflict, particularly the part played by the Hull Corporation, are referred to a thesis by Keith Nolan as submitted to the University of York for the Degree of Doctor of Philosophy in September 2006. It is available on line and is entitled *Municipal Politics and Regional Monopoly: Railways and the Port of Hull, 1840-1922.* The thesis examines *the singular and robust civic involvement in railways and docks at Hull.* It describes an amazing turnabout. After the Corporation's adulation for the HDC and the arrival of the railways in earlier years, there was now outright criticism of those who had invested heavily in the port and railway infrastructure. There were several catalysts for this conflict.

Hull West Dock Company

In 1860 a group of local ship-owners and merchants with the support of the NER and Hull Corporation formed a rival dock company with the title Hull West Dock Company. The prospectus proposed a capital of £400,000 in 20,000 shares of £20 each and stated that the accommodation provided by the HDC had been and still was inadequate for the rapidly expanding traffic. The rival company proposed to construct a dock to the west of the Humber Dock basin and in 1861 promoted a Bill in Parliament for that purpose but it was withdrawn when the HDC successfully promoted its Bill in the same parliamentary session for the construction of Albert Dock. The possibility of a rival undoubtedly spurred the old company into a new phase of dock development which led not only to the construction of the Western Docks but also the enlargement of Victoria Dock and its timber storage facilities which have already been described.

The HDC's Act of 1861 was subject to several conditions, the principal one

of which required the company to consent to the sale and transfer of its undertaking to a public body in the event of Hull Corporation promoting legislation for that purpose and giving security for the payment of the purchase money. In 1866 Hull Corporation, having petitioned unsuccessfully against the HDC's proposal to raise more capital, introduced a Bill for the vesting of the docks in trustees. The Bill was opposed by the HDC and by the principal rate payers who did not want to be saddled with the financial burden of purchasing and maintaining the docks, thereby resulting in a massive hike in local rates. The Bill was lost.

Hull, South & West Junction Railway

In October 1872 a serious blockage of traffic occurred on the NER at Hull causing delays to goods, passenger and fish traffic. The congestion on the line was widely reported in the press as far afield as Scotland and Northern Ireland. This resulted in a vicious attack on the perceived NER monopoly by the merchants and ship-owners under the banner of the Hull Chamber of Commerce and Shipping supported, of course, by Hull Corporation, excepting Alderman John Lumsden (1805-1876) who had just been elected as a director of the NER! At a meeting of the Chamber held on 23 October 1872 Frederick Brent Grotrian (1838-1905), a leading merchant and ship-owner proposed a new railway to Hull. The proposal manifested itself in the Hull, South and West Junction Railway with a capital of £960,000 in 96,000 shares of £10 each. Provisional directors included Grotrian, Christopher Sykes MP and Hull ship-owners Henry John Atkinson (1828-1913) of Wm. Brown, Atkinson & Co and Charles Henry Wilson (1833-1907) of the Wilson Line.

The proposed railway was planned to start on the east side of Hull heading westwards to a point where it turned south and tunnelled for over one and a half miles under the Humber. This is how the prospectus described the route: *The proposed Railway will pass by a tunnel under the Humber, between Hessle and Barton, and by the Valley of the Ancholme to Brigg, and thence via the Manchester, Sheffield and Lincolnshire Railway, to the Great Northern Station at Retford, thereby avoiding delay, and affording a new route between Hull and London, shorter than the existing route by not less than 15 miles. A branch will leave the main line near Appleby, opening a passage over the South Yorkshire Railway to the Great Northern Station at Doncaster, and thence reaching Manchester, Liverpool and other parts of Lancashire.* A short curve was also proposed from the South Yorkshire at Barnby Dun to the Lancashire and

Yorkshire Railway at Askern. Clearly the project was very much dependent upon obtaining running powers over the lines of existing railway companies.

The engineer chosen to build the new line was John Fowler (1817-1898). He had this to say about the proposed tunnel: *The crossing of the River Humber is the only important work upon the main line or any of the branches, and it is satisfactory to know that at the point selected the depth of water is small, the materials extremely favourable, and the total length of tunnel only one mile and five eights. With well-known modern appliances and experience this work can be easily executed, and safe calculations made as to time; and for the cost ample provision has been made in the estimate.* Fowler's estimate of the cost of the entire undertaking was £960,000.

The NER was alarmed and extremely annoyed at the proposal. Its deputy chairman, George Leeman (1809-1882), one-time arch opponent of George Hudson, voiced his anger at the ingratitude of Hull, stressing that the NER had only recently at great expense opened its new and shorter route to London via Goole and Doncaster. The NER naturally opposed the Bill for the new railway but on 23 May 1873 it was passed by committee in the House of Commons. The MSLR and the LYR had petitioned against the proposed running powers over their lines but the MSLR had latterly moved to a more neutral position. The NER set about reinvigorating opposition from the MSLR by giving it full running powers into Hull and supporting proposals for it to build its own goods depot which it eventually did on NER land at Hull Kingston Street. However, when the Bill came before the House of Lords committee on 3 July 1873, the NER concentrated its attack on the feasibility of the tunnel under the Humber. Fowler's design was for a brick lined tunnel only 10ft below the riverbed using a pneumatic caisson for its construction; the method proposed had not previously been used for an underwater tunnel. The HDC's consulting engineer, Sir John Hawkshaw, was engaged to appear for the NER and he asserted that it would be impossible to lay watertight brickwork in those circumstances. After hearing the evidence, the Lords considered that the scheme was too experimental and on 23 July rejected the Bill. On 30 August Hawkshaw was knighted by Queen Victoria at Balmoral. The NER had triumphed much to the chagrin of its opponents but its prowess was not to last for much longer.

Pressure from the Wilson Line

The Wilson Line founded in 1831 by

Borodino (1970grt) was the second of three Wilson Line ships to carry the name. She was launched by Earle's Shipbuilding & Engineering Company of Hull (Yard No.579) on 24 August 1911 and is seen here on the north side of Hull's Albert Dock. When first built she had accommodation for 27 first class passengers. The vessel was sold to the Admiralty on 26 September 1939 and sunk on 27 May 1940 as a blockship at Zeebrugge during the German invasion of the Low Countries. [Hull Maritime Museum]

Thomas Wilson (1792-1869) became Hull's largest shipping company. After Thomas's death on 21 June 1869, two of his sons, Charles Henry Wilson and Arthur Wilson (1836-1909) jointly managed the business with the eldest son, David Wilson (1815-1893) as a non-executive director (Note 37). Charles became a director of the HDC in 1869 and was appointed to the NER Board on 13 February 1874, no doubt with a view to getting him on side following the debacle of the proposed Hull, South and West Junction Railway. From 1869 onwards there was a general deterioration in the relationship between the Wilson Line both with the NER and the HDC. This no doubt also reflected the views of other ship-owners and merchants. With regard to dock accommodation it was argued that the existing docks were not sufficiently deep or wide enough for the next new generation of steamships.

In 1873 the NER proposed to strengthen its position against possible interlopers by proposing a line from Hull through Kirkella to join with its existing line at Staddlethorpe which would have given an alternative route to Hull. Following strong opposition by the Hull Corporation and the Hull Chamber of Commerce & Shipping, the proposal was lost. It was argued that the new line would require several level crossings which would add to an ongoing congestion problem with

regard to road traffic. Behind the scenes those with vested interests did not want to give up on the idea of a competing railway company.

In 1878 the HDC, still under pressure from ship-owners and merchants, promoted an omnibus Bill which included a proposal to purchase some 400 acres of land and construct a deep-water dock at Salt End to the east of Hull and outside the town boundary. Charles Wilson was a keen advocate of the scheme and it had strong support from the NER who would build a line to serve the new dock. True to form Hull Corporation opposed the initiative but following bad publicity agreed not to oppose it provided that the HDC would pursue an alternative scheme on land offered by the Corporation. The HDC did not agree to this and proceeded with its Bill. The preamble of the Bill was proved but due to the opposition from Hull Corporation several onerous conditions were imposed in the Corporation's favour which caused dissention amongst the HDC directors. One of the directors, the wealthiest banker in Hull, Lt Colonel Gerard Smith, proposed that the matter be put to the shareholders who included not only the NER but also the MSLR and the LYR. However, another director successfully opposed this and Smith withdrew his proposal. The board then decided to withdraw the entire Bill without consulting the shareholders. By

the end of the year the plans for the new dock were in ruins.

On 14 December 1878, William Wright chairman of the HDC and a director for some 30 years wrote from Algiers tendering his resignation with effect from the next annual meeting which took place on 3 February 1879. He resigned on the grounds of ill health which was why he was in Algiers recuperating in a warmer climate. His resignation was accepted and he was replaced by Colonel Joseph Walker Pease who, as mentioned above, opened William Wright Dock on 24 May 1880. The change of chairmanship changed the political persuasion of the HDC board. Wright, Charles Wilson and Gerard Smith were staunch liberals whereas Pease was a conservative in every sense of the word. Nolan in his thesis sums the situation up admirably: *The facts, obvious to all, were that the progressive liberals on the Dock Company board, Smith, the wealthiest banker in Hull and Wilson, the largest ship-owner, were both strongly in favour of a new dock. Had Wright stayed at the helm, the dock scheme may have been resurrected, but the appointment of Pease estranged both Smith and Wilson and took the Dock Company back to the days of complacency and inertia. The NER could do little but stand by and watch the Dock Company commit commercial suicide. An era of railway and dock monopoly was about to end.*

Left. Sir John Fowler (1817-1898) was the Engineer for the abortive Hull, South & West Junction Railway which included a brick lined tunnel, one mile 1,100 yards in length under the River Humber. Fowler supported the concept even though the tunnel roof would have been only ten feet below the bed of the river.

Below. The proposed railway tunnel would have gone under the River Humber between Hessle on the north bank and Barton on the south bank, following a very similar alignment to the Humber Bridge seen here. The bridge was formerly opened by HM Queen Elizabeth II on 17 July 1981 but had actually already been opened to traffic some weeks earlier on 24 June. The view looks south and the former Hull & Selby Railway can be seen hugging the Hessle foreshore towards the bottom left of the picture. Barton is to the right on the river's south bank.

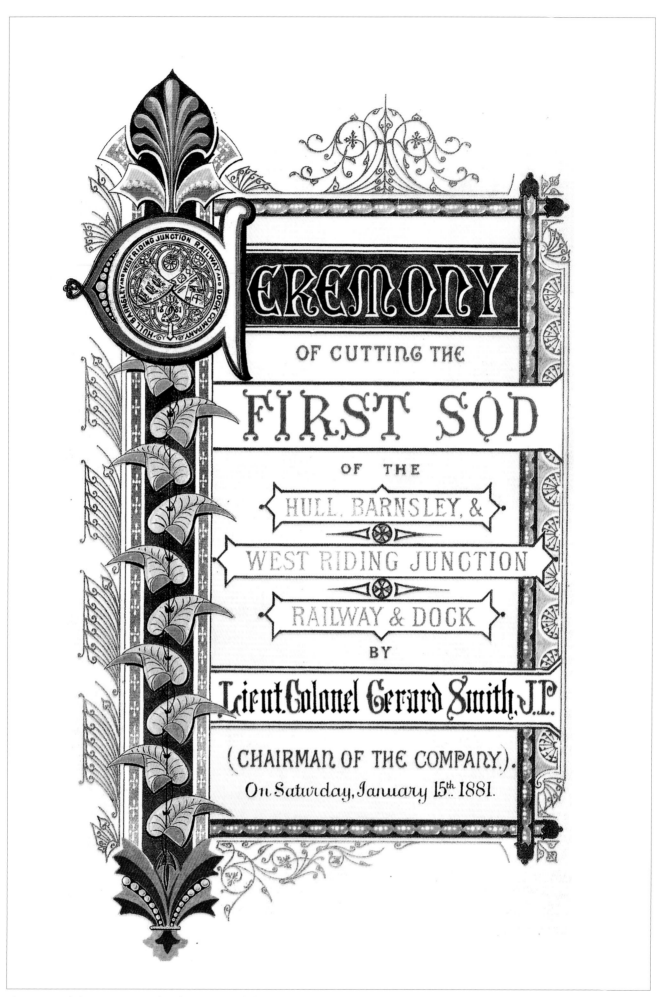

CEREMONY
OF CUTTING THE
FIRST SOD
OF THE
HULL, BARNSLEY, &
WEST RIDING JUNCTION
RAILWAY & DOCK
BY
Lieut. Colonel Gerard Smith, J.P.
(CHAIRMAN OF THE COMPANY.)
On Saturday, January 15th 1881.

The cover of the programme for the cutting of the first sod of the Hull, Barnsley & West Riding Junction Railway & Dock on 15 January 1881. [ABP]

5. Hull and Barnsley Railway

Hull, Barnsley & West Riding Junction Railway & Dock Company

The Act authorising the Hull, Barnsley & West Riding Junction Railway & Dock Company received the royal assent on 26 August 1880, only some 18 months after the Salt End dock scheme was scuppered. This was something very different, not only did it authorise a new independent railway of 66 miles in length, including branches, but also a new deep water dock outwith the control of the HDC. The new dock with a water area of 46½ acres was constructed to the east of Victoria Dock with an entrance from the Humber. It was named Alexandra Dock after Danish born Alexandra, Princess of Wales, whose husband became King Edward VII. Needless to say the leading player in the project was Gerard Smith closely supported by Charles Wilson and other ship-owners, with the full backing of Hull Corporation.

The New Railway

The principal line of the new railway as authorised ran from Stairfoot Junction on the MSLR and from Cudworth on the Midland Railway. Passenger traffic on the line was always meagre, even after the introduction of an express

service to Sheffield in October 1905. Its raison d'être was coal! The line crossed the River Ouse at Drax by means of a large swing bridge and then proceeded to cut its way across the Yorkshire Wolds. Stations east of the River Ouse were located at Howden (24 miles), Eastrington (21 miles), Sandholme (19 miles), Newport (18 miles - Note 38), North Cave (15 miles), South Cave (14 miles), Little Weighton (9 miles) and Beverley Road (1 mile). Barmby to the west of Howden (28 miles) was added later and opened on 1 February 1897. The mileages shown are from Hull Cannon Street which was the terminus for the passenger service. It had three platform roads but was always a very poor relation to its NER equivalent at Paragon. Indeed, it was adapted as a temporary expedient from a carriage shed and remained very little altered throughout its life. The original proposal to have a passenger terminus at Kingston Square was aborted when the cash ran out! There were three tunnels: Weedley (132 yards), Sugar Loaf (132 yards) and Drewton (2,116 yards). Another significant feature was the cutting at Little Weighton which was made through chalk with a maximum depth of 83 feet and a length of about

This marble bust of Lt. Col. Gerard Smith (1839-1920) is displayed in Hull's Guildhall. It was sculptured by William Day Keyworth Jnr (1843-1902) who was born in Hull. He followed the profession of both his father and grandfather and became responsible for a variety of works in Hull, Leeds and elsewhere. Unfortunately in later life he suffered financial problems and committed suicide. [Guildhall: Hull Museums]

Lt. Col. Gerard Smith, with silver spade and polished oak barrow, cuts the first sod on the site of Alexandra Dock with the Mayor of Hull, Alderman John Leake (1831-1895) looking on in his robes. *Although snow covered the ground to a depth of several inches, many thousands of persons assembled to witness the ceremony*. This illustration first appeared in *The Illustrated London News* for 22 January 1881.

This construction scene on the railway towards the western end of the line shows one of Lucas and Aird's Manning Wardle six-coupled saddle tanks with a string of wagons on the lightly laid contractor's temporary track. The engine is equipped with two sets of buffers. The view looks east towards Hull on the site of Upton & North Elmsall station. [Cox/Hull History Museum]

Little Smeaton, looking west towards Barnsdale with a Manning Wardle four-coupled saddle tank, its driver and attendant navvies. The engine is only equipped with dumb buffers. [Cox/Hull History Museum]

An inspection party at a bridge near Norton which includes Lt. Col. Gerrard Smith with his mutton chop side whiskers, seen second from the right. [Cox/Hull History Centre]

three quarters of a mile. The route chosen did not favour loaded coal trains bound for the new dock, as shortly after passing Newport they were handicapped with a seven mile assent at a grade of 1 in 150 terminating at the eastern end of Drewton Tunnel which, at 262 feet above sea level, was the summit level of the railway.

A wonderful official photographic record of the railway construction is deposited with the Hull History Museum. It is attributed to Nottingham photographer Alfred Wilson Cox (1830-1888) but he moved away from Nottingham in 1876 leaving his wife and sons to run the business. The person most likely to have taken the photographs is his son Alfred Cox (1854-1929) who in 1881 was employing two men, two boys and a lady. The boys might well have assisted to carry the heavy cases of glass plates used for the negatives. A number of the images are reproduced here to illustrate the practices and equipment used in the construction of the railway and Alexandra Dock.

The contractors, Lucas and Aird, used a fleet of industrial locomotives to assist in constructing the railway and dock. No less than 28 engines were purchased from Manning, Wardle & Co Ltd of the Boyne Engine Works, Leeds between April 1881 and April 1883. Six were delivered to Cudworth, one to Howden (NER) and the remainder to Hull. There were twelve outside-cylinder 0-4-0 saddle tanks (one of Class E and eleven of Class D); eleven inside-cylinder 0-6-0

saddle tanks of Class K and five outside-cylinder 0-6-0 saddle tanks of Class M. In addition an 0-4-0 well tank was purchased from Kitson & Co Ltd of the Airdale Foundry at Leeds, Maker's No.2363. It was delivered on 3 October 1881 and may have prompted the HBR to purchase six similar engines from Kitsons for shunting Alexandra Dock (see below). The HBR established two principal goods depots at Hull, one at Neptune Street, reached by a branch from Springbank West and North Junctions and the other at Alexandra Dock. Goods traffic was also handled from the outset at Cannon Street and Sculcoates where the British Gas Light & Coke Company Limited had a siding. Other goods facilities were added later to cope with increased demand: Burleigh Street in 1896, Dairycoates in 1905 and Ella Street in 1906. The principal traffic at the latter was landsale coal but the siding also provided access to the Wool Sheds and a connection to the National Radiator Company's private siding. The new railway was always known as the Hull & Barnsley and on 30 June 1905 the name of the company was changed by Act of Parliament (Note 39) to the Hull & Barnsley Railway (HBR) thereby shortening its original cumbersome title. Even the new title was something of a misnomer as the company's lines never actually reached Barnsley!

The engineer for the railway was Sir William Shelford (1834-1905) and the contractor for the construction of the

railway and the new dock was the firm of Lucas & Aird which had been formed in the 1860s by the partnership of Charles Thomas Lucas (1820-1895) and John Aird (1834-1911). They were very experienced in railway and dock work both at home and aboard. The contract with Lucas & Aird was for four years from 1 January 1881 to 1 January 1885. With the exception of the Barry Railway in South Wales, the HBR was the youngest of the major pre-grouping railway companies. The extent of the railway based on its entry in *The Railway Year Book for 1921* is shown on the accompanying map by the late Roger Hateley which shows its connections west of the River Ouse, lines partly owned and leased and lines over which running powers were exercised. It also shows the many collieries directly served by the HBR.

Within the Hull area the line was built on an embankment to avoid the need for level crossings and so the line was well endowed with underbridges both large and small, there being no less than 35 within the city boundary. With the exception of the line from Hull to Selby all other existing railway lines in Hull had to be bridged. Travelling from west to east the first railway to be bridged was the line from Hull to Bridlington just after Springbank North Junction, this was quickly followed by the bridge over the line from Hull Paragon to Cottingham Junction; then came two bridges over significant highways at Newland Toft Lane (now Newland

Construction continues apace through the Wolds – the view looks west away from Weedley down Drewton Dale towards South Cave. The locomotive could well be an 0-6-0 saddle tank built by Kitson & Co Ltd at the Airedale Foundry, Leeds in 1879, Maker's No.1835, but not delivered to Lucas and Aird until 1881, which fits with the construction of the HBR. An official photograph shows it carrying the name *Airedale*. [Cox/Hull History Centre]

The extent of earthworks required at the eastern end of the line is evidenced by this view which looks west through the excavated chalk on the approach towards Drewton Tunnel. [Cox/Hull History Centre]

The HBR crossed the River Hull over this swing bridge which has a bow-string wrought iron lattice span fabricated by Handyside & Company of the Britannia Ironworks, Derby. It was designed by Sir William Shelford (1834-1905), the engineer responsible for the construction of the railway. The bridge is now a listed structure but still carries trains to and from King George Dock. This 1978 view looks north with the original HBR signal box just glimpsed on the right.

Avenue) and Beverley Road. The inaugural 1880 Act specified that the latter bridge had to be of *an ornamental design to be approved by the Corporation, and the piers and abutments to be parallel with the road.* Just after this the line to Cannon Street station branched off at Beverley Road Junction, going over the Victoria Dock branch on a bow-string bridge before reaching the terminus. The double-tracked line to Alexandra Dock carried on beyond Beverley Road Junction to cross the River Hull by a swing bridge designed by Shelford. It has a bow-string wrought iron lattice span fabricated by Handyside & Company of the Britannia Ironworks, Derby with the original hydraulic machinery and mechanical parts manufactured by Sir W.G. Armstrong, Mitchell & Company. The bridge became a Grade II listed structure in 1994 and is still used by freight trains passing to and from King George Dock. After crossing the River Hull the HBR crossed the NER branch to Hornsea, the Holderness Road and then the NER branch to Withernsea. The line entered the Alexandra Dock estate after crossing Hedon Road on a Warren truss girder bridge. That type of bridge was named after James Warren (1806-1908) who in 1848 patented the design which incorporates within its construction equilateral triangles which can carry both tension and compression.

Lt. Colonel Sir Gerard Smith 1839-1920

This man, because of his involvement with the new railway and dock, became the subject of much adulation in Hull

gaining the support of everyone apart from the NER and the HDC and so it is time to learn a little more about him. He was born on 12 December 1839 at Eaton Square, Pimlico, London, the third son of Martin Tucker Smith and Louisa, née Ridley. His father was a politician, banker and a director of the East India Company. Educated at Eton, Gerard Smith joined the Scots Fusilier Guards and in 1862-1864 took part in securing the garrison at New Brunswick, Canada during increasing tensions with the United States resulting from the American Civil War. On 4 May 1871 he married Isabella Chatelaine Hamilton and they had two sons and three daughters. On retirement from the army in 1874, having achieved the rank of Lieutenant Colonel, he became a partner in the family firm, Samuel Smith Bros & Company, bankers in Hull since 1784. He and his family lived in style at Tranby Hall, Hessle supported by a small army of servants. He became a major shareholder and a director of the HDC with his firm acting as that company's banker! His position with the company became so untenable that he had to resign his directorship in 1880. He then became the chairman of the new railway and dock company and as such cut the first sod for the new enterprise in Hull on 15 January 1881. The ceremony took place on the site of the new dock and was carried out during a snow fall. Undeterred, some 7,000 spectators watched as the Colonel cut the first sod using a silver mounted spade and an oak wheelbarrow. The sod

was subsequently divided into slices, enclosed in silver caskets made by a local jeweller and presented to the directors and their friends. There was wild enthusiasm for the new scheme, one banner proclaiming: *York was, London is, Hull will be, through Colonel Smith's exertions, the wealthiest of the three.* Unfortunately, it was not to be.

Alexandra Dock construction

Alexandra dock was designed by the Scottish civil engineer James Abernethy (1814-1896). Its construction required two miles of dock walls enclosing a water area of 46½ acres, two graving docks, a lock 550 feet long and 85 feet wide, a dredged entrance channel, the erection of pumping machinery, the building of transit sheds and the laying of some 12 miles of railway. Abernethy appointed the local Hull firm of Oldham & Bohn to assist him in overseeing the execution of the works. James Oldham (1801-1890) and George Bohn (1839-1922) entered into partnership in 1874 and worked from Imperial Chambers, Bowalley, Lane, Hull. The Resident Engineer was Arthur Cameron Hurtzig (1853-1915) and his Assistant was Abernethy's third son, Harold William Abernethy (1858-1895).

The site for the new dock and surrounding dock estate comprised 192 acres of which 152 acres were below the high water mark. In order to reclaim the required foreshore from the River Humber, an embankment about 40 feet high and 6,000 feet long had to be constructed. However, as the

Left. James Abernethy, CE, FRSE (1814-1896), a Past President of the Institution of Civil Engineers, was responsible for the design of Alexandra Dock. This image appeared in a biography written by his son which was published in 1897.

Below. Construction work underway on the North Wall of Alexandra Dock looking east; the upper portion of the wall, 14ft high, is dressed with Bramley Fall ashlar stone. To the right is a temporary reclamation embankment designed to exclude the tide from the works site. [Cox/Hull History Centre]

contractors required an area where a large labour force could be set to work immediately, temporary banks were formed to exclude the tide from the site of the north quay wall and the graving docks, thus enabling the construction of these works to commence while the outer bank was being constructed parallel to the river. Three more temporary banks were constructed in a southerly direction to link with the ongoing construction of the river bank, so facilitating the excavation works.

A new Priestman steam grab dredger was used to remove the mud overlying the boulder clay on the east, west and south sides of the projected dock, the area for which stretched for some 500 feet out into the River Humber. The exposed boulder clay was then used as the foundation for the protective banks along the foreshore. The banks were formed with chalk sourced from a quarry at Barton-on-Humber on the south bank of the river. The chalk was barged across the river and tipped at low water onto the cleared boulder clay. The tide was finally excluded from the whole of the site in November 1882. The entire workforce was then set to work on the excavation and the masonry walls. The concrete foundations for the dock walls were 51 feet below ground level and the trenches for the walls were 26 feet wide, requiring large timber supports to protect the sides. The excavation was mainly hand-dug, but steam cranes were used to lift out the spoil prior to it being carried away by rail in tipping wagons. The following statistics give an indication of the huge scale of the operation and the materials used.

Excavation	3,350,000 cubic yards
Dredging	661,000 cubic yards
Sand and gravel	400,000 tons
Limestone	50,000 tons
Cement	14,000 tons
Mortar	70,000 cubic yards
Lime concrete	74,000 cubic yards
Cement concrete	88,000 cubic yards
Chalk rubble masonry	144,000 cubic yards
Bramley Fall masonry	136,000 cubic yards
Brickwork	15,000 cubic yards
Chalk stone embankment	293,000 cubic yards
Granite for the lock walls and coping stones	115,000 cubic feet
Dressed Bramley Fall ashlar stone for dock walls	349,000 cubic feet
Rock faced Bramley Fall ashlar stone for river embankment	608,000 cubic feet
Timber for temporary works	1,500,000 cubic feet
Timber in piles and sheeting	390,000 cubic feet
Timber in walings, bracings, etc	92,000 cubic feet
Coal used for power	60,000 tons

The work involved the use of 31 standard gauge industrial steam locomotives, 975 wagons, 37 portable engines, 42 cranes, 24 pile drivers, five steam navvies, two hydraulic navvies and 150 stationary boilers. By mid 1883, the dock bottom resembled a huge marshalling yard with rail tracks snaking everywhere and trains of tipping wagons waiting to ascend the steep rope-worked inclines out of the dock; the excavated material being dumped to form the quays. At one time a maximum of 3,500 men were employed. Work carried on throughout the night with the aid of electric lighting. Readers wishing to learn more about the construction of the dock are referred to the Institution of Civil Engineers Paper No.2208: *The Alexandra Dock, Hull* by Arthur Cameron Hurtzig (Note 40). The total cost of the works, including the lock, the approach channel and the

graving docks was £1,355,392 (Note 41). On 21 May 1885 there was a ceremony to mark the removal of the last portion of earth from the dock. It was performed by Alice Ruth Mary Bohn, née Todd (1844-1922), wife of civil engineer George Bohn of Oldham & Bohn. She used a presentation spade with a teak handle and an inscribed silver shield attached to the centre of the blade (Note 42).

The Lock and Approach Channel
The site for the lock entrance was initially protected by a cofferdam. Work on this commenced in July 1881 and it was completed in June 1882 so enabling the excavation of deep trenches to accommodate the side walls of the lock to commence. In the eastern trench the boulder clay was found at a very suitable level and work proceeded with a remarkable absence of water such that

No.1 Graving Dock under construction; the stepped sides or altars can clearly be seen. [Cox/Hull History Centre]

Left. In 1905 the original cumbersome title was altered by statute to the Hull and Barnsley Railway Company. This was the new heraldic device.

Below. Map of the HBR based on one which appeared in *The Railway Year Book* for 1921. [Courtesy, Susan Hateley]

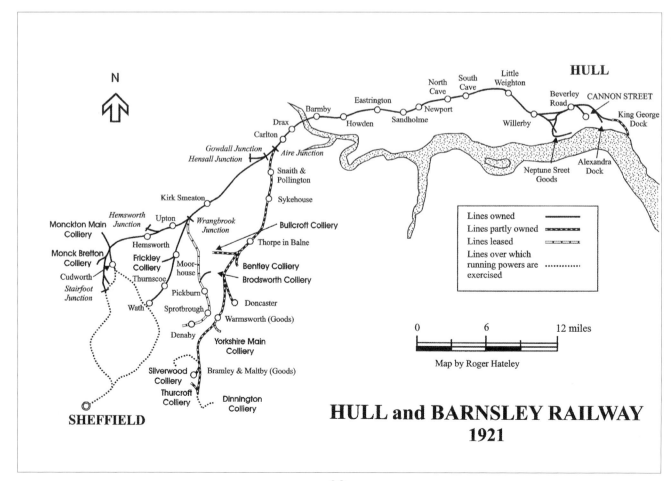

Map by Roger Hateley

HULL and BARNSLEY RAILWAY
1921

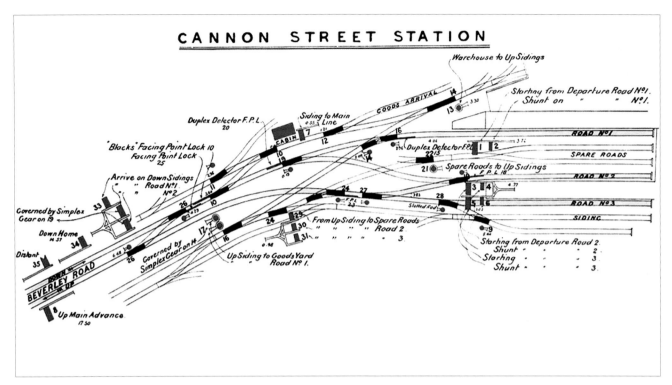

The HBR's passenger station at Hull was at Cannon Street. This signal box diagram displays the layout. [Mick Nicholson collection]

the foundations could be laid quickly and satisfactorily. The situation was just the opposite in the western trench as the boulder clay was much lower. A *blow* occurred at an early stage but the egress of water was quickly staunched before any significant damage occurred. However, as the first length of foundation at the north end of the west trench was being prepared during the evening of 8 April 1883, the bottom of the trench suddenly began to heave and soon the water burst up in two or three places and rapidly filled the trench, mastering the pumps. Large holes also appeared in the adjacent ground. These were staunched by tipping clay puddle mixed with stable litter, straw and bags loosely filled with Portland cement concrete. On investigation using bore holes, it was found that while the bed of clay on which the foundations were laid was generally 15 feet thick, it was only two feet thick in the vicinity of the *blows*. The flow of water was eventually cut off by driving pitch-pine piles, not less than 14 inches square and 50 feet long, to enclose the principal blow-holes and disturbed areas but it was not until September 1884 that the whole of the foundations were rendered secure.

In December 1884 the cofferdam was substituted by a caisson which was 95 feet wide at coping level and 88 feet at the bottom. A double keel of greenheart timber was passed round the caisson which, being dressed very smooth made a water-tight joint with the granite masonry. Once the caisson was in place, the cofferdam was removed and the erection of the lock gates commenced. The gates were constructed of greenheart and there were three sets, each making a mitre at the outer, middle

and inner positions. The gates, capstans and a swing bridge across the lockpit were operated by hydraulic machinery supplied by Sir W.G. Armstrong and Company of Newcastle-upon-Tyne.

The approach channel to the new dock involved dredging some 35 acres of the Hebbles shoal which is mostly composed of very hard boulder clay, with large boulders reaching up to half a ton in weight and smaller stones strewn over the surface. Beds of peat were also found with portions of large ancient trees and hazel nuts! The river bed had to be reduced from an average depth of 3 to 6 feet at low water spring tides down to a level of 12 to 14 feet. At first the dredging was carried out with a double-ladder dredger of 30hp, a single-ladder dredger of 40hp and a steam grab dredger. However, with experience it was found that these vessels could not complete the work in time for the official opening, especially as considerable accretion of mud and silt was constantly going on during the dredging campaign. A 45hp single-ladder dredger hired from the Furness Railway Company was set to work in March 1885 on the very hard material at the lower end of the shoal, while one of the River Tyne's 60hp double-ladder dredgers was set to work at the western end of the shoal. This left the grab dredger to work in the lock bell-mouth and the other ladder dredgers to work in the tideway. The works were thus completed on time. The main approach channel is self-scouring but maintenance dredging is still required within the bell-mouth.

Other Dock Facilities
There were two graving docks: No.1

was 500ft in length on the blocks and 60ft wide; No.2 was slightly larger at 550ft by 65ft. The pumping station for emptying them was situated between the two. They were constructed of masonry throughout and have certainly stood the test of time as both remain in use today, although nowadays they are more commonly referred to as dry docks. A contemporary description said *they were adapted for steamers and sailing vessels of the largest tonnage. Cleaning and painting bottoms, and repairs of every description, can be accomplished with the utmost dispatch* (Note 43). The general quays were initially equipped with 23 1½ ton capacity travelling hydraulic cranes, one 10 ton fixed hydraulic crane, 10 moveable jiggers, 12 small wagon capstans and two 19 ton wagon hoists for coaling, all supplied by Sir W.G. Armstrong and Company. In 1886 a 100 ton capacity steam crane with a fixed jib was installed on the north end of the east quay. It was built by James Taylor & Company of Birkenhead and still survives as a listed structure. A very distinctive feature was the construction of three jetties which jut out from the south side of the dock known as A, B and C Jetties. A fourth jetty stemmed from the centre of the west quay. These greatly increased the length of quayside available, so enabling more ships to be berthed alongside.

Opening of Alexandra Dock
Prior to the official opening of the new dock, two events had been held to mark the filling of the dock with water. This was done using fresh water from the Holderness Drain in the forlorn hope that it would reduce siltation. Of course, as soon as ships started passing through

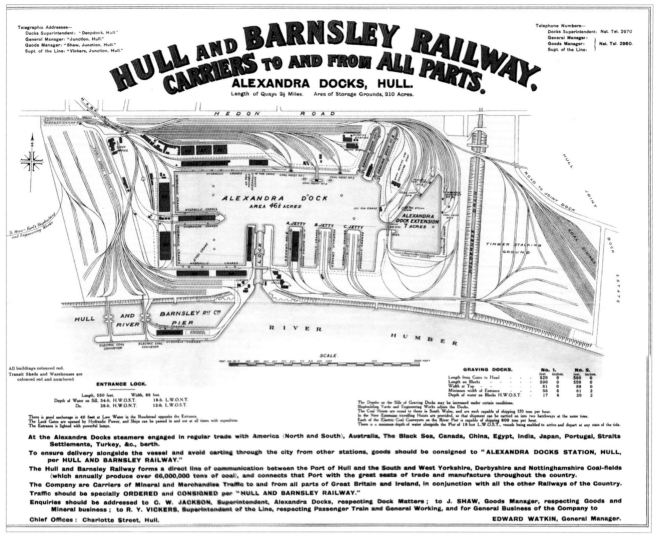

A 1912 HBR plan showing Alexandra Dock, the Extension and the River Pier. Note the reference to the Hull Joint Dock Estate on the right. The new joint dock was under construction at that time but not opened until 1914. Edwin Watkin (1856-1941) was the HBR General Manager from 1905 to 1922. [Courtesy, George Robinson]

A six plank wagon built by Charles Roberts & Co Ltd of Wakefield proudly displays the legend *Continental Route via Hull*. Alexandra Dock became the company's most profitable asset.

70

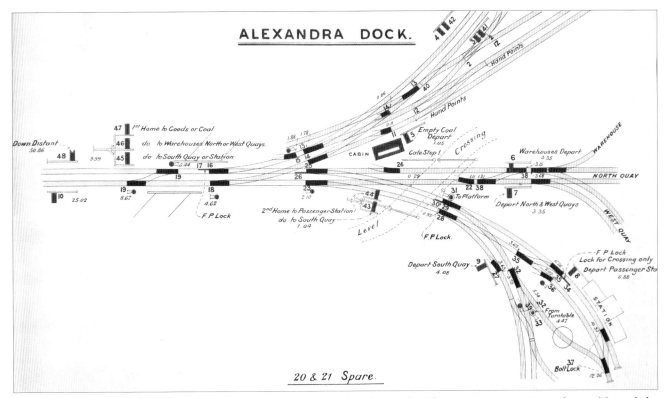

Alexandra Dock signal box diagram illustrating just how complex the dock railway system was. Note the position of the passenger station used by emigrants and the nearby turntable used to turn the main line locomotives.

the lock on a regular basis, the mud and alluvial silt that is constantly suspended in the waters of the Humber also entered the dock. Then, as now, once locking operations are finished on each tide, the mud and silt fall to the dock bottom which thus requires regular dredging.

It had been hoped that the Prince and Princess of Wales would have been available to perform the official opening ceremony but they were unable to accept the invitation. Instead the chairman, Gerard Smith, performed the ceremony assisted by his wife. On 16 July 1885 a small flotilla of vessels left Hull's Minerva Pier heading downstream towards the new dock. They were all dressed overall and were headed by the Wilson Line vessel *Orlando* (Note 44) which carried the chairman and his wife, directors, contractors, engineers and officials of the company, plus members of Hull Corporation. The weather was downcast when *Orlando* and other vessels in the flotilla sailed into the lock at 10.35am. It was reported that *Orlando's arrival was greeted by hand clapping, but the dampness of the weather had somewhat subdued the ardour of the spectators and the cheering was by no means uproarious. This was in spite of the efforts of the band of the Royal Hussars from York who had entertained the waiting crowds.* Then things did not go as planned – the outer lock gates would not close! This was because the amount fresh water supplied to the dock through the town's mains had been depleted in order to put out a fire in a saw mill in Naylor's Row. This resulted in there being insufficient pressure to work the lock gate hydraulic

machinery. High water that morning was at 9.13am and so the crowds experienced the embarrassing spectacle of the *Orlando* and the other vessels lowering themselves in the lock chamber as the tide ebbed away. Instead of coming up they were going down! After a considerable delay and much relief, the outer lock gates were closed. The sluices feeding water from the enclosed dock into the lock were opened and the vessels rose from within the chamber with, no doubt, the chairman and his wife regaining their composure during the process. Once a level had been made, the inner gates were opened and Mrs. Smith, who was situated on the stem of the *Orlando*, cut a white ribbon. *Orlando* and the other vessels then sailed into the vast expanse of the new dock. While the rest of the ships were taking up their positions, an elegant repast of strawberries, accompanied by liberal glasses of champagne, was served on board the *Orlando*. At 12.15pm the party disembarked and walked over a red carpet to listen to a series of speeches which preceded a sumptuous lunch. Alexandra Dock was open for business.

Opening of the railway

In marked contrast to the opening of the dock, there was no official opening of the railway. It opened for goods traffic on 20 July and passenger traffic one week later on 27 July, again without ceremony. However, the stations en route were decorated with flags and flowers, especially so at Howden where 200 people assembled early in the morning to greet the arrival of the first train at 7.12am. The directors did avail themselves of a special train on 10

August which ran through to Barnsley where they attended a banquet in the Public Hall. Prior to the opening, Gerard Smith, in his capacity as chairman, had been out on the line on a number of previous occasions. For example, on 9 January 1884 he travelled from Stairfoot Junction in a *curious train made up of heavy uncushioned carriages* hauled by one of the contractor's locomotives to inspect the works (Note 45). The party included fellow directors, principal officers, the contractors and representatives of the press. After several miles the train stopped and everyone alighted to watch the chairman unlock the line with a silver key presented to him by the contractor's foreman, G. M. Tarry. The party then proceeded towards Hull, crossing the River Ouse by boat to lunch at the new station at Howden, completing their journey to Hull later in the day. A further inspection was made on 29 August that year when the chairman travelled the whole length of the line on the first through train, the gap over the River Ouse having been completed (Note 46). At that point a small ceremony took place when Anna Shelford (née Sopwith), wife of the Engineer, depressed a lever which opened the new swing bridge across the river.

Trade

Alexandra Dock was opened at a time when steam ships were becoming dominant and ever larger in size. One of its main advantages was that it could accommodate the largest vessels then in existence, those vessels remaining always safely afloat while in dock even when fully laden. For this reason deep

Alexandra Dock looking east in 1906 when it was the largest dock in Hull. The steamship *Normandiet* (1369grt), on the left loading coal, was completed in January 1878 as *Sicillian* by E. Withy & Company, Middleton, Hartlepool, Yard No.70. She was built for H. Blaik & Company of Leith, became *Rollon* when sold to French owners in 1899 and *Normandiet* in 1903 when purchased by Danish owners A/S Det Dansk-Franske Dampskibs of Esberg. In 1915 she was renamed *Alfa* when acquired by A/S D/S Absalon of Copenhagen but met her end when she was wrecked at Bempton Cliffs, Yorkshire on passage from Hudiksvall for London with a cargo of timber. Note the Wilson liner in the distance and the silhouette of the 100 ton steam crane. [Charles A. Hill collection]

The ship on the right is the Wilson liner ss *Tokio* (3827grt). She was built by Richardson Duck of Stockton-on-Tees in 1895, Yard No.445. The Wilson liners were known as *Parrot Boats* because of their colourful livery – a green hull and a red funnel with a black top. *Tokio* was sold on 13 December 1911 to the Atlantic Whaling Company of Larvik, Norway and renamed *Polynesia*. On 10 September 1916, the vessel was torpedoed about 50 miles south west of the Scilly Isles by German submarine UB 18 on passage from New York to London with a cargo of oil. [Charles A. Hill collection]

72

This remarkable image dates from 1911 when the eastern extremity of the Alexandra Dock River Pier was still under construction, as evidenced by the piling rigs seen to the top left. The two electrically operated covered coal conveyors seen leading out to the river frontage have just been completed. A HBR wagon is being tipped which must be for demonstration purposes as the ship berthed on the pier is not alongside the nearest conveyor. The ship is wearing the funnel markings of Wm. France, Fenwick & Company Limited whose ss *Stanton* was the first vessel to be loaded on the pier on 25 January 1911. There is a remarkable collection of four-wheeled *timber bogies* in the foreground. These were introduced by the NER in 1870 and subsequently copied by the HBR. The *bogies* were designed to carry seven tons of timber, which used to arrive as loose planks. The planks were stacked on the bogie cross-members and secured with the chains that can be seen awaiting use on most of the *bogies*. The iron-bound dumb buffers were not of normal railway height or width and to move them around the docks from the various berths to the stacking areas, small shunting locomotives were fitted with additional buffers or deeper buffer beams. The LNER later introduced road tractors fitted with steel buffer beams to supersede the shunting engines. A *timber bogie* has survived and is on display at Hull's Streetlife Museum of Transport. [ABP]

sea trading was quickly established with Australia, America, Argentina, Brazil, Canada, Cuba, Egypt, India, Mexico, Russia and the West Indies. The Wilson Line (Note 47) used the dock for its services to Scandinavia with trade to Norway being particularly strong. Emigrants were a significant part of Wilson's business at this time when many thousands of Norwegians and Swedes were leaving for the *New World* in America, escaping from severely depressed economies at home. There was also a surge of Jewish refugees displaced by Tsarist pogroms in the Baltic States. The emigrants were brought to Hull and taken by rail to Liverpool which at the time dominated the transatlantic passenger trade. A station specifically for the emigrant traffic was built at the west end of Alexandra Dock; it comprised a single platform 250 feet in length and was equipped with waiting rooms and the usual conveniences.

Of course, the South Yorkshire Coalfield provided the dock's staple diet with a seemingly inexhaustible supply of steam, gas and house coal for export to foreign markets, shipment coastwise and for ships' bunkers. The table of rates

and charges for goods featured over 800 items but prominent amongst imports were bacon and hams, fruit and vegetables, seeds and grain, meat, sugar, ores, iron and steel, timber and wool. In 1906/1907 the HBR had a brief flirtation with running a shipping service. Two vessels were chartered to operate a twice-weekly service between Hull and Rotterdam but the venture was not a success and was discontinued when the charters expired. Its discontinuance may have been influenced by the loss of two senior HBR employees at sea. The Hull agent for the new service was Charles William Barker Anderson (b.1849) who was the Alexandra Dock Superintendent. He, accompanied by James Barton, HBR Chief Assistant Accountant, were travelling on board the Great Eastern Railway's ferry *Berlin* (1745grt) from Harwich to Rotterdam for a business meeting in connection with the HBR's fledgling service when during the early hours of 21 February 1907 in very stormy weather the ship struck the North Pier at the Hook of Holland and broke in two. Both Anderson and Barton were amongst the 144 passengers and crew who lost their lives. There were only 16 survivors.

The railway was, of course, not the only means of getting cargo to or from the new dock. The Humber keels and sloops navigating the Rivers Humber, Hull, Trent and Ouse, which had traditionally carried cargo to and from the port for transhipment overside to seagoing vessels, were also accommodated in Alexandra Dock. One big advantage to shippers and receivers in transhipping cargo in this way was that the cargo so handled was free from merchandise dues that would otherwise be levied by the dock owners (Note 48).

Locomotives

The vast majority of the traffic for the new dock did, of course, arrive and depart by the new railway. A large fleet of both tender and tank engines was established to handle the traffic with 0-6-0 and 0-8-0 tender locomotives hauling the coal from the collieries and returning the empty wagons. All the locomotives were built by locomotive manufacturing companies and the majority were characterised by having domeless boilers favoured by Locomotive Superintendent, Matthew Stirling (1856-1931). He was born in Kilmarnock and apprenticed at

This 100 ton capacity steam crane, built by James Taylor & Company of Birkenhead, was installed on the north end of Alexandra Dock's east quay in 1886. Here it is unloading a heavy lift from the steamship *Anna Rehder* which carried that name between 1929 and 1947, so this is probably a pre-Second World War view. The ship was built in 1921 by Limhamms Skeppsvarf AB, Limhamm and launched as *Mercia* but completed as *Waterway* for Cory & Blundell. In 1929 she was sold to German ship owner C. Rehder and renamed *Anna Rehder* remaining with that owner until sold in 1947 to the Greek Navy, renamed *Serrai* and converted to a lighthouse tender. The ship was taken off the Greek Navy list in 1971 and sunk as a target in 1975. [Hull Maritime Museum]

The 100 ton crane still survives as a listed structure but is no longer operational. One of its last regular uses was to lift pilot boats out of the water for examination and repair. This view shows it in action in November 1977 unloading former USA Transportation Corps Class S160 2-8-0 No.5820 from the mv *Naleczow* (1968grt) which then operated a regular cargo liner service between Gdynia and Hull. The crane had a fixed jib and the lift is just clearing the ship's coaming with inches to spare. The locomotive was built at the Baldwin locomotive works in Lima, Ohio in June 1945, Maker's No.8758. After the Second World War it worked on the Polish State Railways and when discharged in Hull carried the running number Tr203 474 on two rectangular plates on the cab side. Nowadays the locomotive can be seen in operation on the preserved Keighley & Worth Valley Railway. [Hull & Humber Cargo Handling Co Ltd]

74

One of the three 0-4-0 well tanks built by Kitsons of Leeds and delivered to the HBR in 1886 for work on Alexandra Dock. They bore the running numbers 43 to 45. [Stephenson Locomotive Society collection]

Doncaster to his father Patrick Stirling of Great Northern Railway fame. He was appointed as Locomotive Superintendent of the HBR on 13 May 1885 and remained with the company until his retirement in 1922.

The permanent way on the dock quays featured many curves of tight radius and in order to cope with this situation six 0-4-0 well tanks were ordered from Kitson & Company Limited, Airedale Foundry, Leeds. In spite of Stirling's penchant for domeless boilers, the engines were fitted with domes in accordance with Kitson practice and had Kitson patent valve gear. Although all six engines were ordered simultaneously, because of problems with finance, their delivery was staggered as shown right.

The first three engines differed in that they did not have enclosed cabs and so they must have weighed slightly less than the weight quoted alongside, which is applicable to the last three locomotives. The dimensions are taken from the official Kitson records in the care of the Stephenson Locomotive Society. All six locomotives, which survived until 1922, were kept, along with larger tank engines used for dock shunting, in a wooden two-road locomotive shed located to the west of No.1 Graving Dock. The main HBR locomotive shed was at Springhead. From 1890 this was extended with additional buildings so that the company could overhaul its own locomotives, carriages and wagons.

Finance

Kitson Wks No	Date of Pre-delivery steam test	HBR No
2951	4 February 1886	43
2952	6 February 1886	44
2953	9 February 1886	45
2954	20 December 1888	46
2955	21 December 1888	47
3128	10 January 1889	48

Leading Dimensions

Outside cylinders	14in x 21in
Wheel diameter	2ft 2½in
Wheel base	6ft 4in
Tubes	110 x 1¾in
Heating surface - tubes	382sq ft
Heating surface - firebox	43sq ft
Heating surface - total	425sq ft
Grate area	8.75sq ft
Water capacity	390 gallons
Fuel capacity	15cwt
Boiler pressure	140psi
Total weight	21tons 10cwt

Financial problems had begun to emerge in 1884 before the new railway and dock had been completed. Both the railway and dock works were costing far more than originally anticipated and the company was running out of funds. There was also aggravation between Hull shareholders and those based in London who became increasingly anxious to obtain a return on their investments. On 29 March 1884 James Grierson, General Manager of the Great Western Railway, was engaged to inspect the work and advise on what economies could be effected. On the basis of his report, a further issue of £1,800,000 perpetual preference stock was made. A prospectus dated 16 June 1884 once again described the company's

prospects in glowing terms but the public failed to respond. Doubts about the success of the new venture were setting in and there was talk about amalgamation with other railway companies. On 2 July 1884 all construction works were stopped causing much hardship for the hundreds of men who were discharged. Following the abortive further issue of stock, a Bill was rushed through Parliament to permit further borrowing. Intensive lobbying, professing that the HBR would be a *wreck* unless further money could be raised, resulted in the suspension of standing orders so permitting the Bill to proceed speedily. It received the royal assent on 14 August 1884 (Note 49) and in November that year a further issue of stock was made to the extent of £1,500,000 and this time taken up. The crisis was over and work recommenced on the construction of the railway and dock on 29 November 1884 after a delay of five months.

Charles Wilson, outwardly a keen promoter of the HBR, seems to have played a double role. Once the company had been established he pronounced his hope at the first meeting of the shareholders in 1881 that some day the NER would control all the railways and docks at Hull. That certainly did not enamour him to his fellow directors! Once he realised that the company was running into financial difficulties he reduced his holdings from £10,000 to £100 and resigned his directorship, giving pressure of his other work as the reason. One or other of the Wilson brothers with shipping interests had a

One of the three later Kitson locomotives which had fully enclosed cabs. They carried running numbers 46 to 48, the first two being delivered in 1888 and the last one in 1889. [Robert Humm collection]

seat on the NER board from 1874 to 1909. Charles was first appointed on 13 February 1874, resigning in December 1879 when his involvement with the HBR became plain for all to see, but he was immediately replaced by his brother David who held a directorship until his death on 25 February 1893. Later that year on 20 October, Arthur was appointed to the board remaining as a director until his death on 21 October 1909. Reflecting on those late 19th century commercial manoeuvres, one cannot but wonder whether the Wilsons cleverly used Gerard Smith as a puppet to get their way.

Of course all the difficulties in raising additional capital were quietly forgotten during the celebrations for the grand openings but a financial problem of a different kind soon manifested itself: cut-throat competition. The early history of the new company was riddled with bitter conflict in marked contrast to the rejoicing of earlier years. In an attempt to get business from the South Yorkshire collieries, rates were slashed resulting in similar action both by the NER and the HDC. It became an on-going process such that by the end of 1886 the HBR was driven into bankruptcy and on 6 January 1887 the company went into receivership. During the first seven years of its existence the company only paid one paltry dividend of $3/8$ per cent. Shareholder meetings became increasingly acrimonious with bickering, recriminations, slurs and wrangling,

with at times open attacks on the chairman's character and motives. An Act obtained in 1889 (Note 50) enabled the borrowing powers of the company to be reorganised. New debenture stocks were successfully issued, the whole of the outstanding debt was paid off and the receiver discharged. However, the financial difficulties rumbled on with further talks about working agreements with one or other of the larger railway companies taking place but coming to nothing. The board of directors even approached the NER with Colonel Smith declaring that: *it is only by annexation to a great company or by seeking the aid of a great company's credit, that the ordinary proprietors of the HBR could get any return for their money.* What an about turn! Proposals were actually agreed upon but were strongly opposed by the Hull Corporation and rejected by the HBR shareholders.

In 1892 the HBR opposed two Bills simultaneously promoted jointly by the NER and the HDC for the amalgamation of the two undertakings and for the construction of a new deep-water dock to the east of Alexandra Dock at Marfleet. The proposal had come about following pressure from the fishing industry for more water and quay space and additional facilities for bunkering steam trawlers which were rapidly increasing in numbers. The coal trade also required a greater depth of water on the dock sills for larger and deeper draughted vessels. The HDC could not afford the capital expenditure required

and turned to the NER for assistance but the latter did not have the statutory powers to expend money on an estate it did not own, which brought about the idea of amalgamation. Moreover, rather than spend capital on updating old docks, it seemed opportune to develop a completely new dock. This double whammy was too much for the HBR which petitioned against the Bills on the grounds of unfair competition. Both Bills were lost.

The NER reintroduced a Bill in the following session for amalgamation only, dropping the idea for a new dock. This time the passage of the Bill was frustrated by a prolonged and bitter dockers' strike which brought the port to a standstill for some six weeks and prevented key witnesses from attending the hearings as they dealt with more pressing issues at home. It was not until 1 June 1893 that the Bill came before a select committee of the House of Lords. However, on this occasion there had been advance consultation with the HBR resulting in protective clauses being inserted in the Bill to give the HBR the assurances it required and allay fears of any ulterior motives. The provisions prevented the NER from reducing dock dues below those levied by the HBR, except by agreement or arbitration and also covered the issue of any future new dock with provisions that completely safeguarded HBR interests. It was provided that before the NER could proceed to construct a dock eastward of the River Hull, it had to give notice of its intention to the HBR. The latter, having spare lands adjoining Alexandra Dock, might then require the NER to construct a dock on that site and might further require the new venture to be constructed as a joint undertaking. Clearly the time had come for the HBR to seek co-operation and compromise rather than continue with foolhardy competition. True to form, the Hull Corporation petitioned against the Bill but it was supported by no lesser personages than Charles Wilson and Frederick Grotrian, once arch opponents of NER policy! The House of Lords Committee decided to pass the Bill on condition that within a period of seven years the NER would expend £500,000 on improving the existing docks. The Act received the royal assent on 24 August 1893 (Note 51) and by this means the assets of the HDC passed to the NER, including the Town Docks, Victoria Dock, Albert & William Wright Docks and St. Andrew's Dock. A new dock jointly operated by both railway companies, with a common agreement on the rates to be charged, was eventually built under the Hull Joint Dock Act which received the royal assent on 9 August 1899 (Note 52). It was opened by King George V on 26 June 1914 who named it King George Dock and is described in the following chapter.

Exit the Colonel
Colonel Smith was High Sheriff of Hull in 1880 and became a Liberal Member of Parliament for High Wycombe for the years 1883 to 1885. In spite of the HBR's failings, Hull Corporation always thought highly of him and when he departed in 1895 to take up a new role overseas, held a banquet in his honour. In October 1895 he was knighted and was appointed Governor of Western Australia, arriving there on 23 December that year. He probably breathed a sigh of relief that his involvement with the HBR was over. However, his stay in Australia was not a happy one. He annoyed the Catholic community by holding Masonic functions in Government House and laying foundation stones of public charitable institutions with Masonic rites. Unwisely he also invested in mining and other speculative ventures and was unfortunate in his choice of business partners. Sir Gerald and his co-directors were sued successfully in the Australian Supreme Court in November 1899 for the recovery of an overdraft due to the Bank of New South Wales from the operations of a Coolgardie Hotel, which had gone into liquidation. The Colonial Office was scandalised when the proceedings were published in the press and Sir Gerald was invited to return home, leaving Perth on 22 May 1900. He formally resigned on 30 June 1900. He did not return to Hull. Instead he resumed several commercial pursuits in London, becoming a director of several investment trusts and the Brazilian San

Paulo Railway Company. He died on 28 October 1921 aged 80.

Alexandra Dock Extension
Alexandra Dock was by far the most successful and profitable part of the new enterprise and by 1897 was becoming increasingly busy, so much so that it was decided to build a small extension to the east of the dock. Eight tenders were submitted for the work, the lowest one in the sum of £92,201 submitted by Whitaker Bros Limited of Horsforth, Leeds, being accepted. The dock extension had a water area of seven acres and took the form of an almost equilateral triangle. The walls were 36ft 6in in depth, built of concrete, with the lower portion faced with better quality concrete and the top faced with Staffordshire blue bricks. Approximately 350,000 cubic yards of material was excavated, some of which was used to form foundations for the new permanent way, the remainder being tipped to the east of the Holderness Drain. Although the extension was relatively small in size, it gave an increase of 30% in available quay space. The north-west and eastern quays were reserved for the coal trade and were equipped with four coal hoists, each with its own sidings for loaded and empty wagons. The south quay was reserved for timber and pit props. Hydraulically operated travelling cranes were installed on the south quay and at the southern end of the eastern quay. The opening ceremony took place on 25 July 1899 and was performed by Miss May Poston, daughter of HBR director Charles Poston of Highfield, Stevenage. The first vessel to use the new facility was the Swedish steamer *Axel Johnson* (1517grt), registered in Stockholm (Note 53). As the steamer navigated the passage that led from the main dock to the new extension, its bow touched a white ribbon which was stretched across the water; precisely at that moment it was cut deftly by May Poston using a pair of silver scissors. For many years a swing bridge carrying a single railway track was located at this point.

River Pier
On 26 July 1907 the HBR obtained statutory powers (Note 54) to construct a river pier in the River Humber to the west of the Alexandra Dock lock entrance. The initiative was sparked by the construction of the NER's development of Riverside Quay alongside Albert & William Wrights Docks (see Chapter Six). The pier was designed to foster the near continental trade and was completed in 1911. Two coaling appliances were erected on the pier and were fed by two electrically operated conveyor belts, each capable

of handling 600 tons of coal per hour. The first of the conveyors was brought into use on 25 January 1911 to load the ss *Stanton* (1,097grt) – see Note 55. A ferro-concrete warehouse was built on the pier to accommodate perishable traffic and general merchandise. Electric cranes were installed with electrically operated capstans to move the rail wagons.

HBR harbour craft
The HBR had three dredgers which undertook the maintenance dredging required in Alexandra Dock and also owned three steam tugs *Alexandra*, *Barnsley* and *Hull* for the towage of sea-going ships in the approach channel and for in-dock manoeuvres as required. *Alexandra* and *Barnsley* were built by Earle's of Hull in 1885 and 1886 respectively and *Hull* was built in 1898 by J.P. Rennoldson of South Shields. Details of the tugs can be found in Appendix One.

HBR statistics
The following is a summary of HBR statistical information for the year ending 31 December 1920.

Total capital expenditure to date	£10,241,474
Receipts	£1,517,726
Expenditure	£1,110,842
Route mileage, including share of joint lines and lines worked	106 miles
Locomotives	181
Total coaching vehicles	138
Total wagons	4,827
Number of passengers	336,085
Season tickets	354
Merchandise traffic	924,897 tons
Coal, coke and patent fuel	1,144,179 tons
Other mineral traffic	205,964 tons
Head of live stock, including 18,233 sheep and 3,943 pigs	25,050 head

Springhead, the main HBR locomotive shed in Hull. Class L1 0-6-0 No.29 is at the west end; the engine was built by Kitson, Maker's No.4712, entering traffic in December 1912. It received a new boiler February 1930 and was withdrawn by the LNER as No.2421 in May 1937. Unfortunately it is not possible to identify the tank engine. [Mick Nicholson Collection]

Left. Alexandra Dock in March 1951 looking north west. Dredging is underway near the lock bell-mouth using a bucket dredger and a self-propelled hopper barge. A, B and C Jetties can be seen to the right of the lock and furthermost right, with its triangular shape, is the Alexandra Dock Extension. Above that the two dry docks can clearly be identified as can the two coal hoists on the north wall. Pit props and timber are stacked in the foreground. [ABP]

Below. This 1965 aerial view looks west and illustrates a still very busy Alexandra Dock. The stretch of water running from left to right in the foreground is the Holderness Drain and Holderness Drain South signal box can just be glimpsed to the bottom right. The most prominent coal hoist, on the east side of the Extension, is in use with a good supply of 16 ton mineral wagons waiting to be tipped. Beyond the storage tanks railway wagons loaded with timber await collection and the two dry docks are occupied. To the top left jutting out into the Humber is the River Pier with its two coal conveyors brought into use in 1911. [Ivor Innes Photographers, Hessle]

79

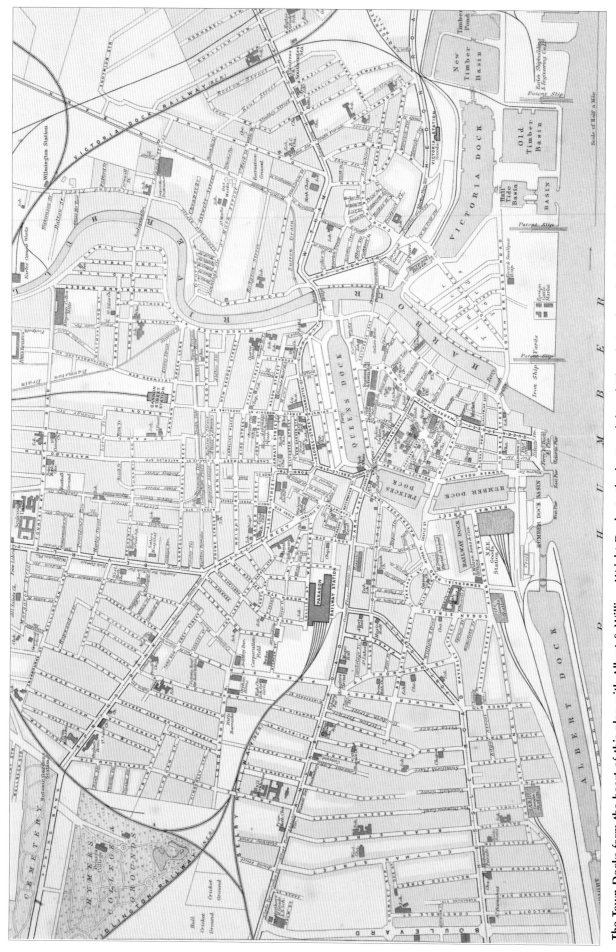

The Town Docks form the heart of this plan with Albert & William Wright Docks to the bottom left and Victoria Dock to the right beyond the River Hull. The main passenger railway termini are clearly marked: the HBR's Cannon Street (top centre) and the NER's Hull Paragon (centre left). Over to the extreme right the Victoria Dock Branch is highlighted showing the positions of Wilmington and Southcoates stations and NER Victoria goods station. The HBR, GCR and NER principal goods stations are clearly marked to the bottom left of the plan.

80

6. The North Eastern Railway 1893-1922

Port Authority

The NER was no stranger to the role of port authority as it already owned Tyne Dock and the docks at Hartlepool and Middlesbrough, together with the coal-shipping staithes at Blyth (North and South) and at Dunston-on-the-Tyne. In addition to the HDC's docks the NER also acquired the splendid Hull Dock Office and a number of harbour craft including dredgers, hoppers, small water boats, dumb barges and the tugs *Active*, *Lively* and *Hercules*. More details of these tugs can be found in Appendix One. The man with prime responsibility for undertaking the NER's dock improvements at Hull was Thomas Monk Newell (1863-1932). The early part of his career had been with the Mersey Docks and Harbour Board at Liverpool but he was appointed as assistant engineer to the HDC in January 1889,

The North Eastern Railway acquired the Hull Dock Company in 1893 and was quick to advertise its new marine assets in Hull. This poster by Percy Home includes St. Andrew's Dock Extension and Riverside Quay opened in 1897 and 1907, respectively. It shows but does not name the HBR's Alexandra Dock but does refer to the new joint dock so that was presumably under construction at the time the poster was produced. On the south bank of the Humber, the Great Central Railway's Grimsby and Immingham docks are completely ignored! Upstream, Goole gets similar treatment. Note the claim that the NER is: *The largest Dock-Owning Railway Company in the World* and that *Hull is the Third Port in the United Kingdom*. Was the NER responsible for giving Hull its *Third Port* label?

shortly afterwards becoming its chief engineer following the retirement of Robert Aspland Marillier. The NER acquired Newell's services on amalgamation and in 1900 made him the engineer responsible for all the NER's ports with the exception of the staithes at Blyth and Dunston. He was based at Hull and remained with the NER until 1913 when he returned to Liverpool to become the Mersey Docks & Harbour Board's engineer-in-chief. Subsequent holders of the NER post were Charles Watson (1872-1915) who was appointed in 1913 and Sir John Rumney Nicholson (1866-1939) who was appointed in 1919. Between 1915 and 1919, i.e. for most of the First World War years, dock engineering work was the responsibility of the NER's Chief Engineer, Cyril Francis Bengough (1864-1931); he retired at the end of 1924.

St. Andrew's Dock Extension

The first major dock improvement undertaken by the NER at Hull was to construct the St. Andrew's Dock Extension to the west of St. Andrew's Dock adding almost another ten acres of water area. Work commenced in 1895 and was progressing well until disaster struck on 15 May 1896. It was planned to utilise the dry dock provided at the west end of St. Andrew's Dock as the entrance to the extension dock. The construction works involved making a dam across St. Andrew's Dock just to the east of the dry dock to hold up the water until the extension was completed. Between 7 and 8am on the morning of 15 May water was seen bubbling under the dam. Within minutes the dam gave way and water rushed into the extension with great force exacerbated by the fact that it was high water time and both sets of lock gates at the St. Andrew's Dock entrance were open. The velocity of the water was such that trawlers, smacks, keels and other smaller craft in the dock broke from their moorings. The smack *Young Greg* smashed against the dam followed by the keels *Friendship* and *Providence*. These stricken vessels slightly checked the rush of water but diverted its course to the south wall of the extension scouring away its lower part which gave way causing the coping to collapse. Amazingly there was no loss of life.

The disaster was a major setback to the progress of works. On 6 January 1897 the *Hull Daily Mail* reported on the state of play as follows. *The obstacles to be overcome in the construction of the St. Andrew's Dock extension are apparently interminable. The smack and coal laden keel which sank in the old dry dock entrance when the extension was flooded have become so tightly wedged from side to side – so much so, in fact, that blasting is necessary to assist the steam crane to tear the wreckage to pieces. With so many unemployed at this*

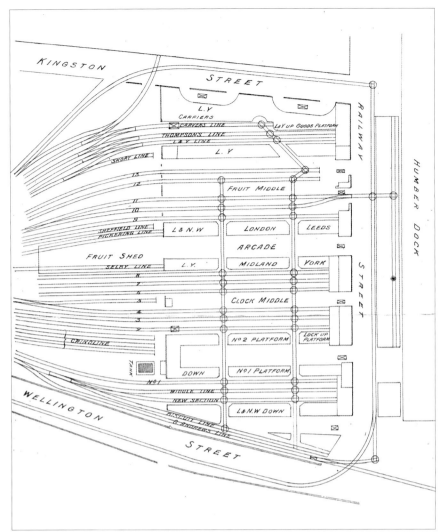

Left. Diagram dating from 1913, showing the layout of the principal NER goods depot fronting Humber Dock, with Kingston Street to the north and Wellington Street to the south. Accommodation allocated to the LYR, LNWR and Midland Railways is clearly marked.

Below. The NER commenced building the Extension to St. Andrew's Dock in 1895 and it was completed two years later. At its extreme west end, there were four slipways which are depicted here. The Hull trawlers on the slips from left to right are H277 *Welsbach* (369grt), H460 *James Barrie* (338grt) and H399. *Welsbach* was built by Cook, Welton & Gemmell of Beverley in 1930, Yard No.550, for F & T Ross of Hull. She served as a minesweeper during the Second World War, going to Fleetwood in 1946 as *Wyre Warrior*. She was broken up at Bruges in April 1955. *James Barrie* was built by Cochrane of Selby in 1928, Yard No.1017, for Newington Steam Trawling Co. She saw war service as a boom defence vessel. In 1947 she was sold to a Norwegian owner and named *Nord Rollnes,* surviving another 20 years before being broken up at Stavanger in 1967. The identity of H399 is unknown. [Hull Maritime Museum]

time of the year, it seems strange that Messrs Kellett, who are the contractors for the St. Andrew's Dock extension, should have found so much difficulty in obtaining sufficient labour. Yet such is the case and it is only quite recently that they have been able to increase their complement of labourers to its requisite efficiency. Neither smack owners nor fishermen will have cause to complain when the St. Andrew's Dock Extension is completed. Many alterations have been made since the first plans were prepared. Now a straight wooden jetty will run right along the North side instead of a slanting stone one, as was first intended, and the herring stage in the north-east corner will be larger, and a decided improvement on the one now in use in the old dock.

The newspaper went on to describe in rather graphic terms an aspect of construction which involved blasting. *There are many points of vantage where the blasting operations may be witnessed without danger. When the charge is laid, the cry of 'Fire! fire!' is raised all round the working. Immediately many whistles are blowing, and everyone climbs up the bank from the dock bottom, and seek shelter of the Humber-bank. To see so many men scaling the dock wall as fast as they can find footing, is a novel sight. When everyone is away from the works, and men are posted at each corner with red flags, another whistle rends the air, and simultaneously the first charge explodes. This is followed by two or three more of a like size, and as each one bursts stones and dirt are hurled hundreds of feet into the air. Blasting and pile-driving is now being carried on day and night.* What a far cry from modern health and safety standards!

The extension, which at its extreme western end included four slipways, opened in July 1897. St. Andrew's Dock and its extension were unique in that all the fishing industry's main activities took place within the dock estate. On the north or *wet side*, vessels landed their catches for auction on the two fish quays, where the merchants' offices and fish processing stands were situated. The fish was despatched to inland markets, initially by rail but later also by road transport, from a loading platform at the rear of the market. On the south and east ends of the dock or the *dry side* the various businesses serving the fishing industry were located including trawler owners' offices, ship repair shops, ship riggers, net and rope stores, an ice factory, a fish meal plant and coaling facilities. Steam trawlers obtained bunkers either direct from craft moored alongside which carried the coal direct from the collieries or from NER shipping appliances which included a 25 ton capacity crane and a 20 ton capacity hoist, both capable of handling 18 wagons per hour. All trimming of bunkers for trawlers was performed by private gangs of trimmers employed by the trawler owners.

Riverside Quay

In 1905 the NER obtained statutory powers to construct a quay on the River Humber alongside Albert & William Wright Docks. The rationale behind this development was to enable vessels employed on the regular short sea continental trades to arrive and berth at almost any state of the tide and avoid the delays encountered through locking in and out of the enclosed docks. The quay was 2,500 ft long and dredging of the river bed was undertaken to give a minimum depth of water at low water spring tides of 16ft, which involved the removal of some two million tons of material. The new works projected into the river at an average distance of 90ft from the old coping line. Slag from Middlesbrough was used to create a bank with a batter slope from the old cope out into the Humber. The slag had a high specific gravity to withstand the scour of the tide and was ideally suitable for pitching the face of the bank. The toe of the bank was secured by sheet piling and the deck of the quay was supported on blue gum and pitch pine timber piles. The quay was provided with several electric travelling cranes from Craven Bros of Manchester with a lifting capacity of 3 tons at a radius of 33½ft and was lit throughout by incandescent gas lamps. Hydraulic power for working capstans for shunting wagons was provided via an ornate brick built accumulator tower which sported a very distinctive clock with four faces. Most importantly a new passenger station was also provided permitting direct transfer from boat train to ship. The passenger service was inaugurated on 11 May 1907 in connection with the Hull-Zeebrugge steamship service run jointly by the NER and LYR with the ss *Duke of Clarence*. Many emigrants from Eastern Europe also used the station after disembarking from Wilson Line vessels which used the new quay as an alternative to berthing in Alexandra Dock. Trains took the emigrants to Liverpool where they boarded ocean liners for the Atlantic crossing to America. The emigrant traffic continued to be very lucrative until the outbreak of the First World War and was again resumed on a considerable scale after 1918 until the early 1920s, when new American legislation drastically limited the number of immigrants. Commencing on 18 November 1918 the quay was used for a very different kind of passenger for on that day the first batch of repatriated prisoners of war arrived on board the triple-screw

steamship *Archangel* (2448grt) – see Note 56. Following that there were several occasions when between 2,500 and 3,000 ex prisoners arrived on a daily basis necessitating the running of six or seven special trains to Ripon where the men were demobbed at the Repatriated Prisoners of War Reception Camp, Ripon South (Note 57).

Riverside Quay quickly became a very important feature of the Port of Hull from both a marine and railway aspect.Every effort had to be made to have the pilot engines at the quay sufficiently early to draw the lines at the specified times and the Traffic Foreman at the quay was instructed not to detain an engine after its specified departure time. Only the traffic which was already loaded at that time was taken, wagons not fully completed had to be left for a subsequent service. The following timetable applicable in April 1913 clearly shows the intensity of the freight service with its variety of destinations.

The new quay was not only used by Hull based shipping services. For example, Goole's Bennett Line vessels started to call there on inward voyages

MAIN LINE DEPARTURE TIME	DESTINATION	LATEST TIME OFF RIVERSIDE QUAY
11.15am	Doncaster	10.30am
11.20am	Normanton	10.30am
5.45pm	York	4.30pm
6.15pm	Leeds	5.10pm
6.40pm	Normanton	5.10pm
7.25pm	Nottingham (GCR)	5.30pm
7.25pm	Birmingham (LNWR)	5.30pm
7.50pm	Wakefield (LYR)	5.30pm
8.30pm	Doncaster	7.00pm
8.38pm	Newcastle	7.00pm
8.45pm	Manchester (GCR)	7.30pm
9.00pm	Bradford (LYR)	7.30pm
9.10pm	Liverpool (LNWR)	8.00pm
9.23pm	Normanton	8.00pm
10.04pm	Sunderland	8.30pm
10.20pm	Milford	8.30pm
11.23pm	Leeds	8.30pm

from Boulogne to discharge fruit and vegetables for the Hull market and quick distribution by rail to all parts of the country. The quay was also used extensively during the Jersey potato season which lasted from the middle of May to the end of June. For example, in 1922 Ellerman's Wilson Line (Note 58) in conjunction with the Goole & Jersey Steam Shipping Company arranged five sailings per week between Jersey and Hull. The average cargo was about 500 tons, consisting of about 10,000 barrels in which the potatoes were shipped. On one particular day two steamers were dealt with at the same berth. The first with 10,830 barrels (498 tons) commenced to discharge at 6.00am and finished at 11.00am; the second with 9,000 barrels (410 tons) commenced at 1.00pm and completed at 6.30pm. A total of 232 railway wagons were loaded with barrels of potatoes at Riverside Quay on that day in addition to another 204 wagons loaded with butter, bacon, margarine and fruit (Note 59).

The Riverside Quay opened in 1907 was an instant success. It enabled vessels employed in the regular short sea continental trades to arrive and berth at any state of the tide and avoid the delays encountered by locking in and out of the enclosed docks. A new passenger station was provided so permitting direct transfer from train to ship. The passenger service was inaugurated on 11 May 1907 in conjunction with the Hull-Zeebrugge steamship service run jointly by the NER and LYR. The ship used on the service was the Goole registered twin screw steamer *Duke of Clarence* (1458grt) seen on the left. Its two sets of triple-expansion engines could generate a speed of 19 knots. The accumulator house with its distinctive clock tower in Albert Dock forms the backcloth.

The Riverside Quay passenger station with a NER 4-4-0, designed by Thomas William Worsdell and built at Gateshead, ahead of a four coach passenger train. The two private owner coal wagons nearest the camera belonged to Michael Whitaker Limited, coal factors and exporters with a head office in Leeds.

The Wilsons & North Eastern Shipping Company Limited was incorporated in March 1906 in anticipation of its services using the new Riverside Quay. One of the vessels in the fleet was the steamship *Cito* (819grt) seen here about to dock at Hull. She was built by Earle's of Hull, Yard No.452, in 1899 but had a sad ending. On 17 May 1917 the ship was sunk by gunfire from German torpedo boat destroyers twenty miles east of the Noord Hinder light vessel while on passage from Hull to Rotterdam. The master, George Watson Orme (1859-1917) and nine of his crew were killed. They are commemorated on the Tower Hill Memorial, London. [Hull Maritime Museum]

NER shipping services

Unlike the LYR which operated extensive shipping services from Goole and the GCR which did the same from Grimsby, the NER was a late comer to the plethora of shipping that used the River Humber. The *Duke of Clarence*, mentioned above, was built by Laird of Birkenhead (Yard No.582) in 1892 for the Fleetwood to Northern Ireland service operated jointly by the LYR and the LNWR. With a gross register tonnage of 1434 and two sets of triple expansion engines giving a speed of 19 knots she was a valuable acquisition to the fleet. The vessel was acquired outright by the LYR in June 1906, re-fitted and re-boilered by Cammell, Laird & Company and transferred to Goole registry in March 1907 in readiness to operate the

inaugural service from Riverside Quay. Prior to the first voyage the ship was berthed in Albert Dock and open to invited guests for inspection. These included local councillors, representatives of the fruit and fish trades and railway officials. A contemporary advertisement proclaimed that the ship was fitted with electric light, baths and all modern conveniences for the comfort of passengers (Note 60). The saloons and state rooms were amidships and separate cabins were provided for ladies. Passengers were looked after by experienced stewards and stewardesses. The ship's master was Captain William Mason (1859-1912) of Goole, *a skilful and courteous commander, whose personality will do much to ensure the success of the*

service (Note 61). Being a LYR/NER joint venture, the ship had a house flag that was unique – blue and red in alternate quarters, having in white in each corner, one letter of the initials L.Y.N.E. Following Goole practice, the funnel colouring was yellow with a red band and black top. The Hull-Zeebrugge service operated during the summer months carrying passengers and cargo and when not employed on that service the *Duke of Clarence* operated elsewhere. The service was suspended in August 1914 at the start of the First World War but was resumed in 1920 when on 16 May that year the *Duke of Clarence* was the first passenger steamer to enter Zeebrugge Harbour since the declaration of peace (Note 62). In 1928 the ship undertook several cruises from Hull around Britain before being taken out of service for breaking up in 1930.

The Wilsons & North Eastern Railway Shipping Company Limited was incorporated in March 1906 by Thos Wilson & Company Ltd in association with the NER. The joint enterprise was clearly sparked by the presence of the new Riverside Quay which gave much greater operating flexibility for the continental services from Hull to Antwerp, Ghent, Hamburg and Dunkirk. The Wilsons and NER funnel colour was made up of the familiar red and black-topped Wilson funnel, with a narrow white band to reflect the NER interest. The house flag was white with three white bells inside a red circle. During its independent existence the company operated a total of 13 ships,

Funnel marking for the *Duke of Clarence* and its distinctive house flag. [Mick O'Rourke]

The NER acquired the Hull & Netherlands Steamship Company Limited in 1908 and at the grouping of the railways in 1923 the company was vested in the LNER. The last ship built for the shipping company was actually ordered by the LNER and built by Earle's of Hull in 1929, Yard No.674. Named *Melrose Abbey* (1908grt) she is seen here in Humber Dock with LNER lighters 15 and 26 identifiable near her bow. [Hull Maritime Museum]

Although Hull Joint Dock (later named King George Dock) received Parliamentary approval in 1899, construction did not commence until 1906. This view dated 31 January 1907 shows how the contractors, S. Pearson & Son Limited, tipped spoil to reclaim the foreshore on the north bank of the River Humber in order to create a southern boundary for the new dock estate. The contractor's locomotive, a Manning Wardle 0-6-0 saddle tank, has propelled the wagon to the point of tipping. The wagon has then been chocked to prevent any further movement while the locomotive with the aid of a steel wire rope and pulley block draws back, thereby tipping the wagon to which the rope has been connected. [ABP]

The contractor's dumb buffered wagon No.78, showing the operation in greater detail. The tipping could only take place at times of low water. [ABP]

the first seven of which were transferred from the Wilson Line fleet. The *Otto* was the first vessel used in 1906 followed by the *Cito, Bruno, Hero, Truro, Juno* and *Dynamo* which were transferred between 1906 and 1910. The first new ships built for the company, *Hull* and *York*, came from the Caledon yard at Dundee in 1907. In April 1915 *Hull* was sold to the North of England Protection & Indemnity Association but was re-acquired at the end of the First World War. Earle's of Hull built *Darlington* and sister ship *Harrogate* in 1910 and 1911, respectively. They had a speed of 15 knots and attracted a considerable volume of passenger traffic, the so called *Wilson's Boat Express* train becoming something of an institution in connection with them. *Harrogate* became a Great War casualty. The company continued to exist after the grouping of the railways in 1923 and two more ships were added shortly afterwards. *Selby* built by J. Duthie Torry Shipbuilding Company of Aberdeen joined the fleet in 1922 and *Harrogate* built by Ramage & Ferguson Limited of Leith was added in 1925, taking the name of the ship lost

during the First World War. More details of the fleet can be found in Appendix One.

The NER was clearly benefitting from its shipping involvement as in 1908 it expanded its interests by acquiring the Hull & Netherlands Steamship Company Limited. That company was formed in 1894 and had strengthened its fleet in 1907 by the delivery of four new vessels which no doubt aroused the NER's interest in its acquisition. Two of the new ships, *Rievaulx Abbey* and *Kirkman Abbey* were built by Earles of Hull, the other two, *Whitby Abbey* and *Jervaulx Abbey* were built by William Gray & Company of West Hartlepool. These ships featured in a new daily service between Hull and Rotterdam departing at 6.15pm every weekday, with a saloon return fare of £1 and completing the sea passage in less than 12 hours (Note 63). Other older ships also acquired were *Sea Gull, Swallow, Swan* and *Swift*. The latter was immediately renamed *Selby Abbey* reflecting the change of ownership and the new naming policy. She also participated in the new Rotterdam service. The last ship to be built for the

company, which at grouping was vested in the LNER, was named *Melrose Abbey* and built by Earle's of Hull. She was delivered in February 1929. Further details of the ships acquired can also be found in Appendix One. The funnel colour was buff with a black top and the house flag was a white pennant bearing a red St. George cross with a black ball in the middle.

King George Dock

In the 1898 parliamentary session the NER presented a Bill for dock improvements at Hull which included a proposal to extend Victoria Dock eastwards in order to provide more accommodation for the ever expanding timber trade. The expansion was dependent upon the acquisition of a strip of land owned by Hull Corporation known as the *Western Reservation* which lay between Victoria Dock and the HBR's Alexandra Dock. The HBR countered the NER proposal by depositing a Bill to acquire the same area of land in order to extend the Alexandra Dock estate westwards. Hull Corporation having leant towards the NER proposal sought to impose on the NER an obligation to abolish the numerous level crossings around Hull. This was an extremely costly exercise and so the NER suggested that the Corporation should fund half the cost of the work, which it refused to do. This tussle resulted in the NER abandoning the Bill. Instead it fell back upon the arrangements sanctioned in principle by parliament back in 1893 when the NER acquired the HDC whereby a dock could be constructed jointly with the HBR to the east of Alexandra Dock at Marfleet. An agreement was entered into with the HBR for the construction of the new dock with the HBR granting to the NER running powers over its line to the new

The flag and funnel colours adopted by the Wilson & North Eastern Shipping Company Limited. [Mick O'Rourke]

Left. Several structures, like the one shown here, were erected in the River Humber to lift the contractor's materials and equipment. They were powered by electrically driven winches with the electricity supply generated by temporary windmills. This view looks west and the ship silhouetted between the structure and the tipping operation is probably leaving Alexandra Dock. [ABP]

Below. This scene depicts the construction of the wooden western approach jetty to the entrance lock. The 0-6-0 saddle tank is a product of the Hunslet Engine Company Limited of Leeds. [ABP]

A view from the lock bottom showing the inner set of gates. [ABP]

dock in exchange for the NER granting running powers for the HBR to access Paragon Station. Accordingly a Bill was deposited in the next parliamentary session to effect the proposals. Hull Corporation opposed the Bill in each House but without success and so the Hull Joint Dock Act 1899 came into being on 9 August that year (Note 64). At long last the NER and HBR were working in harmony. However construction of the dock, which was estimated to take seven years, did not commence until 1906 when statutory powers were obtained to extend the timescale.

The construction, maintenance, working and management of the new dock were undertaken by the Hull Joint Dock Committee consisting of three NER directors and three HBR directors. The chairman was appointed by the members on an annual basis such that a representative from each company held that office in alternate years. The cost of constructing and working the dock was borne by the two companies in equal proportion. The total cost of construction was nearly £3m. The joint engineers with overall responsibility were Thomas Monk Newell for the NER and Richard Pawley (1857-1940) for the HBR. The contractors were S. Pearson & Son Ltd. Sir John Wolfe Barry (1836-1918) and Arthur Cameron Hurtzig acted as consulting engineers, Hurtzig had, of course, been resident engineer for the construction of Alexandra Dock. The resident engineer was William Ebdon (1875-1959) of the NER. As built, the dock had a water area of 52.5 acres. The main basin, accessed by a lock from the Humber, was 1,000ft by 1,050ft and there were two arms: the north-west arm, 1,350ft by 325ft and the north-east arm 1,356ft by 450ft. The south west and south east arms were added later.

The total area of land reclaimed from the foreshore was about 206 acres all of which was formerly flooded at high water. The method adopted for the reclamation was by tipping earth banks onto the mud; the banks were constructed to enable the land to be reclaimed in portions. The first or inner portion, comprising about 30.5 acres, embraced the site of the north-west arm and a corresponding width of the main dock basin. The completion of this bank and exclusion of the tide enabled an early start to be made on the permanent works. Other banks were then constructed to embrace the remaining portions of the dock and the site of the entrance lock. The excavated material was used as fill for the quays, other storage areas and as a base for the railway sidings.

The dock walls were constructed of concrete and faced with Staffordshire blue bricks to a depth of 12 ft below cope level; the height of the wall from the dock bottom is 44ft. The walls were coped with granite and cast iron horn bollards were installed. Owing to unsatisfactory foundations, timber wharfing with a stone faced slope was used along the south side of the north east arm. The timber utilised for this was Tasmanian blue gum. Access was and still is gained by an entrance lock from the River Humber with three sets of mitre gates at the outer, middle and inner positions. The lock is 750ft long with a width of 85ft. The depth of water in the dock originally ranged from 31ft to 38ft depending upon the tidal cycle as, at that stage, there was no provision

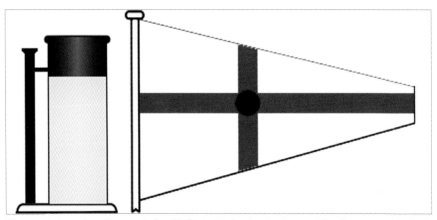

Flag and funnel colours of the Hull & Netherlands Steamship Company Limited. [Mick O'Rourke]

The lockpit after flooding as seen from the River Humber with its three sets of gates: outer, middle and, in the far distance, the inner set. The lock is 750ft long and 85ft wide. The Dock Master's house is under construction on the left and an accumulator tower is being erected on the right. [ABP]

This view, taken from a similar aspect in 1950, shows the King George Dock lock in everyday use. Note the Dock Master's house on the left and the accumulator tower behind the tug's funnel. The tug *Forto* (180grt) owned by Ellerman's Wilson Line is assisting the same company's *Rinaldo* (2957grt). The latter vessel was built by William Gray & Co Ltd of West Hartlepool, Yard No.1188, in 1946 and remained in the Ellerman's fleet until sold in 1967 to Greek owners and renamed *Emerald*. She changed hands on two further occasions before arriving in Split, Yugoslavia for demolition in September 1974 as *Midas*. The tug was another build by Cook, Welton & Gemmell of Beverley, Yard No.649. She was launched on 12 November 1938 and completed the following January. After a very brief spell in the ownership of United Towing, she arrived at Blyth for breaking up in June 1968. [Ivor Innes Photographers, Hessle]

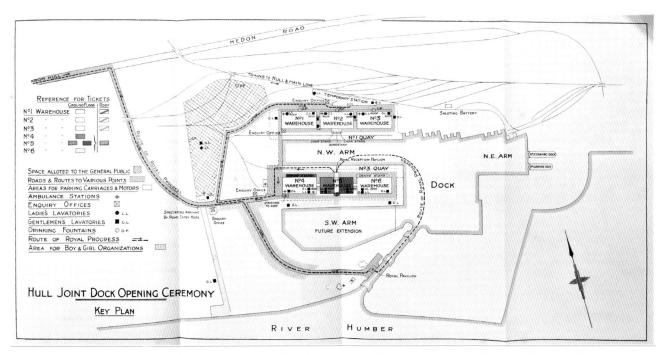

King George Dock was so named on 26 June 1914 when it was opened by King George V. This is the key plan for the opening ceremony. The King and Queen Mary arrived at Hull Paragon station at 11.55am but travelled to the dock in open horse drawn carriages after being received by the Mayor. They boarded the Trinity House yacht *Irene* at the entrance lock at 1pm for the short trip to No.3 Quay where the formal ceremony took place. They did not stay for lunch and departed from the temporary station, to the north of No.2 Warehouse, at 2pm. [Hull History Centre]

for impounding water from the river Humber. Impounding pumps were installed later in 1964. The dock was the first in the country to employ electricity to power the cranes and all the machinery. There was no steam generating plant and the hydraulic machinery for operating the lock gates and the sluices was powered by electric motors. The electricity was supplied by Hull Corporation at 440 volts direct current.

Six ferro-concrete transit sheds were provided on the north-west arm: Nos.1, 2 and 3 Sheds on 1 Quay and Nos.4, 5 and 6 Sheds on 3 Quay which was opposite. All these sheds had flat asphalted roofs which could be used for the storage of cargo and those on 3 Quay each had a double storey. The roof tops of these sheds were equipped with 30cwt capacity electric travelling cranes supplied by Craven Brothers (Manchester) Limited. The electric travelling quay cranes ranged from 3 to 10 tons capacity; the 3-ton cranes were built by Royce Limited, Manchester and the 7-ton and 10-ton cranes were built by Craven Brothers. All the quay cranes had a track gauge of 15ft. A self-propelled electrically operated floating crane was provided with a lifting capacity of 80 tons. The coaling appliances were situated on the north side of the north-east arm where ships berthed in an echelon formation. It was originally intended to install three electrically driven belt conveyors, each capable of loading at the rate of 800 tons per hour and three hydraulic coal hoists, each with a shipping capacity of 500 tons per hour. In practice it seems that only two conveyors and two hoists were installed

and it may well be that the onset of the First Word War curtailed the installation of further coaling appliances. Each appliance had its own separate set of sidings for loaded and empty wagons and gravity working was used to maximum advantage. The sidings were connected to a new rail link which bridged Hedon Road on a Warren truss skew bridge and connected with the H&BR's high level line to Alexandra Dock at Bridges Junction. There was also another more southerly link to Alexandra Dock which crossed the Holderness Drain between the two docks. These new lines were jointly owned by both railway companies. Two dry docks were provided at the eastern extremity of the new dock, the more northerly one was 562ft in length and 72ft wide and the other 460ft in length and 66ft wide. Both dry docks had a depth of 28ft 4in on the sill at high water ordinary spring tides (HWOST).

Formal Opening

The formal opening, which took place on 26 June 1914, was a very grand affair with the records showing that there were over 13,000 guests! An elaborate souvenir brochure was produced with illustrations by marine artists Charles Edward Dixon (1872-1934) who undertook the coloured images and Frank Henry Mason (1875-1965) who used black and white. According to *The Railway Magazine* (Note 65) nine special trains carrying guests were run to a temporary station erected on the north side of the dock. There were three trains from London, two of which ran direct with the third also serving Grantham, Newark, Doncaster and Goole. The

others were as follows: one train from Birmingham serving Burton-on-Trent, Derby, Chesterfield and Cudworth; another from Liverpool serving Manchester, Rochdale, Mirfield and Wakefield; another from Bradford serving Leeds and Selby; another from Newcastle and Darlington which also carried Scottish guests; a train from Sunderland serving West Hartlepool, Stockton, Middlesbrough, Northallerton, Thirsk and York and, finally, one from Willerby & Kirkella station on the H&BR. Guests coming from a distance were served with breakfast on the outward and dinner on the return journey. In addition special trains were run to convey the catering staff, military, bandsmen and others making a total of 16 specials run in connection with the ceremony. Thirteen different kinds of special railway tickets had to be printed to cover the various journeys. Many of the trains were made up of the largest and newest first-class dining cars and saloons and were hauled by NER 4-6-0s over the NER system, though the train from Birmingham via Cudworth was worked in by a HBR locomotive.

The Royal train conveying King George V and Queen Mary started from Retford at 10.45am and was attended by the General Manager of the Great Northern Railway, Charles Hastings Dent (Note 66) and the General Manager of the NER, Sir Alexander Kaye Butterworth. It was worked by a new NER 3-cylinder simple superheated Atlantic No.2164 (Note 67) and arrived at Hull Paragon Station on time at 11.55am. Their Majesties had some official business to attend to in the City of Hull after which they travelled to the

The ferro-concrete grain silo that stood at the extreme west end of the north-west arm of King George Dock; it was not brought into use until 2 June 1919. The silo was designed to hold 43,000 tons of imported grain and the four spouts shown here demonstrate how the grain was loaded into river craft. [Hull Maritime Museum]

This is the north-west arm of King George Dock in 1954 looking west towards the grain silo. The deep sea ship on the left is Blue Funnel Line's *Jason* (10125grt). She was built in 1950 by Swan Hunter at Wallsend-on-Tyne, Yard No.1775, remaining in service until 1972 when she was scrapped. The three tugs to the right are *Norman* (222grt), *Rifleman* (292grt) and *Seaman* (369grt) owned and operated by United Towing of Hull. They were all built by Cochrane of Selby in 1929, 1945 and 1924, respectively and allocated Yard Nos.1047, 1302 and 943. [Ivor Innes Photographers, Hessle]

dock in open horse drawn carriages. It was a fine sunny day. Their arrival at the lockpit at 12.50pm was announced by a bugle fanfare and they were received by the chairmen of the two railway companies: the Right Hon Lord Knaresborough of the NER and William Shaw Wright of the HBR. Those presented included the chairman of the Hull Joint Dock Committee, Sir Hugh Bell, Bart and the members of that committee together with the contractors and consulting engineers. The directors of both railway companies were also presented, together with their general managers and their engineers who had overall responsibility for constructing the new dock. At 1pm their Majesties boarded the Trinity House yacht *Irene* (543grt), a twin-screw steamer normally used for lighthouse inspections (Note 68). They then steamed around the dock for 15 minutes before arriving at 3 Quay which is the quay opposite the present Zeebrugge Passenger Terminal used by P&O Ferries.

The cruiser HMS *Shirmisher* (Note 69) was present in the dock together with eight destroyers of the Seventh Destroyer Flotilla. The *Hull Daily Mail* commented that *the freshly painted black destroyers were in grim contrast with the bright dresses of the ladies on the grandstands*. The royal dais was positioned in the centre of 3 Quay in the front of 5 Shed and was surrounded by two grandstands in front of 4 and 6 Sheds to accommodate some of the guests; others were grouped in seats around the dais and on the flat roofs of the double-storey sheds. Still more guests together with the bandstand and the choir stands were housed on the opposite quay.

At precisely 1.32pm the King proceeded to the front of the dais, declared the dock open and named it King George Dock. There was then a fanfare of trumpets and drums and a Royal Salute of 21 guns fired by the 2nd Northumbrian Brigade, Royal Field Artillery. Then, rather oddly, their Majesties did not stay for lunch. They left by motor car for the Royal train which departed from the temporary station at 2pm. Luncheon for an amazing 3,900 special guests was served on the first floors of 4 and 6 Sheds. In spite of its new name, the dock for many years continued to be known as Joint Dock and was often referred to as such in the 1970s when I was there employed by a stevedoring company as an operations manager. Many of those so calling it did not know why! King George Dock did not become fully operational until 1 August 1914, just three days before war was declared on Germany. The new dock did not enjoy a happy beginning.

First World War and Afterwards
Following the onset of the Great War, the Government took overall control of all railways in return for the payment of a fixed dividend. The NER

management knew that a large number of staff wished to enlist but remain together. On 8 September 1914 a circular was sent to all male employees of military age inviting them to enlist in one of the reserve companies of the North Eastern Railway Battalion, Northumberland Fusiliers and almost by return there were nearly 3,000 applications. The formation of the company, which became the 17th (Service) Battalion Northumberland Fusiliers (NER Pioneers), began immediately and the first detachment arrived at King George Dock on 22 September. With the consent of the HBR, two of the two-storey transit sheds, Nos.5 and 6, were converted for use as barracks and placed at the disposal of the battalion which had assembled by 1 October. The officers' quarters were on board the NER owned Hull & Netherlands steamship *Rievaulx Abbey*, which was berthed alongside. The dock with its open spaces was an ideal place for training the troops providing ample space for drill, manoeuvres and firing ranges, etc. It was well situated on the eastern fringe of Hull and troops could soon reach the coast where they built and manned coastal defences.

The docks at Hull suffered very little damage during 1914-1918 but eight Zeppelin raids between June 1915 and August 1918 caused much damage to housing and over 160 Hull citizens lost their lives. As previously mentioned, the raid on 5 March 1916 blew out the glass in the roof over Paragon Station. While the docks were more or less unscathed, the war played havoc with trade and many ships were lost or seized including three in which the NER had a direct interest (see Appendix One). The war caused delay in completing the planned installations at King George Dock. For example, the grain silo at the extreme west end of the north-west arm was not brought into use until 2 June 1919. It was constructed of reinforced concrete by Henry Simon Ltd of Stockport and had a capacity to hold over 43,000 tons of imported grain which was stored in 288 bins, each of which held 150 tons. Three ships could be discharged simultaneously.

The NER's principal First World War memorial is at York and was unveiled on 14 June 1924 by Field Marshal Lord Plumer (1857-1932). The following year a bronze memorial tablet was erected at the entrance to Alexandra Dock to commemorate the memory of the 183 men of the Hull & Barnsley Railway who died from injuries received during the war. It was unveiled on 9 May 1925 by Colonel Charles William Trotter, CB (1865-1931) who was the company's last chairman. The memorial was his idea and he made a generous contribution towards its cost with other contributions coming from former HBR employees. The Colonel had been inspired by the NER's memorial at York and wanted to recognise HBR staff that had also lost

their lives. The Bishop of Hull led the memorial service which was attended by relatives of the deceased, former HBR staff and directors and officers from the LNER. As a consequence of the A1033 Hedon Road Improvement Scheme, which was subject to a public enquiry in 1993 and subsequently implemented, the HBR memorial was removed for safe keeping and is now on display at Hull's Streetlife Museum of Transport.

Salt End Jetties
An integral part of the Port of Hull is the jetty installation at Salt End where bulk liquids are handled. The NER shrewdly purchased a large tract of land (187 acres) known as Salt End Pasture about one mile to the east of King George Dock and its Act of 1909 authorised the company to construct a branch railway from the Hull to Withernsea line to give access to the land. Moreover, it also authorised the construction of a jetty out into the Humber, which had its root on the recently purchased land. On 16 July 1909 an agreement was made with the HBR by which the latter, subject to sanction by parliament, was granted an option to acquire a half share in the proposed jetty and the connecting railway. The HBR exercised this option in 1913 and the relevant powers were granted in the Hull & Barnsley Railway Act which received the royal assent on 15 August that year (Note 70).

The catalyst for the Salt End initiative was the growing increase in motor transport and the recognition that there was no place where motor spirits could be landed and stored on the east coast north of Thames Haven and Purfleet. Storage tank facilities were provided for motor spirit, kerosene, lubricating oil and heavy oil. Molasses and chemicals came later. Initially there were about 25 storage tanks with holding capacities of 5,000 tons and 6,680 tons. They were fed by pipe lines along the jetty and the ships' pumps were utilised to effect the discharge.

Construction of the first Jetty, known as No.1 Jetty, commenced in January 1913. It was a timber structure extending 1,500ft into the river with a depth of water at its head of 30ft at low water ordinary spring tides (LWOST) which meant that it could accommodate the largest tankers then afloat at any state of the tide. The NER undertook the dredging utilising the company's bucket hopper dredgers *David Dale* and *Lord Joicey*, both named after NER directors (Note 71). The first ship to discharge at the jetty was the motor tanker *Artemis* (3809grt) which arrived on 27 May 1914 with a part cargo of benzene from Roumania. The *Artemis* completed earlier that year by N.V. Nederlandsche Scheepsbouw-Maatschappij of Amsterdam (Yard No.126) survived until 1953, having been renamed *Felania* in 1938. The proposed rail connection with

King George Dock looking east in 1953. The deep sea ship on the left is Blue Star Line's mv *Adelaide Star* (12037grt), a refrigerated cargo liner, built by John Brown & Co Ltd, Clydebank in 1950, Yard No 657. She was in service for 25 years before arriving in South Korea in June 1975 for breaking up. The deep sea ship to the right on 3 Quay is *Ravello* (8452grt) built in 1941 by Cantiere Riuniti, Palermo, Yard No.140, for Italian owner Achille Lauro G & C of Naples. She survived the Second World War and was broken up at La Spezia in May 1971. The tug near her stern is United Towing's *Scotsman* (222grt) built by Cochrane at Selby in 1929, Yard No.1040. In 1964 she was rebuilt and converted to a motor tug, lasting until broken up at Hull by Albert Draper in 1972. The two tall appliances to the stern of *Adelaide Star* are coal conveyors, followed by the two coal hoists in the far distance. [Ivor Innes Photographers, Hessle]

King George Dock looking west. The ship with the list is loading coal from one of the electrically operated coal conveyors. The east end of 3 Shed can be seen above the conveyor. The ship on the left is one of the Danish East Asiatic Company's four-masted motor vessels that an exhaust pipe instead of a funnel. In the Far East, the locals using pidgin English called them: *Four sticks no puff-puff.*

the Hull to Withernsea line was not made, instead the two railway companies accessed the jetty by a joint line extended from the new railway serving King George Dock. By 1921 occupiers of the new site were the Asiatic Petroleum Company (Shell), the Anglo Mexican Company (Shell Mex) and British Petroleum (BP). The venture was extremely successful such that a second jetty was constructed to the west of the first jetty by the LNER in 1928. The ownership of the site and the jetties subsequently passed to the BTDB and to ABP, the present owners.

Organisation of Freight Traffic Working

The NER's organisation and freight traffic working arrangements employed at Hull in April 1913, i.e. before the opening of King George Dock and the onset of the First World War, is illustrated by the diagram on pages 98-99. The following commercial and operating staff reported directly to the District Superintendent: Mineral Traffic Agent, Yard Master (Hull West), Yard Master (Hull East) and the Dock Superintendent. The following key members of staff reported to the Dock Superintendent: Fish Traffic Agent, Dock Traffic Agent (Western and Town Docks), Dock Traffic Agent (Victoria Dock), Dock Masters (Western, Town and Victoria Docks), Quay Master, Riverside Quay. The Dock Traffic Agents were responsible to the Dock Superintendent for the landside operations including the control of quays, cranes and warehouses and they were also responsible to the two Yard Masters for all services in connection with loading, unloading and shunting railway wagons on the dock lines. The Dock Masters were responsible for marine related tasks including the working of the locks, sluices, swing and lift bridges, mooring of vessels and the movement of lighters and other craft in the docks to avoid any obstruction to the sea going vessels. The Quay Master at Riverside Quay had responsibility for both marine and landside operations. It is interesting to note that at this time in addition foreign going ships, there were many regular coastwise services northwards to Newcastle, Leith, Grangemouth, Kirkcaldy, Dundee and Aberdeen and southwards to Boston, Wisbech, King's Lynn, Great Yarmouth, Ipswich, London, Southampton and Bristol. As with the foreign going services they were assigned to particular docks and berths.

So prior to the opening of King George Dock most of the NER's coal shipments took place in Albert and Victoria Docks. The speed of loading with the major appliances was quite remarkable but, of course, operational difficulties did sometimes prevent the maximum tipping speeds

shown opposite from being achieved. This could involve breakdowns or shunting difficulties in bringing in the full wagons and getting away the empties. At busy times additional shunting locomotives could be taken from other duties and used to lead the coal to the dock sides and take the empties away. Everything possible had to be done to prevent a stoppage to the loading of ships. All coal loaded at the NER's docks was trimmed by the railway company's staff but in the case of loading bunkers, private gangs of trimmers could be employed by the shippers. In St. Andrew's Dock many trawlers took bunkers direct from small craft. Insofar as Victoria Dock was concerned the Drypool Foreman arranged which locomotive was to work particular loads of coal and return empties. Owing to heavy local weekday passenger traffic only two trains of empty coal wagons could be worked from Victoria Dock between 8.00am and 10.00am. There was a further restriction on Mondays in that the empties could not be despatched until the Hornsea and Withernsea cattle trains had passed off the branch, even if this was after 10.00am.

Hull only became publicly known as a coal port in 1885 following the opening of Alexandra Dock by the HBR. However, during the previous year 631,454 tons of coal was shipped through the HDC's coal handling appliances. Indeed in 1891, just two years prior to its acquisition by the NER, the HDC handled 1,015,551 tons which must have been a record. However, by 1910 the total coal shipped through the port had increased to 4,500,000 tons, of which 2,800,000 tons went through Alexandra Dock. Just prior to the First World War the overall annual total shipped exceeded 6,000,000 tons, a quarter of which went into ships' bunkers!

Coal for shipment

Appliance	SWL (Tons)	Wagons Tipped per hour
ST. ANDREW'S DOCK		
Hoist	20	18
No.49 Crane	25	18
WILLIAM WRIGHT DOCK		
No.46 Crane	40	20
ALBERT DOCK		
No.1 Hoist	20	50
No.2 Hoist	20	35
No.3 Hoist	20	35
No.4 Hoist	25	55
No.23 Crane	40	20
No.32 Crane	40	20
No.33 Crane	25	28
No.34 Crane	40	20
No.42 Crane	40	18
HUMBER DOCK		
Hoist	20	28
No.41 Crane	25	18
RAILWAY DOCK		
No.16 Crane	20	8
No.21 Crane	25	28
VICTORIA DOCK		
No.1 Hoist	20	20
No.2 Belt Conveyor		55
No.3 Belt Conveyor		55
No.26 Crane	40	10

Timber traffic

For moving timber from the quaysides to the storage yards or direct to the merchants' yards, the NER introduced a fleet of basic four-wheeled trucks known as timber bogies that were unique to timber operations at Hull. Their introduction was prompted following the increasing use of steamships as timber carriers. The sailing ships that had carried timber hitherto berthed end on to the quays, whereas steamships berthed alongside occupying more quay space but enabling the timber to be discharged more rapidly. The discharged timber had to be moved away from the quays very quickly to avoid congestion and the bogies solved the problem. The NER used them mainly at Victoria Dock but the HBR copied the design and used them on the Alexandra Dock estate. Hundreds were built up until the outbreak of the Second World War. Each bogie was wooden framed and designed to carry 7 tons of timber. The ends of the two longitudinal beams of the frame were fitted with iron plates and acted as dumb buffers. The timber was stacked on three wooden cross members and roped or chained down to hooks positioned on either side of the bogie frame. Each bogie had its own number. The shunting locomotives were fitted with an additional set of dumb buffers to match those on the timber bogies which were for internal use only. The bogies were also moved by capstans and much care had to be taken to avoid damage to the timber by rough shunts.

The custom at the port was that all sawn timber cargos (consisting of deals, battens and boards), pit props and mining timber were placed to quay or on bogies at the receivers' request. The dockers carrying the loose timber off the ships wore leather saddles over their shoulders to protect them from injury. Telegraph poles, pitch pine and other large timbers were usually discharged using the ship's derricks. Traffic from the timber yards for despatch over the NER main lines was either loaded direct at the yards or carted to the timber loading facility at Drypool. An allowance was made to the merchants if they loaded the wagons but the NER was directly responsible for roping or chaining all loads and for sheeting when required. Pit props were usually discharged direct from ship to quay where they were sorted and loaded up for forwarding by rail.

The job of loading timber to rail from the timber ponds was split between the NER's railway staff and the dock department staff. The latter were responsible for loading timber that had been stored in the ponds by the dock department, telegraph poles for Staddlethorpe and traffic for stations within a short distance from Hull. Railway labour was employed in all other cases, including timber traffic delivered in the dock waters at

King George Dock's two coal hoists.

The ship being manoeuvred in King George Dock by United Towing steam tugs *Irishman* (222grt) and *Seaman* (369grt) had a fascinating history. She was completed in 1909 by Sir Raylton Dixon & Company of Middlesbrough as *Vasari* (10117grt), Yard No.539, for the Liverpool based Lamport & Holt Line. In 1928 she was sold to Hull's Hellyer Bros, renamed *Arctic Queen* and converted as a vessel to support line fishing for halibut off Greenland which was done from small boats (dories) that can be seen suspended from the ships davits. The photograph was taken between 1929 when *Irishman* was built by Cochrane's of Selby, Yard No.1041 and 1935 when *Arctic Queen* was sold to Russian owners at Vladivostok and converted to a fish factory ship, surviving until 1979 when in February that year she arrived at Kaohsiung, Taiwan for breaking up. [Hull Maritime Museum]

the ships' side for direct forwarding. The reference to Saddlethorpe relates to the creosote works commissioned there in 1907 by Richard Wade & Sons (Note 72). The works had a private siding which received trains of telegraph poles and railway sleepers on a daily basis for treatment. The poles arrived wet as they had been stored in the ponds and so they were stacked in the open for about a year before being impregnated with creosote under steam pressure. The works survived until 1970.

Fish

It was not until 1883 when St. Andrew's Dock opened that the fishing industry could at last unload the trawlers onto the market and transfer the fish straight away into waiting fish trains. The NER had three outlets to reach its customers located outwith its own system. Fish vans for London, the South East and East Anglia were handed to the GNR at Doncaster – indeed the GNR also had running powers to York for such traffic which were frequently used. Other fish traffic went to Normanton for onwards conveyance by the Midland Railway to the East and South Midlands and also to the LYR for northern destinations. Last, but certainly not least, much fish traffic went to Leeds for transfer to the LNWR. The NER's main rival was, of course the HBR which established its Billingsgate fish station on the south side of West Dock Street between West Dock Avenue and Harrow Street. There were two loading lines each holding 24 vans. During the early 1900s, five fish trains a day left this station; two to Carlton for the LYR, two through trains for the Midland Railway and one general purpose through train which ran if required. Loaded fish vans were also attached to NER and HBR passenger trains as the need arose.

Other Perishable Goods

In 1913 butter, margarine, bacon and eggs were discharged from vessels arriving from Copenhagen (Railway Dock); Gothenburg (Albert Dock); Rotterdam (Riverside Quay) Amsterdam and Harlingen (Humber Dock); Finland and Riga (Victoria Dock). Discharging commenced between 11.00pm and midnight. The traffic from the Rotterdam boat was loaded direct to rail vans at Riverside Quay and that from the Finland and Riga vessels at Nos.1 and 2 Sheds at Victoria Dock. The butter, margarine and eggs from the remaining boats was carted to the English Street Warehouse and loaded up there; the bacon was carted to the general warehouse in Railway Street. The following trains were run at the approximate times stated, the actual time of departure taking place as soon as loading operations were finished:

The trains as far as possible comprised vacuum braked stock and special care was taken to ensure that the vans were clean. Special attention was given to the loading of 25 ton vans with butter and bacon. The traffic had to be carefully

FROM	TIME	DESTINATION
Manor House Yard	1.50am	Leeds
Manor House Yard	3.50am	Normanton
Victoria Dock	3.50am	Normanton
English Street	4.00am	Leeds and Normanton
Riverside Quay	5.00am	Leeds and Normanton

sorted according to consignments and the whole of each consignment kept together.

Fruit and vegetable traffic was accommodated at No.35 Shed on the south side of Albert Dock. Oranges and lemons were imported as full ship loads, consisting of 20,000 to 30,000 loose cases at any one time. The cases were delivered to stages on the ship's deck by the shipowner, from whence they were barrowed by gangs of men employed by the merchant to the shed, subsequently being delivered by the merchant to the receiver's 'rully' (local name for a horse drawn flat-bed cart). Onions from Alexandria were also accommodated in No.35 Shed but were dealt with on the upper storey so as not to taint the fruit. Slings of 6 or 8 bags were delivered from the ship's hold to the deck. They were then craned to the upper storey of the shed for weighing, each bag being tagged with its individual weight. They were then stowed to mark in the shed, subsequently being barrowed to an opening in the shed floor, where the bags were shot down a chute on to rullies below.

Hull played a surprising role in growing the British banana industry. In 1902 Elders & Fyffes adopted Manchester as the northern port for its Caribbean banana business, transferring it to the Merseyside port of Garston with effect from 1 January 1912. However not all the fruit discharged at Manchester and Garston was destined for consumption at home. As early as 1905, consignments were sent to Hull by train for onward shipment to Holland and Norway. The experiment was successful and as demand grew the package and carriage arrangements were improved. Initially the bananas for trans-shipment were stacked in returnable crates but as the business developed they were placed in specially designed 'lift vans' built by Hull carpenters. These vans which held between 60 and 80 bunches (Note 73) were slung into the ships' holds to be returned empty in due course. Connecting shipping services from Hull to Belgium, Denmark, France, Germany, Holland, Sweden and Norway thus provided a catalyst for further growth in the banana trade until such time as direct shipments to the continental ports became feasible.

Grain and seed traffic

The flour milling industry at Hull grew to become one of the largest and most up-to-date in the country, the industry providing a market for all the principal grain producing countries of the world. Prior to the opening of the King George Dock silo in 1919, all grain in NER docks at Hull was discharged from ship to craft moored alongside. It was then conveyed to a dock or private warehouse for storage, to one of the creeks for forwarding by rail or direct to its destination by inland navigation. If the grain arrived in bulk it was put into in 4 and 5 bushel bags in the ship's hold. The former were weighed before being tied and lowered into the craft alongside; the 5 bushel bags were weighed and then ripped before being shot via a chute into the craft.

Hull also secured the reputation of being the largest centre in the world for seed crushing and oil extraction, a successor to the old industry for refining whale oil. At its peak over 30 crushing and extracting mills were located in Hull and the surrounding district, importing large amounts of oil bearing seeds, nuts and kernels. As a consequence Hull became one of the foremost producers of subsidiary products such as cattle, pig and poultry foods, edible fats, margarine and soap.

Other commodities

The above is just a snapshot of some of the main cargos handled at Hull in the early 20th century. Both the NER and HBR also handled large quantities of wool in bales, iron and steel, chemicals and general cargo. There was also a lairage and slaughterhouse located to the south of Victoria Dock for foreign cattle and sheep; 700 head of cattle could be accommodated or 500 cattle and 1,400 sheep. There was also a major slaughterhouse to the north of Railway Dock on land occupied in recent years by retailer *Toys R Us*.

Shunting operations

Much shunting was carried out in yards and on the docks using horses and capstans but the steam locomotives were the principal motive power providers for shunting movements. Sharp curves abounded on the dock lines and so it is not surprising that the NER, like the HBR, made good use of 0-4-0 tank engines with short wheelbases. Between November 1871 and November 1875 the NER purchased eleven 0-4-0 saddle tanks from three different makers: six from Manning, Wardle & Company of Leeds, one from Hawthorns & Company of Leith and the remaining four from Black, Hawthorn & Company of Gateshead. They were of the makers' standard types and became known as NER Class 900. Two of the Manning Wardle locomotives were delivered to Hull. They belonged to the maker's Class H and carried NER Nos.959 (MW 467) and 997 (MW 573) being despatched on 22 September 1873 and 25 November 1875, respectively.

A fine array of motive power in the NER Dairycoates shed yard in 1913 with a line up of 0-8-0 goods tender engines to the right. The leading 0-8-0s are Class T1 No.769 on the right and 764 on the left. They were built at Darlington in August 1911 and were withdrawn in December 1946 and November 1948, respectively. This is a posed view as all the locomotives have specially whitened buffer and cylinder covers. There is one interloper in the form of a Lancashire & Yorkshire Railway 0-8-0 tender engine which is the second locomotive from the left. [Mick Nicholson collection]

Above. A cast iron number plate from timber bogie 01040.

Left. The NER made extensive use of timber bogies. Five of them are in use here having been stacked with loose timber discharged from a vessel berthed in Drypool Basin using the ship's derricks. The photograph was taken in 1950. [Ivor Innes, Photographers, Hessle]

Below. An unidentified NER Class K 0-4-0 (later LNER Class Y8) tank engine at work in Victoria Dock circa 1900. There were five members of the class all built at Gateshead in 1890 specifically for use on the docks at Hull. [Robert Humm collection]

FAMOUS RIVER SERIES - GRIMSBY

THE HUMBER

SAILINGS TO AND FROM ALL PARTS OF THE WORLD

HULL – BRITAIN'S THIRD AND CHEAPEST PORT

GRIMSBY–WORLD'S PREMIER FISHING PORT

IMMINGHAM – DEEPEST DOCK ON EAST COAST

ADJACENT HOLIDAY RESORTS – CLEETHORPES AND WITHERNSEA

LONDON AND NORTH EASTERN RAILWAY

In 1923 the LNER acquired control of all the docks in Hull, together with the Ports of Grimsby and Immingham. This 1932 poster by Frank Henry Mason (1876-1965) advertises the LNER's strong presence on the River Humber and encourages holidaying at Cleethorpes on the south bank and Withernsea on the north.

7. The London and North Eastern Railway 1923-1947

Grouping

The LNER not only brought together all the docks and railways at Hull under one unified control but also the competing Ports of Grimsby and Immingham and their associated railways. The Lincolnshire assets were owned and operated by the former Great Central Railway (GCR) which also became a constituent part of the LNER. Like the NER, the GCR also operated extensive short sea shipping services and the ferry service from Hull to New Holland and so these maritime activities also became part of the LNER empire. The only Humber port installation of any significance that escaped the net was the upriver Port of Goole which remained under the control of the Aire & Calder Navigation. Other important constituent railway companies within the LNER group were the Great Eastern Railway, the Great Northern Railway and two Scottish companies, the latter being the North British Railway and the Great North of Scotland Railway.

Rationalisation and Improvements

The former HBR Cannon Street station witnessed its last passenger train on 13 July 1924. From the following day all former HBR passenger services were diverted to Hull Paragon over the newly completed spur at Spring Bank. The station master, Arthur Ferdinand Richardson (1863-1926) issued the last ticket; as a booking clerk he had issued the very first ticket when the railway opened on 27 July 1885. The station carried on as a goods station. A great deal of soft fruit was handled there, especially during the strawberry season. For example, on 1 July 1924 17,345 packages were handled with sales taking place on the platforms (Note 74). The locomotive shed at Alexandra Dock was demolished in December 1927 but locomotives continued to be allocated there and stood in the open. With effect from 1 January 1932 the former HBR passenger service was withdrawn between South Howden and Cudworth.

The LNER did much to improve the facilities at St. Andrew's Dock to cope with increases in the fish trade. After a fire in 1929, the whole of the No.2 Fish Market had to be rebuilt; following that, work started on the reconstruction of the No.1 Fish Market so that by 1933 both markets were up to date and Hull was handling a larger fish tonnage than any other port in the country. Landings of trawl fish in 1932 amounted to 206,568 tons and in addition to that were 25,960 tons of Norwegian herrings and 6,000 tons of fish from other sources. In the same year a record shipment of 710,887 tons of coal as bunkers for trawlers was recorded (Note 75).

Soon after grouping, the LNER became interested in small four-wheeled vertical boiler locomotives manufactured by Sentinel Waggon Works (1920) Ltd of Shrewsbury. The drive was transmitted by chains to the 2ft 6in diameter driving wheels. Advantages lay in economy and their suitability for one-man operation. Initial trials were encouraging and between 1925 and 1933 a total of 56 locomotives had been acquired – 24 single speed versions of Class Y1 and 32 examples of the two-speed version of Class Y2. The engines were not necessarily intended to replace the older 0-4-0 tank engines. In many cases they replaced shunting horses or were engaged on light duties previously undertaken by larger engines. One of the engines was specially modified to work on Victoria Dock by removing the ballast weight in order to keep the overall weight down to 14 tons. The locomotive was built in 1926, Maker's No.6735, but was not taken into LNER stock as No.19 until January 1929. At the end of 1931, Hull's allocation was seven Sentinel locomotives as detailed overleaf.

This Valentine's multi-view postcard of Hull's docks was posted on 30 July 1928 to an address in Anglesey. King George Dock rightly has centre stage, Riverside Quay features as does Queen's, Prince's and Albert Docks but Alexandra Dock is strangely omitted.

SHED	CLASS	LNER No	SENTINEL No/DATE
BOTANIC GARDENS	Y1	19	6735/1926
	Y1	108	7839/1929
DAIRYCOATES	Y1	106	7838/1929
	Y1	187	7848/1929
	Y3	90	7141/1927
	Y3	193	7851/1929
SPRINGHEAD	Y3	117	8476/1931

On completion in 1927, No.79 of Class Y1 (Maker's No.7138) and No.90 of Class Y3 (Maker's No.7141) went to Hull where they were tried on duties intended to economise on pick-up goods workings. From Dairycoates one worked as far as Brough, shunting at Hessle and Ferriby on the way and setting empty and full wagons to be collected by the following pick-up goods train. At Brough the engine shunted the yard and then, after the goods had arrived, it shunted the train whilst the goods' engine took water. The Sentinel then returned to Hull, again shunting at Ferriby and Hessle on the way back. A similar working was introduced on the former HBR line as far as North Cave. However, the Brough working had ceased by 1932 and the North Cave working by 1934. At the end of the LNER regime in 1947 only four Sentinels were allocated to Hull. Class Y1 No.8151 (ex-187) was at Botanic Gardens and acted as the Stepney goods yard pilot and the following members of the same class were at Dairycoates: Nos.8137 (ex-79), 8139 (ex-19) and 8140 (ex-100, Sentinel 7837/1929); two of these shunted at Victoria Dock as and when required.

In 1935 the LNER introduced a Pullman service from Hull Paragon to London King's Cross which completed the journey in 3½ hours, then the fastest service passengers had ever enjoyed between the two cities. There was one stop at Doncaster where the four Hull Pullman cars were attached and detached to the *Yorkshire Pullman* which ran between Harrogate and London. In the timetable for the period 3 July to 24 September 1939, the one in operation immediately prior to the Second World War, departure from Hull was at 11.30 am arriving at 3.00pm. The working in the opposite direction left King's Cross at 4.45pm, arriving Hull at 8.15pm. It was clearly assumed that Pullman passengers would spend at least one night in the capital! The Pullman cars were the property of the Pullman Car Company Limited and a supplementary

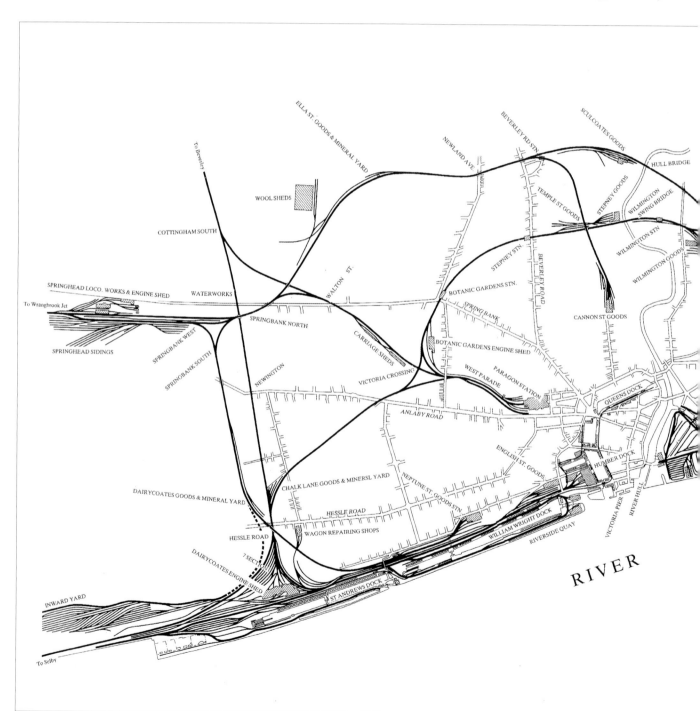

fare was charged for each single journey at a cost of 6s 0d for first class passengers and 3s 0d for third class. Meals and refreshments were served at every seat.

On 9 December 1935 a new mechanised inward goods yard was opened at Hull with an entrance from Hessle Haven Junction on the old Hull and Selby line. Hitherto the traffic had been handled in a small marshalling yard consisting of nine sidings with a shunting neck that would accommodate no more than 27 wagons. With the large number of docks and terminal points, plus the branch lines, inward traffic could only be partially marshalled in the old inward yard and many of the wagons had to be taken to other groups of sidings, including those on the docks, for second sorting and distribution. The new yard had 30 sidings and six tandem reception sidings each of which could

accommodate 100 wagons. Each of the 30 sidings could accommodate a minimum of 70 wagons and those sidings together with the reception and departure lines totalled to 24½ miles of track. The new yard marshalled inward traffic from all directions with the exception of that from the former HBR route. In the centre of the group of reception lines was an additional line used only by the hump engine for the purpose of getting around the train to propel it over the hump. A shunter uncoupled the wagons into *cuts* in accordance with the sequence of sidings into which the wagons were to be shunted. There were four groups of sidings, each group accessed via a hydraulically operated retarder operated by a brakesman from the control tower. The point switching by means of compressed air was also operated by

one man from a desk in the control tower. It was very much a state of the art installation capable of dealing with 3,000 wagons per day (Note 76).

As mentioned in Chapter One, the LNER closed Queen's Dock in 1930. The infilling commenced on 14 August that year using foundry waste, dredgings and other materials but the task was not completed until 1934. The dock was sold to Hull Corporation at a cost of £117,000 and is now the very attractive present day Queen's Gardens. When the NER acquired the Hull Dock Company in 1893 it also acquired the Hull South Bridge Company and responsibility for maintaining the south bridge over the River Hull. Both the NER and the HDC were authorised to subscribe to the bridge company and did so and under the Hull Docks Act 1877 certain powers, rights and privileges were vested in the

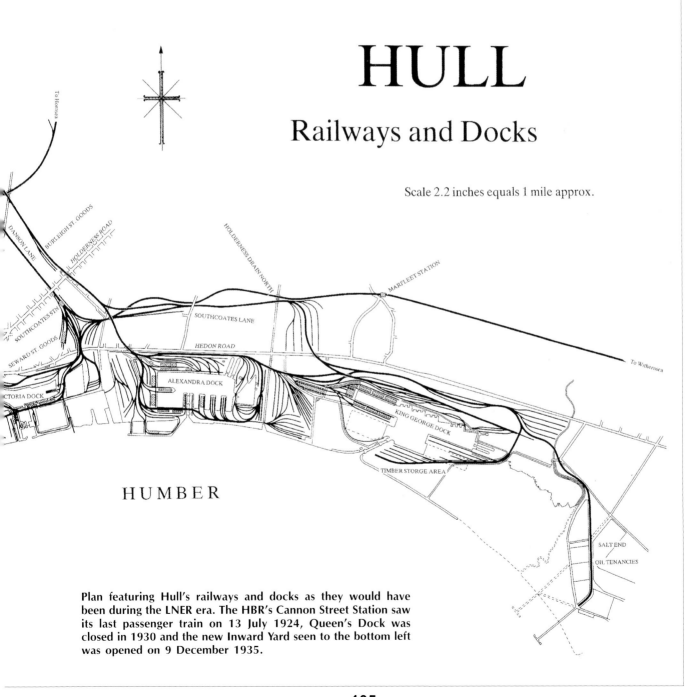

HULL

Railways and Docks

Scale 2.2 inches equals 1 mile approx.

HUMBER

Plan featuring Hull's railways and docks as they would have been during the LNER era. The HBR's Cannon Street Station saw its last passenger train on 13 July 1924, Queen's Dock was closed in 1930 and the new Inward Yard seen to the bottom left was opened on 9 December 1935.

A November 1935 view of the railway approach towards Hull. The lines in the centre of the photograph to the right of Dairycoates West signal box follow the route of the old Hull & Selby Railway which was the first line into Hull, by this time carrying goods traffic only. The lines veering way to the left take passenger trains to and from Paragon Station and those running across the picture over the diamond crossings are the up and down goods lines from Hessle Road to St. Andrew's Dock Junction. The vans assembled on the right are in the Outward Yard. The ships on the horizon to the right are trawlers on the slipways at the west end of the St. Andrew's Dock Extension and the building with the tall chimney to the left of them is the Hull Fish Meal Factory. Dairycoates locomotive shed is on the horizon to the left of the signal box and two old NER carriages can be seen on the siding to the extreme left in use as permanent way staff vehicles. The picture, with the freshly ballasted track, was taken to illustrate the re-modelled junction to accommodate the new Inward Yard located behind the camera to the left. The new yard came into operation on 9 December 1935. [Mick Nicholson collection]

This winter scene looks in the opposite direction away from Hull. The sheds in St. Andrew's Dock are to the left and Dairycoates locomotive shed is to the right of the junction. [Hull Maritime Museum]

The LNER has stamped its ownership of No.2 Fish Quay on the sheds in the St. Andrew's Dock Extension. The view looks east with the Hull Fish Meal Factory and its pungent smell on the right. [Hull Maritime Museum]

HDC and subsequently passed on to the NER which became the holder of all the shares in the bridge company. At grouping in 1923 the bridge company was vested in the LNER. The condition of the bridge gradually deteriorated and the LNER entered into discussions with Hull Corporation over its closure which focussed on the ownership of the bridge passing to the Corporation, a proposal which was eventually rejected. The bridge was closed permanently on 31 December 1934 but remained in situ for ten years before being demolished in 1944. The Hull South Bridge Company, although defunct, was not finally dissolved until 6 August 1947.

Humber Ferries
Railway interest in ferries across the Humber was instigated by the Great Grimsby & Sheffield Junction Railway which, along with other railway companies, amalgamated to form the MSLR in 1847. The MSLR was renamed the Great Central Railway (GCR) on 1 August 1897 and as such became a constituent company of the LNER in 1923. By this means the LNER acquired the ferry service and the ferries that the GCR operated between New Holland on the Lincolnshire coast and Hull. The five ferries acquired were all shallow-draughted paddle steamers and two were quickly scrapped in 1924, these were *Magna Charta II* (116grt) built in 1872 by T. Charlton of Grimsby (Yard No.6) and *Grimsby II* (351grt) built by Earle's of Hull in 1888 (Yard No.314). The former was used by the LNER as a

tug prior to scrapping. The other three vessels which continued to run the service were *Cleethorpes* (302grt), *Brocklesby* (508grt) and *Killingholme* (508grt). *Cleethorpes* was built by Gourlay Bros. Ltd of Dundee in 1903 (Yard No.209) and remained in service on the Humber until 1934 when she was sold to the Redcliffe Shipping Company Ltd for pleasure cruises on the Firth of Forth from Leith and renamed *Cruising Queen*. She did not perform well on this duty and was scrapped the following year. *Brocklesby* and *Killingholme* were both built by Earle's of Hull in 1912 (Yard Nos.583 and 584). They were *...about the ugliest monstrosities imaginable, each being double-ended, very broad and with a ridiculous chimney-like funnel abaft the paddles* (Note 77). An unusual feature was the slinging of the lifeboats over the paddleboxes.

Killingholme had been employed for the opening of King George Dock in 1914 and during World War One all three of these surviving paddle steamers had operated as seaplane tenders. *Brocklesby* remained on the Humber until 1935 when she too was sold to the Redcliffe Shipping Company for pleasure cruising on the Firth of Forth; she was renamed *Highland Queen* but again proved to be unsuccessful in Scottish waters and was sold for scrapping in Germany the following year. In 1928 the LNER augmented the ferry fleet with the transfer of the paddle steamer *Frodingham* (218grt). Originally named *Dandy Dinmont*, she was built by A. & J. Inglis of Glasgow in 1895 (Yard

No.237) for the North British Railway for operation on the River Clyde. She worked on the Humber until 1936 when she was sold to breakers in Ghent, Belgium.

A great change took place in 1934 with the introduction of two brand new coal burning paddle steamers and improvements to the pier terminals at Hull and New Holland by the provision of floating pontoons. The two identical new vessels were built by William Gray & Company Ltd of West Hartlepool (Yard Nos.1059 and 1060) and were named *Tattershall Castle* (550grt) and *Wingfield Castle* (550grt) to represent the Lincolnshire and Yorkshire sides of the river. Tattershall Castle is some 12 miles north east of Sleaford and Wingfield Castle in Suffolk was the ancestral home of the famous De la Pole family which was closely connected with the early history of Hull. The new pontoons, each 150ft long and 50ft wide, were connected by hinged bridges to the New Holland Pier on the Lincolnshire bank and to Victoria Pier at Hull. The Hull pontoon was built by the Furness Shipbuilding Company Ltd at Haverton Hill Yard on the River Tees and was towed around the coast to Hull. The bridges were 23ft wide with a central roadway 10ft wide for vehicles and livestock with passenger footways 5ft wide on either side. Both bridges and pontoons were covered over to give protection from adverse weather. The maximum gradient of the hinged bridges at low water spring tides was 1 in 9 in both cases whilst at high water the approach to and from the

LNER Class Y8 No.561 (ex-NER Class K) 0-4-0 tank engine, with accompanying match trucks, shunts Hull's fish docks in 1931. The locomotive was turned out of Gateshead Works in June 1890 and was withdrawn in September 1936. [Patrick Ransome-Wallis/Mortons Media].

The route out of Hull Paragon station on 6 May 1937. It was an LNER publicity shot taken in connection with the 1938 route relay interlocking and colour light signalling scheme. The building under construction on the left is the new panel box brought into use on 24 April 1938. Shunting in the background is an ex HBR 0-6-0 tender engine which was amongst the last of that company's tender engines to remain in service. [Mick Nicholson collection]

Above. This image taken on the same day as the last but a little further away from Paragon Station, also looks west; it shows the NER signal gantry erected in 1904 spanning four tracks with no less than 22 arms. West Parade Junction is just beyond and the Bridlington line can be seen veering to the right under Argyle Street Bridge. [Mick Nicholson collection]

Left. Hessle Road level crossing in LNER days looking east towards Hull city centre with two electric trams in the distance. The view is taken from the former HBR embankment that took its high level tracks to Neptune Street goods station away to the right. The train of empty wagons on the level crossing is coming off the Western Docks having tipped its load of coal. Wagon 6736 belongs to Chatterley-Whitfield Collieries Ltd of Tunstall, North Staffordshire. The tramway along the Hessle Road lasted longer than all the other tramway routes, not being replaced by trolleybuses until July 1945. [Hull Maritime Museum]

HULL: BRITAIN'S CHEAPEST PORT

DIRECTLY SERVES AN INDUSTRIAL AREA OF 13,000,000 PEOPLE

FULL PARTICULARS AS TO FACILITIES AND CHARGES FROM DISTRICT GOODS MANAGER L·N·E·R HULL; OR FROM REPRESENTATIVE FOR DOCKS & OVERSEAS TRADE, 87 GRACECHURCH STREET, LONDON, E.C.3.

LNER 1929 poster illustrating Alexandra Dock and its River Pier by artist Henry George Gawthorn (1879-1941), who was born in Northampton. He commenced his career as an architect but later turn to pictorial art and graphic design. He produced many posters for the LNER but on this occasion rather overdid the use of blue. The muddy waters of the Humber are never quite like that!

pontoons was virtually level. The new facilities were a vast improvement on the previous arrangement whereby motor vehicles had to craned on and off the ferries. The new vessels had more room for vehicles and were equipped with refreshment buffets for the passengers. Of course the newcomers heralded the departure of *Cleethorpes* and *Brocklesby* but *Killingholme* survived until July 1945 being used as a standby vessel and for excursions on the Humber which were very popular prior to World War Two. The LNER ordered a third new paddle steamer for its Humber ferry service just prior to the outbreak of war. It was named *Lincoln Castle* (598grt), built by A. & J. Inglis of Glasgow (Yard No.1024) and delivered in 1940 with provision for 914 passengers and 20 cars. *Lincoln Castle* and the two ferries built in 1934 passed to the British Transport Commission with effect from 1 January 1948 and their subsequent history is dealt with in Chapter Eight.

Associated Humber Lines

Associated Humber Lines (AHL) was an organisation created in May 1935 to manage the various railway shipping

services based on the Humber ports. The services concerned were not only those inherited by the LNER from the NER and GCR but also those operated by the LMS from Goole. The services involved are summarised thus:

Hull & Netherlands Steamship Company Ltd wholly owned by the LNER.

Wilsons and NER Shipping Company Ltd, with the LNER as majority shareholder.

Former GCR services operating from Grimsby.

LMS services from Goole operated by the Goole Steam Shipping Company Limited and the LMS service from Goole to Copenhagen.

The ownership of the vessels remained with the railway companies and AHL had no involvement with the operation of the ports, control of which remained with the LNER in respect of Grimsby, Immingham and Hull and with the Aire & Calder Navigation in the case of Goole. The Humber ferry service remained under the direct control of the LNER. The funnel colour of vessels managed by AHL was buff with a red band touching a black top with the letters AHL in black on the red band.

The house flag was blue with the letters AHL in red on a central white disc with the letter A above HL. The organisation survived under various ownerships until November 1971 when its operations ceased. Its history after 1948 is covered in Chapter Eight.

Hull's Docks in 1939

Once established the LNER produced an annual trade publication containing up-to-date information on all its ports with plans and illustrations. The thirteenth issue covered the year 1939 and it seems very appropriate to extract from that publication all the information relevant to Hull's docks and other marine installations as they were immediately prior to the outbreak of the Second World War. What follows are direct quotes from the 1939 publication. The text is in the present tense as it was in 1939 and apart from a few minor punctuation and spelling changes to suit modern day presentation, remains exactly the same.

****

'In order to gain a clear perspective of the Hull Docks, it is convenient to begin at the **St. Andrew's Dock**, at the western extremity of the dock estate. The St. Andrew's Dock, with its extension, covering a water area of nearly 20 acres, is devoted entirely to the fishing industry, an exceptionally important one in view of the fact that it supports nearly one-fifth of the population of Hull [approximately 320,000 in 1939]. The quantity of fish landed at Hull in 1937 was 328,207 tons, as compared with 319,612 tons in 1936. The whole north side of St. Andrew's Dock is reserved for the landing and marketing of fish. There are two markets, both of which have been rebuilt, giving a total length of 3,300 feet with a width of 90 feet. Concrete office boxes have been provided on both markets, for the merchants and a block of offices has been built between the two markets, which contain accommodation for the post office, fish merchants, banks and the railway company. The premises are also the site of the Hull Fish Merchants' Club. Facilities are provided at the south side of the dock for the supply of coal, ice and provisions to trawlers and extensive alterations are at present taking place in order to increase the coal-shipping facilities. The appliances for the coaling of trawlers have a maximum capacity of 460 tons per hour. Last year [1938], 805,893 tons of coal was shipped. At the west end of the dock there are four slipways and a fifth is available by

means of one of these being provided with the most modern side slipping mechanism; beyond the slipways an extensive area is provided for fish-drying purposes.

'The **Albert and William Wright Dock** has a water area of 30 acres. Double-storey sheds are provided for the accommodation of hard fruit cargoes, which are discharged direct into the shed and loaded into rail wagons under cover. The dock also possesses a conveniently situated cold store. This dock is noteworthy for the number and variety of its handling appliances. The grain warehouses, transit sheds and modern two-storey sheds for fruit and provisions cover an area of quay level of 52,000 square yards and a total floor area of over 20 acres. There is excellent coaling equipment, consisting of three hoists and five cranes. A graving dock opens from the west end of the Albert and William Wright Dock of 501 feet in length, gate to head and a width at its entrance of 50 feet, the depth of water on its sill ranging from 16 feet to 20 feet. This graving dock is equipped with two side berths each 150 feet long, over blocks.

'A feature of considerable interest in the vicinity of the Albert and William Wright Dock is the **Riverside Quay**, which was

constructed by the then North Eastern Railway Company and opened in 1907, with the object particularly providing facilities for passengers, fruit and provision traffic. The quay is 2,500 feet in length, though the space available will admit of its extension to more than double this length as and when necessary. The Riverside Quay is undoubtedly one of the most important components of the Hull dock system. In crossing the river by the ferry service from New Holland, one cannot fail to be impressed by its general appearance and its fine cranage and warehousing installation. The quay varies from 85 feet to 100 feet in width and it has a depth of water alongside enabling vessels to berth at all states of the tide and discharge their cargoes direct into rail wagon or transit shed. For the passenger traffic the quay is equally valuable, as it enables vessels to depart on a time schedule and not be dependent, as they are in many of the docks, on the state of the tide. As already indicated, in the design and construction of the quay particular attention has been given to the requirements of the fruit, vegetable and provision trade, for which extensive accommodation is provided. Fruit sales are held within a few yards of the point at which the fruit is landed and fruit purchased by out-of-town buyers can

The NER was quick to oust the former HBR Kitson 0-4-0 well tanks from Alexandra Dock, scrapping the lot in 1922 just ahead of the formation of the LNER. They were replaced with NER 0-4-0 tank engines. No.985, seen here at Alexandra Dock in 1933, was actually one of five Class Y7 engines built at Darlington in 1923. Amazingly the locomotive is still with us. It was allocated LNER number 8088 in November 1946 and became British Railways 68088 after nationalisation. The locomotive was transferred to BR Eastern Region Departmental Stock in June 1948 as No.34 and was subsequently sold in November 1952 to the National Coal Board for work at Bentinck colliery in Nottinghamshire. In 1964 it was purchased from the NCB by the Y7 Preservation Society and has since spent time operating on the North Norfolk Railway and at the Beamish Museum.

Only twelve HBR locomotives came into British Railways ownership, the majority being withdrawn by the LNER. Here in 1925, outside the dilapidated shed at Alexandra Dock, is ex HBR Class G3 0-6-0T No.114 as LNER Class J75 No.2495. It was built by the Yorkshire Engine Company, Meadow Hall Works, Sheffield, Maker's No.658, in January 1902. Its boiler was renewed in December when it was fitted with a new domeless boiler built at Darlington, seen here equipped with Ross 'pop' safely valves. The locomotive was withdrawn in May 1937. [Laurie Ward collection]

LNER Class J73 0-6-0 No.545, ex-NER Class L, rests between duties at Alexandra Dock with a fellow classmate and a tiny Austin Seven Type R 'Top Hat' saloon with the registration number OF1238 owned by the railway photographer H.C. Casserley (1903-1991). The locomotive was built at Gateshead in December 1891. It was originally equipped with steam brakes only but in June 1915 was fitted with a Westinghouse brake, condensing gear, screw coupling and train heating apparatus for hauling heavy gun trains along the north-east coast as a defence against enemy bombardment during the First World War. There was also an extra Westinghouse pump intended to lift water from streams when the normal supply was not available. The condensing gear was removed circa 1919 and a vacuum brake ejector was fitted in November 1928. The engine was renumbered 8356 in March 1946 and in July that year all the remaining extra equipment was removed. From then on the engine reverted to a steam brake only and had a three-link coupling; the BR number 68356 was applied in September 1948. The locomotive survived for another ten years being withdrawn in August 1958 and scrapped the following month.

In 1929 timber imports began to fall away dramatically at the start of the trade depression. As a result of this, the LNER Class Y8, ex NER Class K, 0-4-0 tank engines allocated to Hull spent long periods in store at the former HBR locomotive works at Springhead. Nos.561 and 562 are seen there on 4 June 1933. They were withdrawn in September 1936 and May 1937, respectively. [Robert Humm collection]

be loaded direct to wagon for conveyance to destination. At the west end of the quay has been built a fine passenger station, whence passengers may pass direct to the boats. The station includes Customs examination and waiting rooms and booking and telegraph offices. The thirteen travelling cranes on the Riverside Quay are actuated by electricity. Ten of them are of 3 tons and three of 30cwt capacity.

'Passing from the Riverside Quay we come to what are described as the Town Docks, situated as they are towards the centre of the city. They are the **Prince's, Railway and Humber Docks**, providing a total water area of 18 acres. Although they are fairly old, these docks are well equipped for the handling of coal and general cargoes and fulfil an essential purpose in the accommodation of vessels engaged in the coastwise and Continental trades. Adjoining the Humber Dock is the Kingston Street Goods Station, the largest and most important of Hull's goods stations. Other goods depots situated close to the dock are English Street and Neptune Street, whilst subsidiary stations serving the city are at Wilmington, Drypool, Stepney and Cannon Street.

'Though the **Victoria Dock** was built as long ago as 1850, it is an exceptionally fine dock, covering, with its basins, a water area of about 25 acres. Utilised primarily for the timber trade, the dock also regularly accommodates vessels engaged in the Finnish, Riga and Danzig

trades, as well as the coal trade. The coal-handling appliances include an electric belt coal conveyor, capable of shipping 650 tons an hour. The dock is surrounded by extensive timber grounds with adequate siding connections, this accommodation covering an area of over 140 acres. An extension of the accommodation and facilities at Victoria Dock has recently been carried out and three additional bogie berths have been provided and equipped, as well as additional standage sidings and storage area. [Note that there is no mention of the timber ponds indicating that they had fallen out of use. A pond was mentioned in the 1937 publication.]

'Built in 1885, the **Alexandra Dock** provides many up-to-date facilities. Its water area, including that of its extension, amounts to 53½ acres. The entrance lock is 550 feet in length and 85 feet in width, the depth at high water springs being 32 feet 6 inches. It possesses 2½ miles of quayage and the storage ground in the vicinity amounts to 210 acres. By reason of its size and depth the dock can accommodate the large ocean-going steamers, maintaining services with North and South America, Australia, Black Sea ports, Canada, India, Egypt, China, Japan, West Coast of Africa and the Straits Settlements. It is used extensively for the exports of coal and also machinery, agricultural implements, chemicals, iron and steel and other manufactured goods. Its imports consist of timber, which arrives in large

quantities, provisions, grain, seeds, wool, iron, molasses, sugar and frozen produce. Noticeable features of this dock are the four jetties with adequate cranage and rail connection. There are no fewer than twelve warehouses immediately adjacent to the quays, including a cold store of 180,000 cubic feet, which is extensively used for the accommodation of frozen products from the Dominions and South America. Of special interest is the manner in which the dock has been laid out for dealing with coal traffic. The dock is equipped with six hydraulic hoists, each capable of shipping at the rate of from 400-500 tons an hour. One of these hoists is equipped with a Handcock Anti-coal Breaking appliance. There are 72 cranes (including one of 100 tons capacity) used for the handling of general cargoes. The dock possesses two well-equipped graving docks: No.1 being 528 feet in length, gate to head and 56½ feet in width at the entrance, with a depth of water on the blocks of 17 feet 9 inches at HWOST and 11 feet 9 inches at HWONT and No.2, 580 feet long, gate to head and 61 feet wide at the entrance, with a depth of water on the blocks of 20 feet 3 inches at HWOST and 14 feet 3 inches at HWONT.

'In addition to the aforementioned facilities at the Alexandra Dock, there is a **River Pier** 1,300 feet in length, with a depth of 18 feet at low water on spring tides, enabling moderate sized vessels to arrive and depart at all states of the tide. This pier is used regularly for the

113

LNER Class Y8 No.559 was renumbered as 8090 in June 1946 and is seen here at Dairycoates Shed in April 1947. It was withdrawn the following year in November without receiving its British Railway's number. [H.C. Casserley]

shipment of coal and general cargoes. It is equipped with two electric belt conveyors, each capable of shipping 600 tons of coal an hour. For general cargo purposes the pier possesses eight electric jib cranes of a capacity varying from one-and-a-half to five tons.

'The **King George Dock** is the largest on the north-east coast and its equipment is on the most modern lines. The whole of the site which it occupies, with the exception of about 20 acres, was reclaimed from the foreshore, which was formerly flooded at high water, the total area of land to be so reclaimed being in the neighbourhood of 206 acres. The dock has a water area of nearly 53 acres and provision has been made for future extension to 85 acres. Access to the dock is gained by an entrance lock, 750 feet long and 85 feet wide and divided into two pens of 250 and 500 feet respectively, the depth at high water springs being 39¼ feet. There are two graving docks of modern construction with a 25 ton electrically operated crane. No.1 graving dock is 466 feet 6 inches long, gate to head and 66 feet wide at the entrance, with a depth of water on the sill of 28 feet 4 inches at HWOST and 22 feet 4 inches at HWONT. No.2 graving dock is 568 feet 3 inches long, gate to head and 72 feet wide at the entrance, with a depth of water on the sill of 28 feet 2 inches at HWOST and 22 feet 4 inches at HWONT. The dock possesses six capacious reinforced concrete transit sheds, situated on the north-west arm. These sheds, three of which are double-storeyed, have a total

capacity for 63,000 tons of general goods and have flat asphalted roofs, equipped with 30 cwt travelling cranes, which can be used for storage purposes. In addition to the warehouses, a large reinforced concrete granary has been provided as the western end of the dock. This installation has a capacity for 40,000 tons of grain. By means of belts, working in ferro-concrete tunnels underneath the quays, three grain ships can be discharged simultaneously. Two electrically driven elevators and floating weighing machines have been introduced to supplement the facilities for the discharge of grain at the silo. The weighing machines work mechanically and weigh one ton of grain at a time and the portable elevators work at the rate of 100 tons per hour. The coal-shipping appliances are situated on the north side of the dock and the arrangements are such that berths can ultimately be provided for six vessels. There are two electrically-driven belt conveyors, each capable of loading at the rate of 800 tons per hour and two hydraulic coal hoists having a shipping capacity of 500 tons per hour. In connection with these coaling appliances, high and low-level nests of sidings have been provided, which enable advantage to be taken of gravity working and each has its separate set of sidings for loaded and empty wagons. The dock is equipped throughout with 57 electric cranes, ranging from 30cwt to 80 tons, the 80 tons appliance being a self-propelled electrically-operated floating crane.'The LNER has two deep-water piers at **Salt End** on the River Humber

for the importation of oil in bulk. Facilities are also provided for dealing with molasses in bulk. The largest type of oil tanker afloat can be safely accommodated. The principal oil companies of the country have erected extensive storage tanks at Salt End and oil can be pumped direct from the overseas vessels to these tanks; 1,000 acres of land for this and other industrial purposes are available in the immediate vicinity. Extensive premises and plant have been built for the distillation of industrial alcohol from molasses.'

****

World War Two
The Riverside Quay and Nos.17 and 26 Warehouses are burning furiously. There are large fires in timber storage grounds at Victoria, Alexandra and King George Docks. There is a large crater in the Withernsea Branch near Southcoates Station blocking both lines. The H & B high level approach to Alexandra and King George Docks is blocked by bomb damage at Ella Street and an unexploded bomb near Bridges Junction. Lighters are on fire and sinking in Albert and Alexandra Docks. A parachute mine has blown up the rail entrance to Railway Street Goods Station. The foregoing was typical of the summaries issued by the LNER District Intelligence Office. Hull and its docks and railways suffered badly from bomb damage during the Second World War. There were 82 raids during which bombs were dropped, approximately 1,200 people were killed and some 3,000 injured. No.3 coal conveyor in Victoria Dock was severely

In 1934 the LNER upgraded the Humber ferry terminals at Hull and New Holland by the provision of floating pontoons and the purchase of two new coal burning paddle steamers *Tattershall Castle* and *Wingfield Castle*; a third similar vessel, *Lincoln Castle*, was added in 1940. This 1954 view shows *Lincoln Castle* berthed at Hull alongside the floating pontoon. Humber Dock is to the middle left with a ship berthed alongside the former NER/LNER covered goods station; Prince's Dock is in the middle distance. The mouth of the River Hull is seen to the right with a barge on the mudbank near to the Central Drydock. [Ivor Innes Photographers, Hessle]

damaged in 1941 and although the LNER authorised expenditure to repair it in 1947 nothing was done and the BTC agreed in 1953 that it should be demolished.

From the beginning of the war there was a gradual reduction in the trade of the port from 9 million tons of cargo handled in 1939 to the lowest point of only 3 million tons handled in 1942. The heavy enemy attacks on the east coast and the danger to shipping in the North Sea led to the diversion of as many ships as possible to the west coast. Hull handled an enormous tonnage of stores and ammunition for the United States Forces based in this country, including in the final stages thousands of tons of bombs. In the weeks immediately preceding *D Day*, 6 June 1944, a substantial number of ships destined for the beach-heads were loaded *with great enthusiasm* by a combined force of dockers and military stevedores. By 1945 the port's annual tonnage of cargo handled had increased to 5.5 million tons (Note 78).

An unusual locomotive movement during the early months of 1940 was the transfer of Class Y8 0-4-0 side tank No.559 from Dairycoates to the military railway at Spurn Head, which was isolated from the main line railway system. The locomotive ran to Patrington station on the Withernsea branch were it was craned onto a low loader and hauled by two LNER tractors – a Fordson shunting tractor and a three-wheeled Scammell 'mechanical horse'.

On arrival at Kilnsea the locomotive was winched down a ramp on to the Spurn Head Railway (Note 79).

Riverside quay which was built mainly of timber was destroyed by fire during an air raid in May 1941. The AHL passenger services from the quay had ceased in September 1939. The final services were twice weekly to Rotterdam departing at 6.30pm on Wednesdays and Saturdays, returning on Thursday and Sunday mornings and a once weekly service to Hamburg (Sandthor Quay) also departing at 6.30pm on Wednesdays with the return service arriving on the following Monday morning. Connecting train services ran from and to Paragon Station.

On 16 August 1946 a temporary facility was brought into use to accommodate the B.A.O.R. (British Army of the Rhine) leave service from Cuxhaven. It consisted of six 'Mulberry' pontoons of the type used during the invasion of Normandy. They were moored along the face of the damaged quay but their berthing face of 1,200ft was further from that of the destroyed Riverside Quay so as to ensure a minimum depth of water of 21ft at all states of the tide. The pontoons were fitted with spuds resting on the bed of the river which were raised and lowered mechanically to suit the level of the tide. Dolphins were built between each pair of pontoons to give additional moorings and added security against the strong tidal flows experienced in the Humber. Bailey bridges provided the connection

with the shore. The first vessel to berth at the temporary facility on 16 August was the steamer *Empire Lance* with 1,300 men who boarded trains alongside. Five ships were used on the service with one arrival and one departure daily. Hitherto the leave boats had berthed in King George Dock requiring the men to be moved by road to Paragon station. By the end of 1946 approximately 120,000 service personnel had disembarked and about 38,000 prisoners of war embarked on their way back to Germany. Riverside Quay was subsequently rebuilt as described in the following chapter (Note 80).

Wingfield Castle (550grt) was built in 1934 by William Gray & Company Ltd of West Hartlepool, Yard No.1060. She is seen here complete with a brass band with all her passengers enjoying an excursion on the Humber. Such outings were very popular during the summer. The paddle steamer was withdrawn from service in 1974 but is now a beautifully restored non-operational exhibit in the Museum of Hartlepool. [Ivor Innes Photography, Hessle]

Lincoln Castle (598grt) at Hull in 1952, was the last of the three paddle steamers ordered by the LNER. She was built by A. & J. Inglis of Glasgow, Yard No.1024, and delivered in 1940. The ship was withdrawn after a boiler failure in February 1978 but unlike her two sisters has not survived. After several attempts to preserve the vessel she was broken up at Alexandra Dock, Grimsby in October 2010. [Ivor Innes Photography, Hessle]

Riverside Quay was destroyed by fire during an air raid in May 1941 but on 16 August 1946 a temporary facility was brought into use to accommodate the B.A.O.R. (British Army of the Rhine) leave service from Cuxhaven. Six *Mulberry* pontoons of the type used during the invasion of Normandy were moored parallel to the damaged quay to provide a new berthing face. The arrangement can be seen on the left with *Bailey* bridges providing connections to the shore. Hitherto the leave boats had to berth in King George Dock but this temporary arrangement enabled the troops to gain direct access to the awaiting trains. Albert Dock with its distinctive accumulator house and clock tower forms the backdrop. The view looks west. [Hull Maritime Museum]

The second half of the 20th Century brought about big changes for the port of Hull. This evocative 1950 scene of the newly built Ellerman's Wilson Line steamer *Rialto* (5005grt) assisted by tugs in the River Humber, masked the dock closures and industrial unrest that were to follow a decade or so later. [Ivor Innes Photographers, Hessle]

8. Nationalisation 1948-1982

Organisational changes

As a consequence of the Transport Act 1947, nationalisation of the railways, railway-owned ports and the most of the canal system took effect from 1 January 1948 when the British Transport Commission (BTC) came into being as the organisation with overall control. It established a Railway Executive and a Docks & Inland Waterways Executive (DIWE). The latter took immediate responsibility for the Port of Goole and the Aire & Calder Navigation but the ports of Grimsby, Immingham and Hull were not transferred from the Railway Executive to the DIWE until 1 January 1949 (Note 81). The old HDC Dock Office was established as the headquarters for the Humber ports with a Chief Docks Manager in overall charge. The traffic management was decentralised with Docks Managers for Hull and Goole and a Port Master responsible for Grimsby & Immingham. With effect from 1 October 1953, the DIWE was abolished and the BTC took direct control through a Docks & Inland Waterways Board of Management. Yet another arrangement was introduced on 1 January 1955 when the docks were divorced from the waterways and managed separately through a Docks Board of Management responsible directly to the BTC. That situation prevailed until 1 January 1963 when, by virtue of the Transport Act 1962, the BTC itself was abolished and replaced by the Railways Board, the British Waterways Board and the British Transport Docks Board (BTDB), each being an autonomous organisation. Goole, Hull, Immingham and Grimsby became four of several BTDB ports located around the UK coast. Examples of annual cargo throughputs at Hull during the nationalised era are given in Appendix Two. The total throughput in 1962, the final year of the BTC's existence, was 8,536,000 tons of which only 357,000 tons was export coal and coke.

British Transport Commission – Reconstruction and modernisation

As previously mentioned, Hull in particular had suffered severely from enemy bombing, leaving a heavy burden of war damage repairs and reconstruction in addition to improvements necessary to bring the port up to date with more modern facilities. One particular aspect of the changing times was the emphasis being placed on improved road access to the various berths to cope with the increasing use of road transport. King George Dock was given special attention in this regard by reconstructing and widening of the main road on the north side of the dock. The old setts bedded in chalk were removed and replaced with reinforced concrete with a rolled asphalt wearing surface. The south roadway at Alexandra Dock to the west of the lock entrance received similar treatment. The dock railway system, which then totalled 190 miles of running lines, quay lines and sidings, also received attention. The most important project in this regard was the doubling of the running line from King George Dock to Salt End in anticipation of

Victoria Dock in 1964 still crowded with ships discharging timber to rail wagons and timber bogies, empty rakes of which can be seen in the foreground ready for use. In 1950 the Docks & Inland Waterways Executive authorised the construction of a further 800 timber bogies, such was the demand. The nearest ship *Sonny* (2255grt) was built as *Mongolia* by William Gray & Co Ltd, West Hartlepool, Yard No.1218, and was renamed when acquired by Norwegian owners in 1955. The vessel was sold again in 1969 and on two further occasions before arriving at Villanueva y Geltrú, Spain for breaking up in December 1973. The vessel *Olsztyn* (1923grt) discharging alongside the quay had a fascinating history. She was one of the 'Hansa A' class of steamers built during the War by the Nazi Government, some in German yards and others in occupied countries. This one was built in Holland in 1945 at Werf De Noord, Alblasserdam, Yard No.604; she was completed in Flensburg as *Imkenturm*. In 1945 she was taken by the UK as a war prize and named *Empire Gantry* but passed the same year to Russia as *Feodosiya*. The Russians passed her to the Polish Government in 1947 as *Olsztyn* in which guise she became part of the fleet operated by the Polish Steamship Company until broken up at Bruges in January 1972. [Ivor Innes Photographers, Hessle]

The 1950s saw the decline of commercial traffic in the Town Docks. This 1955 view shows the J. Marr & Son Ltd trawler *Thornella* (793grt) fitting out in Prince's Dock. She was built by Cook, Welton and Gemmell of Beverley, Yard No.906, launched on 20 May 1955 and completed on 22 September that year. The British Railway's sign to the left advertised a direct train service to Boothferry Park station for Hull City football matches and combined rail/road excursions to Chatsworth, Buxton and Burnsall in Wharfedale. Boothferry Park station opened on 6 January 1951 and closed at the end of the 1985/1986 football season. The distinctive building to the right above the double cream phone box, a distinctive feature of Hull, was constructed by the North Eastern Railway as offices circa 1905 and became known as Monument Buildings because of its close proximity to the Wilberforce Monument which was repositioned in 1935. The building survives as a listed structure.

increased petroleum traffic. Work on this project was completed in 1950 and involved the construction of a reinforced concrete bridge across the Old Fleet Drain. Another interesting aspect of the dock rail operation was the decision taken in February 1950 to construct 800 rail bogies for the timber operations (Note 82). Prior to the 1939-45 War an amazing number of 3,612 bogies were in use at Hull for the conveyance of sawn wood from ships to the storage grounds. Due to obsolescence and war damage the stock had been reduced to about 1,900 of which 500 were over 50 years old and life-expired. The cost of the 800 new bogies was £31,375 and it was agreed that the Railway Executive would undertake the work utilising second-hand materials. On 31 July 1951 the DIWE approved the purchase of four additional diesel driven rubber-tyred road shunting tractors for use at Hull at a total cost of £4,000 to replace shunt horses and worn out electric capstans (Note 83). Similar appliances had been introduced by the LNER and proved successful where rail lines were flush with the quays.

However, the most pressing need was for covered storage and transit shed accommodation to replace warehouses and sheds destroyed during the war. Out of a pre-war total of some 60 warehouses and sheds only 33 remained intact after enemy action. The number

of effective shed berths had been reduced from 56 to 25. The first steps were to construct a number of sheds at the more important berths, the ground space being substantially the same as that occupied by the former buildings but so as to provide new covered accommodation in the shortest time the new builds had only single storeys and steel frames. New sheds were quickly provided in Albert, Humber, Victoria and Alexandra Docks. A re-craning scheme was devised for King George Dock costing nearly £1 million. It was decided to abandon the existing direct current supply and convert to alternating current taking supplies from the Yorkshire Electricity Board via a new sub-station. The scheme involved ordering 45 new electric level luffing travelling cranes; they were designed for a lifting speed of 150ft per minute with 6 tons on the hook and 300ft per minute with a load of 3 tons.

Two of the most important improvement schemes completed during the BTC regime applied to King George Dock and concerned the reconstruction and modernisation of the southern and northern quays of the north east arm. The southern quay which had become known as 12 Quay was tackled first. The original construction comprised a timber piled structure 1,320ft in length, built over a stone-pitched slope. It had given good

service since its completion in 1914 but there had been a gradual deterioration in the timber decking and a large number of steel joists carrying the crane tracks had been replaced; the main timber blue gum piles were still in excellent condition. However, the structure as a whole was inadequate to cater for locomotives or higher capacity modern cranes. The decision was therefore made to undertake the quay's complete reconstruction using reinforced concrete piles with a beam and slab deck. The quay was equipped with crane tracks and two lines of railway. A contract was placed for the work in April 1952 at a cost of £210,000 and the new facility was handed over for traffic in April 1954. Interestingly, the original timber piled structure was retained below deck level to form a complete fendering system independent of the new concrete quay work. The quay improvement scheme was the first major step towards modernising King George Dock, the only dock that could accommodate increasingly larger and deeper draughted ships.

The second quay improvement scheme, authorised in 1960 at a total cost of £4.75 million, was much more ambitious. It involved the removal of all the coal exporting facilities on the north side of the dock, the removal of the echelon berthing arrangements and their replacement with some 3,000ft of

Humber Dock in 1956 and the former railway-owned steamships *Bury* and *Melrose Abbey*, both displaying the funnel markings of Associated Humber Lines (AHL). AHL was created in May 1935 to manage the various railway shipping interests based on the Humber Ports, becoming a limited company in 1957. *Bury* (1634grt) was built by Earle's of Hull, Yard No.569, for the Great Central Railway in 1911; *Melrose Abbey* (1908grt) was also built by Earle's, Yard No.674, but much later in 1929. *Bury* was taken out of service in June 1958. *Melrose Abbey* was laid up in 1959 but subsequently sold to Greek owners and named *Kritti*. She was broken up in Piraeus in 1984 after being laid up there for some 18 years. The vessel at the far end of the dock lettered 2 PILOT was built by Cook, Welton & Gemmell of Beverley in 1944, Yard No.726, as HMS *Calvay* – one of the of the Isles Class of naval trawlers used as minesweepers and patrol vessels. She was sold in 1946 to the Humber Pilots Steam Cutter Co Ltd, converted to a cruising pilot vessel and renamed *Wm Fenton*. As such she worked outside Spurn in the Humber approaches boarding and landing pilots as required. She was sold for breaking up at Blyth in October 1975. [Ivor Innes Photographers, Hessle]

Plan of King George Dock from 1955. The coal conveyors and hoists are still present on the north side of the dock with its echelon berthing arrangements, the south west arm awaits development for use by North Sea Ferries and Queen Elizabeth Dock had still to be constructed. The Salt End oil jetties are shown to the bottom right.

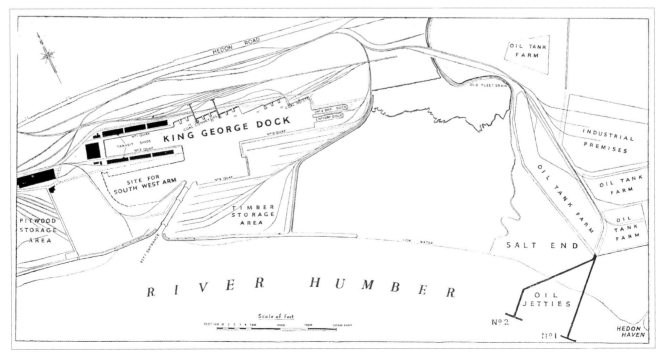

121

This early 1950s view of the north-west end of King George Dock features the Ellerman's Wilson Line vessel *Rialto* (5005grt) which was built by Swan, Hunter & Wigham Richardson Ltd, Walker-on-Tyne, Yard No.1860, and completed in April 1949. She remained with Ellerman's until June 1970 when she was sold to Cypriot owners and renamed *Sandra* but only traded for a further year when she was sold to Chinese ship breakers for demolition at Whampoa. As built, the vessel had accommodation for twelve first class passengers. The ship is berthed by No.1 Shed on 1 Quay and is working cargo to or from rail wagons and vans using the original electric travelling cranes and also overside to craft using the ship's gear. The railway sidings to the top left of the picture are fully occupied by full and empty wagons. [Hull Maritime Museum]

King George Dock in the early 1950s, an animated scene on 3 Quay with all three forms of transporting cargo to and from the dock well illustrated, although motor transport is only playing a small part. Steel wire rod in coil is either going to or from the British Waterways barge and the same commodity can be seen in rail wagons along the quay next to the double storey transit sheds. The *American Inventor* (8431grt) was a Second World War US Navy C2 Class attack cargo ship. She was built by the Federal Shipbuilding and Drydock Company, Kearny, New Jersey in 1944 as USS *Theenim* (AKA-63) and saw action the following year during the assault on Okinawa. She was decommissioned in 1946 and renamed *American Inventor* in merchant service with United States Lines, becoming *Pioneer Surf* in 1959. From 1965 she operated under the flag of Farrell Lines, Inc as *Australian Surf* and then from 1969 as *Surfer* before being broken up at Kaohsiung, Taiwan in April 1970. [Hull Maritime Museum]

additional straight sided quay. The scheme also included the provision of six new large transit sheds and an extension to the grain silo increasing its capacity by 50% and the provision of an impounding station. The latter, still in use today, is designed to maintain a constant water level in the dock by pumping water from the River Humber, so permitting vessels of up to 25,000dwt with a draught of up to 33ft to be kept afloat at any berth irrespective of the state of the tide. The development scheme was officially inaugurated on 25 November 1963 by Vice-Admiral John Hughes Hallett CB, DSO (1901-1972), who was the Parliamentary Secretary to the then Minister of Transport. Hallett was the naval commander during the Dieppe Raid of 1942.

A more protracted and somewhat controversial improvement scheme was the reconstruction of Riverside Quay. The DIWE at its meeting held on 28 November 1950 agreed to recommend to the BTC the reconstruction of the quay and the south side of Albert Dock at an estimated cost of £1.75 million.

Earlier that month the Commission's first chairman, Lord Hurcomb (1883-1975), had visited Hull commenting that whilst the scheme warranted high priority, such large expenditure on new facilities could only be undertaken if the project was remunerative, producing a good return on the investment. It took over a year for the Commission to approve the scheme in principle subject to certain conditions. The proposal then dragged on and on involving discussions with the Hull Chamber of Commerce and Shipping, the Hull & District Wholesale Fruit and Potato Buyers' Association and Hull Corporation. The stumbling block was the very point that Lord Hurcomb had raised and it was not until the end of 1955 that a contract was let following agreement with the Hull traders and shipowners to pay an extra £134,000 in increased charges as soon as the first instalment of the work had been completed. The work involved the rebuilding of the quays in concrete and the provision of sheds for fruit and vegetables discharged on the riverside

and for handling general cargo on the south side of Albert Dock. The new quay, 1,065ft in length, was provided with three sheds each with a floor area of 288ft x 82ft 6in and nine 7½ ton capacity semi-portal electric travelling cranes. Four transit sheds were erected on the south side of Albert Dock together with eight semi-portal cranes. The reconstructed Riverside Quay was formally opened by Mary, Princess Royal and Countess of Harewood (1897-1965) on 12 May 1959. She was the wife of Henry Lascelles, 6th Earl of Harewood and daughter of King George V. It had taken eight and a half years for the scheme to come to fruition.

The original jetty installation at Salt End consisted of No.1 and No.2 timber jetties built in 1914 and 1928 by the NER and LNER, respectively, each providing a single berth for tankers up to 17,000dwt, plus loading facilities at the rear of No.2. Jetty for barge traffic engaged on bunkering services. After a life of over 40 years, the No.1 Jetty had not only become seriously decayed but also inadequate for the growing needs

In the 1950s, Saunders-Roe Limited secured a contract to supply 620 single deck buses and components to Autobuses Modernos SA, Cuba. They were built at the firm's Beaumaris factory, Anglesey, North Wales. Three of those buses can be seen as deck cargo on this ship loading for Cuba in King George Dock in 1951. A further chassis loaded with components is being carefully dipped into one of the ship's holds. The ship on the opposite side of the dock is the Elllerman City Line passenger/cargo liner *City of Paris* (10902grt). She was built by Swan, Hunter & Wigham Richardson Ltd at Wallsend, Yard No.1129, launched on 24 December 1920 but not completed until February 1922. She survived for another five years after this photograph was taken, arriving at Newport, South Wales for breaking up by John Cashmore Ltd on 24 February 1956. [Ivor Innes Photographers, Hessle]

Unloading bagged grain to rail wagons at 3 Quay, King George Dock in the early 1950s, using one of the original 3 ton capacity electric travelling cranes supplied by Royce Limited, Manchester. Note the large number of bags in the sling and that the wagons are being sheeted prior to being moved off the dock. [Ivor Innes Photographers, Hessle]

The 2315grt *Norinda* berthed (on the left) at 12 Quay, King George Dock in 1955. A contract to refurbish the quay was placed with the Yorkshire Hennebique Contracting Co Ltd in April 1952 and completed in April 1954. The view looks west and the two coal hoists seen on the north side of the dock demonstrate that they are still in use, as are the two coal conveyors further along the quay. *Norinda* was built in 1952 for Swedish owners and had three changes of name and owner before being broken up in Piraeus in 1985. The ship to the right behind the display of United Towing tugs is *Welsh Trader* (7897grt) built in 1954 by William Pickersgill & Sons Ltd, Southwick, Yard No.331, for Trader Navigation Co Ltd, London. Note the distinctive letter 'T' on the funnel. She had no less than ten owners and six names before being broken up in Kaohsiung, Taiwan in June 1980. [Ivor Innes Photographers, Hessle]

These cars assembled for export in 1958 are parked to the rear of the double storey transit sheds on 3 Quay, King George Dock. There are two Vauxhall Victors at the bottom right; from the bottom left there are four rows of MG Magnettes, one MGA Coupe and then a batch of Triumph TR2s. Beyond them come Ford 100E Estates, Standard 10s and finally Morris Minors – all built in the UK! The quayside sports new cranes but the original ones still remain on the shed roofs. The south west arm of the dock to the left has still to be developed for use by North Sea Ferries. [Ivor Innes Photographers, Hessle]

of the oil and chemical companies operating at Salt End. The BTC therefore decided to replace it with a new concrete jetty with two jetty heads which became known as No.1 Jetty and No.3 Jetty, each capable of accommodating vessels of up to 27,500dwt. Barge berths were also provided at the rear of No.3 Jetty. The cost of the whole scheme was £1.3 million, including the pipelines and the dredging. There were a total of 57 pipelines which because of their large number were carried on pipe bearers at three levels throughout the new structure which also carried a 10ft wide footway for pedestrian access. The dredging was undertaken by the Humber-based bucket dredgers *David Dale* and *Oliver Bury* which were served by three steam hoppers. *David Dale* had been used by the NER for the dredging works for the original No.1 Jetty (see Chapter Six); *Oliver Bury*, also named after an LNER director, was built in 1929 by Lobnitz & Company, Renfrew (Yard No.951). The new berths were dredged to a depth of 36ft below MLWST.In plan the new structure assumed a Y-shape, the stem of which ran in parallel with the existing No.1 timber jetty, just to the east. The new structure for most of its length was supported on 16in square reinforced concrete piles founded on a firm stratum of boulder clay. The new jetty heads were founded on steel Rendex foundation columns driven as

bearing piles on to hard chalk at an average depth of 60ft below dredged level.

The contract for the works commenced on 19 May 1958 and the first pile was driven on the following 26 July. The original No.1 Jetty had to be kept in service until the most eastward of the two new jetty heads (No.3) had been commissioned which took place on 10 August 1961. The old No.1 Jetty was then demolished and replaced by the new westward jetty head which was completed on 9 November 1962. The original No.2 Jetty remained in service until demolished in 1977.

British Transport Docks Board
The British Transport Docks Board (BTDB) came into being on 1 January 1963. It was responsible for 31 ports which included the Humber ports of Hull, Grimsby, Immingham and Goole. Its other operational ports in Scotland, England and Wales were: Ayr, Barrow, Barry, Burntisland, Cardiff, Fleetwood, Garston, Grangemouth, Hartlepools, King's Lynn, Lowestoft, Lydney, Methil, Middlesbrough, Newport, Plymouth, Port Talbot, Silloth, Southampton, Swansea, Tayport and Troon. The remaining five ports, Alloa, Bo'ness, Burry Port, Charlestown and Penarth, had already been closed to commercial shipping. The BTDB Headquarters was established in Melbury House, Melbury Terrace, London, NW1 in offices which

from one aspect overlooked Marylebone Station. That is where I commenced my port industry career on 20 April 1970, little realising that I was destined to be in charge of the Port of Hull for some 16 years! Although the operational docks acquired appeared to be relatively successful under the BTC system of accounting, the published figures for 1962 included only a limited amount for depreciation and nothing at all for interest on capital. This was immediately rectified in order to put the BTDB activities on a sound financial footing and pay the interest due on its prescribed capital debt of £84 million.

So far as Hull was concerned the BTDB era was characterised by a serious decline in traffic and a corresponding loss of profitability. Initially, this was brought about by declining tonnages of coal and conventional cargo and latterly by endless industrial disputes and strikes resulting in the loss of the port's good reputation and traffic being transferred elsewhere. The tonnage throughput at Hull in 1963, the first year of BTDB operation, amounted to almost 9.5 million tons, boosted by an unexpected sharp increase in coal and coke exports to 1.3 million tons; by 1979 total throughput had dropped to 3.5 million tonnes! There was a continuing decline in railway traffic on the docks following the cessation of coal exports and the total transfer of fish traffic to road. The last fish train ran in 1965, the service having

This rake of loaded rail wagons on the opposite side of the sheds shown in the previous illustration, features Ford Consul cars and Ford 100E vans. The tugs *Yorkshireman* and *Riflemen* berthed alongside each other at the east end of 3 Quay were owned by United Towing. *Rifleman* has featured in a previous illustration. *Yorkshireman* was built by Earle's of Hull in 1928, Yard No.672, for work as a tug and excursion vessel. She was based at Hull but for the summer season went north around the coast to Bridlington Harbour to operate pleasure cruises for holiday makers, being capable of accommodating up to 400 passengers. She returned to the Humber after the end of each summer season and survived until 1965 when she was sold for breaking up in Belgium. [Ivor Innes Photographers, Hessle]

Grain being loaded to craft in March 1961 via one of the four spouts from the grain silo located at the west end of King George Dock. *Robrix* (292grt) was Dutch built in 1937 for Robert Rix & Sons; she was sold in June 1963 and subsequently had several more owners and names. As *Young Ann* she returned to Hull in April 1974 to be broken up by Albert Draper & Son Ltd on the Victoria Dock slipway. The Rix business continues today as J.R. Rix & Sons Ltd. [Ivor Innes Photographers, Hessle]

King George Dock looking east on 6 February 1957. The Cyrillic (Russian) alphabet has shown the nearest ship to be *Volkhovges* (5597grt) built at Nosenko Shipyard, Nicolayev in 1956 and registered to the Murmansk Shipping Company. She is discharging grain via a land based suction elevator and one of the three floating suction elevators originally built for the Ministry of Transport. The craft receiving the grain is the Hull registered *Ibis*, No.9 in the fleet owned by CWS Ltd. The tug *Yorkshireman* is scurrying across the dock and the deep sea ship astern of the Russian vessel is Ellerman's *City of Durban* (13345grt) built by Vickers Armstrongs Ltd at the High Walker Yard in 1954, Yard No.123. She was sold to Greek owners in 1971 and broken up at Kaohsiung, Taiwan where she arrived on 30 March 1974. [Ivor Innes Photographers, Hessle]

to Kingston House Tower in Bond Street in the interests of greater efficiency. In my opinion this was a disaster as the occupation of the new building was subject to the payment of a rental, everyone was located in offices which were tantamount to little boxes with no interaction and the new administrative centre was several miles away from the main operations at the eastern docks. The lease came to an end shortly after my arrival in Hull as Port Manager in 1987 and one of my first decisions to incur capital expenditure was to relocate the office in a new build on the King George Dock estate with easy access from Hedon Road. We no longer had to pay the rent and, more importantly, we needed to be seen by customers and staff on the doorstep of our modern day operations! The new office, known as Port House, was built quite cheaply using the foundations of a building which once housed the Humber Tidal Model – a mechanical interactive model simulating the bed of the River Humber which had become obsolete in the new age of computers and information technology. The old Dock Office was sold to Hull City Council and very appropriately it is now the Hull Maritime Museum.

The next docks for the closure treatment were the Albert & William Wright Docks which were closed to commercial shipping in October 1972. However, in this case, after discussions with the British Trawler Owners Federation, it was decided to refurbish the docks for the fishing industry which would be transferred from St. Andrew's Dock and St. Andrew's Dock Extension. The latter facilities were closed to shipping on 3 November 1975 but the refurbished facilities were not formally inaugurated until 27 February 1976 when the Rt. Hon. Frederick Peart MP, Minister of Agriculture Fisheries and Food, performed the task. In 1986, Associated British Ports (ABP), as

been previously reduced to one train a day – a far cry from the nine trains a day that ran at the close of the LNER era. That approximated to around 350 loaded vans a day or about 1,400 tons of fish, with additional vans added to passenger trains. The period also witnessed a revolution in cargo handling with the introduction of unitised cargo in the form of pre-slung and pre-packed timber, palletised cargo, containers and the introduction of roll-on/roll-off ships. The large numbers of dockers formerly employed were no longer required which led to a large surplus of unwanted labour. Inevitably, this was the period of dock closures and industrial unrest but somewhat ironically it also saw the country's last major enclosed dock development with the opening of Queen Elizabeth Dock in 1969.

Dock Closures
By the 1960s, the Town Docks had become obsolete. The last commercial sailing took place in August 1967 when the mv *Deben* (500grt) sailed from Humber Dock. The ship was a typical Dutch coaster built by Boele's Scheepswerven & Machinefabriek N.V. at Boele's, Holland in 1966 for Blue Star Line Ltd, Yard No.1023. After several

changes of owner and name the ship as *Abdoulah 1* was listed as lost on 8 September 2001. By 1969, Humber Dock together with Prince's Dock and Railway Dock had been closed. In 1973, all three docks were sold to Hull City Council for £500,000. Humber and Railway Docks now form part of the Hull Marina which was opened on 1 May 1983. Part of Prince's Dock forms an attractive water feature complimenting the *Prince's Quay* shopping centre which was built on stilts over the remaining part of the dock and opened on 15 March 1991. Following the closure of the Town Docks the BTDB decided to close Victoria Dock. The entrance to this dock from the River Hull had been closed in 1964 and complete closure followed on 1 February 1970. In 1987 the whole of the derelict Victoria Dock estate was purchased by Hull City Council. Subsequently the whole of the dock area has been transformed into a private housing estate known as *Victoria Dock Village*. Work commenced in 1988 and was completed in the late 1990s. Another symbolic happening occurred on 10 March 1972 when, after 100 years, the old Dock Office was vacated and the staff from there and various other locations scattered throughout the city transferred

This 1961 view looking west illustrates the new sheds and semi-portal electric travelling cranes provided on the south side of Albert Dock and for Riverside Quay which was badly damaged during World War Two. The sheds serving Riverside Quay, known as A, B and C Sheds are to the left. D shed on the south side of Albert Dock can be seen in the distance. Note the rail shunting tractor at the bottom right. [Ivor Innes Photographers, Hessle]

The reconstructed Riverside Quay was formally opened on 12 May 1959. This view looking east shows the Ellerman's Wilson Line vessel *Borodino* (3206grt) discharging provisions from Denmark at the new facility on 9 November 1959. *Borodino* was built in 1950 by Ailsa Shipbuilding Co Ltd, Troon, Yard No.468. She remained with the Ellerman's fleet until sold for breaking up at Bruges in July 1967. The 7½ ton capacity cranes were constructed on the semi-portal principle to create more space for handling cargo on the narrow quayside. [ABP]

David Brown 30D tractors were manufactured between 1953 and 1957 at Meltham Mills, West Yorkshire. Several of their breed are clustered around the jetties on the south side of Alexandra Dock awaiting export. The 3 ton capacity quayside cranes were built by Cowans Sheldon of Carlisle and note that the roadway still contains the original sets. *Teano* (1580grt) was an Ellerman's Wilson Line vessel launched by Henry Robb Ltd of Leith, Yard No.439, on 10 December 1954. She was sold in 1968 and from then on had a chequered history. In 1977, when named *Ocean Duchess*, she was beached at Bahrain following an engine room fire when inward bound with a cargo of tea from Colombo. The vessel was completely gutted and declared a total loss, following which she was sold to Pakistani shipbreakers for demolition at Gadani Beach. The other ship prominent in the picture is *St. Helena* (7210grt). She was a standard 'Liberty ship' design by Bethlehem-Fairfield shipyard, Baltimore, Yard No.2357, built as *Samloyal* in 1944 for the British Government. From 1947 she was registered at Newport, South Wales as *St. Helena* and operated by the South American Saint Line until broken up at Belgium in January 1963. [Ivor Innes Photographers, Hessle]

successors to the BTDB, commenced a multi-million pound scheme to fill in St. Andrew's Dock and its Extension with dredged material in order to turn the former estate into a leisure and retail park known as *St. Andrew's Quay*.

Railway Closures

On 1 August 1955, the BTC's Railway Executive withdrew the passenger service on the former HBR line between Hull and South Howden but at that stage the coal traffic from South Yorkshire pits moved along the line much as before. However, on 1 December 1958, the former HBR main line was closed to through goods and mineral traffic between Little Weighton and Wrangbrook Junction with trains diverted to other routes. A pick-up freight from Hull to Carlton ran until 4 April 1959 when the whole line between Little Weighton and Wrangbrook Junction was closed completely. From 4 July 1964 the pick-up freight service

from Hull to Little Weighton also ceased; the goods depot at Hull's Cannon Street survived for another four years but that too closed on 3 June 1968. As a mainline railway the HBR had gone but Alexandra Dock, its greatest asset remained open for business. In 1957 diesel multiple units were introduced on the Hornsea and Withernsea branches but did not encourage sufficient extra traffic and both branches lost their passenger traffic with effect from 17 October 1964, that decision having been taken by the newly formed British Railways Board (BRB). Goods services on both branches lingered on until 30 April 1965. The Victoria Dock branch closed in 1968.

Just prior to the 1923 grouping of the railways, the NER had 348 steam locomotives stationed at Hull which amounted to 16% of its entire stock (Note 84). All steam engines were transferred away from the former HBR engine shed at Springhead on 29

November 1958 and the former NER Botanic Gardens shed closed to steam on 14 June 1959, prior to conversion for diesel traction. The end of Hull's steam power came on 25 June 1967 when the last two engines in regular traffic, Class B1 4-6-0 No.61306 and Class WD 2-8-0 No.90009, were transferred away following the closure of Dairycoates locomotive shed to steam engines; it closed completely on 21 September 1970. Diesel power had become the order of the day. Rail traffic on the docks, once the principal means of carrying imports and exports, was dwindling away. However, shunting locomotives continued to be allocated to Alexandra Dock until 27 October 1963; they were stabled in the open air over the pits in the two roads which had originally been inside the wooden shed demolished by the LNER in 1927. After 1963 the location was still used as a signing-on point for engine crews until 1982 with diesel-electric shunters stabled there overnight.

Alexandra Dock in 1962 showing off the newly concreted quay along the north wall with its flush rail tracks. The view looks east with 32 Shed in the distance and the storage tanks of United Molasses to the left. A shunting tractor is parked to the left and would be used to position the wagons exactly as required to facilitate direct discharge of the slings of timber into the wagons. *St. George* (5205grt) was built in 1936 in Germany as *Guinean* by Howaldtswerke of Hamburg for the United Africa Company which was owned by Unilever. Under Hitler's restrictions the company's Deutschmark earnings could not be accessed and so it had ships built in Germany to use up the funds. Post-war, Unilever's shipping arm was renamed Palm Line so *Guinean* became *Kano Palm* only to become *St. George* when sold to Greek owners in 1954. Ten years later she was sold again as *Susanne Eureka*, becoming *Mok Tat* in 1966 before being broken up at Kaohsiung, Taiwan in November 1967. [Ivor Innes Photographers, Hessle]

The decline of rail traffic on the docks accelerated when coal export traffic ceased in the 1960s. Here a loaded wagon is being tipped onto one of the two coal conveyors located on the north side of King George Dock. Both conveyors had gone by the close of 1963 even though that year saw an unexpected increase in coal and coke shipments. A diesel electric 0-6-0 shunter can just be glimpsed on the embankment to the right behind the lamp standard. [Ivor Innes Photographers, Hessle]

This 1970 aerial view shows the extent of the dock closures. The Town Docks in the foreground are devoid of traffic as is Victoria Dock seen towards the top right beyond the River Hull which closed on 1 February 1970. Above that Alexandra Dock is still operational and the only other transport activity is the railway goods yard abutting onto the closed Humber Dock at the bottom of the picture and one of the Humber paddle steamers with its red funnel to the right of the picture. Unusually, it is berthed on the East Pier as its normal berth astern of the vessel lacks its pontoon which must have been away for repair. [Tony Ward, Topcolor Fotoworx, Hull]

Associated Humber Lines

AHL was acquired by the BTC along with the railways and docks in 1948. In 1957 AHL became a limited company with the title Associated Humber Lines Limited. The BTC owned 91% of the shares with the remainder being held by Ellerman's Wilson Line. All the vessels managed by AHL at that time were transferred to the new entity, including four that had been ordered by the BTC between 1954 and 1957. A fleet renewal programme was then put into place with no less than eight new vessels being built for AHL Limited during 1958/ 1959 for its Humber services. In 1963 control of AHL Limited was transferred to the Transport Holding Company. The latter was a government owned company created under the Transport Act 1962 to administer a range of transport, travel and engineering companies previously managed by the BTC. It came into existence on 1 January 1963. A further change occurred in 1969 when control of the company passed to the National Freight

Corporation (NFC). Following severe competition from short sea container and roll-on/roll-off services AHL Limited went into a loss making situation. In February 1971 the NFC announced that it was seeking a buyer for the company but hopes to sell it as *a going concern* failed to materialise and the operation was closed later that year in November. Latterly the company had only four ships, the sister ships *Melrose Abbey* (3169grt) and *Bolton Abbey*, cargo-passenger motor vessels operating on the Hull-Rotterdam route and the sister ships *Leeds* (1113grt) and *Wakefield*, cargo-only motor vessels operating on the Hull-Antwerp route.

Hull-New Holland Ferry

On 1 January 1959 AHL Limited acquired the responsibility of managing the Hull-New Holland ferry service but the ownership of the three paddle steamers ordered by the LNER prior to the Second World War remained with the BTC. From 1963 ownership passed to the British Railways Board but the

ferries continued to be managed by AHL Limited until November 1971 when the company ceased trading. For the next decade the ferries were operated by Sealink UK Limited, a subsidiary of British Rail. *Tattershall Castle* was withdrawn in 1973, *Wingfield Castle* in 1974 and *Lincoln Castle* in February 1978 following a boiler failure. Latterly the service was operated by just one vessel, the mv *Farringford* (489grt) which had been built by William Denny & Bros of Dumbarton (Yard No.1402) for the Southern Railway's Lymington-Yarmouth Isle of Wight service and launched on 31 March 1947, becoming BTC property in 1948. She was towed to the Humber in 1974 and after undergoing modifications was put into service. Her ownership was transferred to Sealink UK Limited in 1979 and she performed the very last ferry crossing on 26 June 1981, just two days after the opening of the Humber Bridge. *Farringford*, which had diesel-electric engines, was broken up at Silcock's Basin, Hull in 1984. *Tattershall Castle* has

During the 1950s the docks still relied heavily on rail traffic as evidenced by this array of semaphore signals in 1952, in a view from Hedon Road on the north side of Alexandra Dock. The name of the signal box was Graving Dock. A coal hoist can be seen to the left of the picture and the tall building between the box and the signals is an accumulator tower. Unlike the railway, it still exists as a listed structure and has recently been restored by ABP for use as part of a visitor centre. Graving Dock signal box closed on 27 July 1968. [Mick Nicholson collection]

Alexandra Dock continued to have an allocation of steam locomotives and was regarded as a sub-shed of Springhead 53C, even though the building itself on the dock had been long demolished. As at 31 August 1950 no less than 24 tank engines were allocated to Alexandra Dock, the most common types being Class J72 0-6-0 side tanks of which No.68676 takes centre stage in this 1951 view. The engine was built by the NER at Darlington Works in December 1898 and survived until withdrawal in September 1960.

Eleven engines are 'on shed' at Alexandra Dock (in reality locos stabled on the tracks in the open) in the 1950s. Prominent in the foreground are Class J72 0-6-0 tank engines Nos.68747 and 68753. They were built by the LNER at Doncaster in November and December 1925, respectively and withdrawn October 1961 and August 1960. The ships forming the backdrop are under repair in Nos.1 and 2 Drydocks.

survived and is now a floating pub and restaurant in London moored on the River Thames, likewise *Wingfield Castle* is now a beautifully restored but non-operational exhibit in the Museum of Hartlepool, and has become a top maritime attraction in the town where she was built. *Lincoln Castle* was not so lucky, after several vicissitudes, she was cut up in Alexandra Dock, Grimsby in October 2010.

North Sea Ferries
The inauguration of the first roll-on/roll-off ferry service from Hull took place on 17 December 1965, which saw the maiden voyage of North Sea Ferries' mv *Norwave* (3540grt) to Rotterdam. The ship could accommodate 235 passengers, 65 lorries or semi-trailers and 60 cars. The maiden voyage was not without its difficulties. HM Customs prevented several semi-trailers from being loaded as the relevant documentation had been held up in the Christmas post and the voyage out and back was accompanied by a force 10 gale! So violent was the ship's rolling motion that several trailers broke free from their shackles but fortunately damage was only nominal. The return voyage was even worse such that the ship was forced to heave to for four hours. However, the lessons learnt on the outward voyage meant that more attention had been paid to the lashing and securing of the trailers. Apart from the snags caused by the extreme weather there was nothing but praise for the new

service which initially left Hull on Mondays, Wednesdays and Fridays with departures at 6.00pm. Arrival in Rotterdam was at 8.00am the following day. It was planned to increase the sailings to every weekday once *Norwave's* sister *Norwind* entered service the following year. The two ships were built by Weser AG Werk, Seebeckwerft, Bremerhaven, Yard Nos.898 and 899. The *Norwave* was British registered and had a British crew whereas the *Norwind* flew the Dutch flag and was manned by Dutchmen. They wore a very distinctive black and orange livery.

North Sea Ferries (NSF) was a consortium of six shipping companies – two British – two Dutch and two German. The new Hull terminal for the service was not fully completed at the time of the maiden voyage but it was opened by Barbara Castle, Minister for Transport on 9 May 1966 by which time sister ship *Norwind* was also operating on the route. The terminal which was funded by the BTDB cost £1.4 million and was located on 5 Quay, King George Dock. It provided a second berth for a ro/ro service to Gothenburg operated by the England/Sweden Line, a consortium of Ellerman's Wilson Line, Svea Line and Swedish Lloyd. Each of the three lines agreed to provide a ship to operate the service which was predicted to be capable of handling a weekly quota of 3,600 passengers, 900 cars and about 10,000 tons of cargo. Swedish Lloyd's mv *Saga* (7889grt) performed the first sailing on the day

Barbara Castle opened the new terminal (Note 85).

Almost one year later in November 1966 Ian Churcher, NSF General Manager, reported that: *Despite the effects of the six-week* [UK] *seamens' strike, which halved their services and cost them £100,000, and the refusal of Hull dock labour to work at weekends, North Sea Ferries carried over 10,000 freight units (containers, trailers or flats) since the opening of the service in December 1965.* He said that NSF thought highly of the way in which the Hull labour force dealt with loading and unloading the vessels but the lack of port labour on a Saturday limited the Friday departure from Rotterdam to self-drive vehicles and this was obviously restricting traffic (Note 86). In spite of early problems with Hull dockers, the NSF service went from strength to strength. Not so the Swedish ro/ro service which had a very short life. It soon became clear that the limited demand for passenger and car ferry facilities to Sweden, other than in the summer months, was making the consortium uneconomic. Swedish Lloyd's *Saga* was withdrawn from the service in 1967, followed by Svea Line's *Svea* (7883grt) in 1968 (Note 87). Thereafter, Ellerman's Wilson Line's *Spero* (6916grt) – see Note 88 - maintained the service but she was an expensive ship to operate and losses mounted such that the service ceased completely on 1 April 1972. *Spero* was re-employed by Ellerman's Wilson on a new service from Hull to Zeebrugge but

The 1960s saw many WD 2-8-0s engaged on local trip workings. Almost at the very end of steam operations, No.90695 is passing Alexandra Dock signal box on 20 April 1967, about to cross over Hedon Road, seen to the left. The view looks east. Although not apparent from the photograph, the train is made up entirely of loaded tank wagons from the Salt End complex. The locomotive was built by Vulcan Foundry Ltd, Newton-le-Willows, Lancashire in December 1944, Maker's No.5182. It was withdrawn in September 1967. The signal box closed on 27 May 1974. [Mick Nicholson collection]

No.90467 alongside the coaling stage at Hull (Springhead) the principal locomotive shed of the former Hull & Barnsley Railway. It closed on 1 December 1958. The locomotive was built by Vulcan Foundry in May 1944, Maker's No.5063 and was withdrawn in November 1963. [Mick Nicholson collection]

90352 with a train of empty 16 ton mineral wagons ex the coal roads passes King George Dock Junction signal box in the 1960s. The locomotive was withdrawn in June 1967. It was built by the North British Locomotive Company Ltd of Glasgow in August 1944, Maker's No.24954. The signal box was closed on 27 May 1974. [Mick Nicholson collection]

that too failed and the ship was sold to Greek owners in April 1973 and renamed *Sappho* (Note 89).

The Devlin Report

Decasualisation of the dock labour force took effect from 18 September 1967 following the publication of the Devlin Report which reported on a Committee of Enquiry into employment within the port transport industry (Note 90). The committee was chaired by Patrick Arthur Devlin (1905-1992). Its recommendations, inter alia, proposed that all dockers had to be allocated to a particular port employer under a licensing system with the port authority acting as the licensing authority. Hitherto, the Hull general stevedoring companies, like those in many other ports, had very few regular men and, when they had a ship to work, took extra men from a pool of labour administered by the National Board Labour Board (NDLB). Men would assemble at the NDLB's call stand and the stevedoring companies' foremen would pick the men required for the job, many of whom were known favourites and referred to by Devlin as *blue-eyed boys* who received preferential treatment. Insofar as Hull was concerned the report stated that there were 4,731 men and 90 employers on their respective registers but added that 65 of the employers hardly operated at all and quite a few of the rest were only casual employers. The report

highlighted a bitter division between the Transport & General Workers Union at Hull and the National Association of Stevedores and Dockers, commonly known as the *Blue Union*. Another recommendation was that the number of port employers should be greatly reduced in the interests of achieving a cohesive workforce capable of coping with the rapidly changing cargo handling methods. The NDLB remained in being to administer the registers, control recruitment, training and discipline with 50% employer and 50% employee representation on its national and local boards.

In Hull the recommendations of the Devlin Report resulted in the formation on 4 March 1968 of the Hull & Humber Cargo Handling Company Limited (Hull & Humber), a wholly owned subsidiary of the BTDB which at that time was the port authority. It was in effect a merger of rival companies which included J. H. Dickinson Ltd – the largest general stevedoring company in Hull; Hull & East Coast Stevedores Ltd mainly handling timber; Humber Stevedores Ltd and P.E. Holland. Andrew Brett who became a senior accountant with the BTDB and its successor ABP was very much involved with the merger and recalls that the exercise came across as more like *bailing out the stevedores* than a means to achieve more harmonious relationships and improve efficiency. Subsequent companies also acquired by Hull & Humber were Jacobs, Larvin

(Stevedores) Limited, Cargo Operations Ltd and Hull Superintending & Tallying Company Limited. North Sea Ferries and EWL continued to provide their own labour under separate licences.

Industrial unrest in the docks

The years 1969 and 1970 were very difficult years for the BTDB financially. In 1969 the Board as a whole produced a deficit of £0.8 million with another loss of £1.6 million the following year which was greatly hampered by a three-week national dock strike in July. The overall position in 1971 was much better with an operating surplus of £7.6 million but at the beginning of 1972 the Managing Director, Stanley Johnson CBE, 1912-2007, (Note 91), was prompted to issue the following message to all staff. *Looking ahead, the future is far from clear insofar as international trade is concerned and it is as well to be aware that there will be problems to be faced. Competition becomes keener and, increasingly, customers will select their ports not on direct financial benefits alone but on the quality of service we provide. In this situation there is no possible place for one-day strikes and other such misguided activities which have so sadly affected one or two of our ports during the past year.* Hull was one of those ports.

In 1969 Hull produced a loss of £500,000; this was followed by a loss of £950,000 in 1970, £900,000 in 1971 and almost £1.5 million in 1972. These losses were of such magnitude that drastic measures had to be taken to cut costs

Shunting on the dock estate was performed latterly by British Railways 0-6-0 diesel-electric locomotives – later designated Class 08. In 1963 a clutch of them stand in Alexandra Dock where HBR 0-4-0 Kitson well tanks once stabled. The so-called Alexandra Dock engine shed closed on 22 October 1963 but was retained as a signing on point. Alexandra Dock was closed to shipping on 30 September 1982 and the railway serving it was officially closed on 31 December that year. [Mick Nicholson collection]

This view looks towards the old Hessle Road signal box and level crossing on 6 January 1962. The bridge carrying the former Hull & Barnsley Railway to Neptune Street goods station away to the right will shortly be demolished and trains from the ex-HBR route diverted onto new goods lines yet to be laid to the left. The new arrangement with a new road bridge to replace the level crossing was implemented on 10 October 1962. The locomotive is Class J39 0-6-0 No.64943 which was built by the LNER at Darlington April 1939. It is performing some of its last duties as it was withdrawn in November 1962. The line curving away to the left is the main line to Hull Paragon station. [Mick Nicholson collection]

Dairycoates shed on 10 June 1967; it closed to steam engines later that month. The only occupant appears to be WD No.90478. It saw a little more work after being transferred away from Hull to West Hartlepool but was withdrawn in September 1967. [Mick Nicholson collection]

and it was against this background that the decisions to close Victoria Dock and the Albert & Wright Docks were taken. Falling throughputs of cargo did not really impact on Hull until 1968 when coal exports dropped by 700,000 tonnes and petroleum imports by 500,000 tonnes. The opening of the new export coal terminal at Immingham and new oil refineries developed there and on the Tees, where ships of up to 44ft draught could be accommodated, resulted in the permanent loss of coal exports at Hull and greatly reduced the importation of refined petroleum products. However, several other factors were also coming into play. The containerisation of the Australian wool trade based on Tilbury, deprived Hull of its wool imports and other deep-sea traffics. Moreover, the increasing size of dry bulk carriers operating at lower freight rates encouraged the transhipment of cargoes at continental ports to small vessels capable of discharging at private river wharves on the River Humber which, unlike Hull, were not subject to the National Dock Labour Scheme. This Scheme, introduced under a Labour Government in 1947, was designed to protect dock workers but became a great inhibitor to modernisation. It was administered by the NDLB and several local boards, including one covering Hull and Goole. Each board consisted of 50% trade union and 50% employer representation. The system, which effectively gave the unions an absolute veto over dismissal and total control of

recruitment and discipline, became progressively abused by militant dock workers of which Hull certainly had its share. Because of the ramifications of the scheme, the management of the day became unable to manage and effect the reductions in the manpower required commensurate with modern cargo handling methods. Because of this the port was simply unable to compete with ports that were not subjected to the Scheme like the growing container port of Felixstowe and the private wharves on the Rivers Humber, Ouse and Trent, all of which were thriving at Hull's expense. In 1968 a Humber Harbour Reorganisation Scheme was implemented whereby the Humber Conservancy Board was abolished and the BTDB became the conservancy and pilotage authority for the Humber and parts of the Rivers Trent and Ouse (Note 92).

In January 1971, Sir (Edward) Humphrey Browne CBE (1911-1987) became a member of the BTDB board and on 1 May that year he was appointed as chairman. His background was the coal industry and he was once director and chief mining engineer of Manchester Collieries Limited from 1943 to 1946 where an industrial locomotive *Humphrey* was named after him (Note 93). He was deputy chairman of the National Coal Board from 1960 to 1967 and held several directorships in private companies. During an interview in July 1972 he said that he had, with one exception, visited all the BTDB ports and

amongst dock workers of all grades he had encountered good manners and friendliness. The individual registered dock workers had been helpful and sensible but he added that collectively people often behaved differently to the way they behaved as individuals. That was exactly my experience with Hull's registered dock workers, many of whom were highly skilled and could stow a deep sea general cargo ship with precision so that the maximum amount of cargo was loaded in a safe and seaworthy manner. However, when it came to the annual wage negotiations and disputes, the collective approach was always followed, led by the militant shop stewards.

Queen Elizabeth Dock
Amidst mounting losses, disappearing traffics and industrial unrest Her Majesty the Queen opened the south east arm of King George Dock on 4 August 1969 and named it Queen Elizabeth Dock. The royal party arrived at Hull aboard the Royal Yacht *Britannia* which berthed in the new dock early that morning. The ceremony took place before an audience of 1,200 guests in one of the new quayside transit sheds. Two Ellerman Lines ships in dock, *City of York* (13345grt) and *City of Lancaster* (4949grt), due to load cargo for South Africa, were garlanded with the white and red roses of the Houses of York and Lancaster. The occasion formed part of a six-hour visit to Hull by the Queen, Prince Philip and Princess Anne.

Brush BR Class 47 diesel-electric locomotive being lifted on board the Yugoslavian registered steamer *Kolasin* (7176grt) with a floating crane in King George Dock in 1965. Ten such locomotives were delivered to Cuba using Yugoslavian ships between 1965 and 1966, some via Hull others via Tilbury. Following the Cuban Missile Crisis, it became difficult for Cuba to buy new railway equipment because of the United States embargo. There was some secrecy about the deal to avoid upsetting the USA and so all ten locomotives were painted in the same livery as BR Class 47s to avoid undue attention. They were actually derivatives of the Class 47 as they were fitted with LVA24 Vee engines as installed in BR Class 48s. While to all intents and purposes they were built at Loughborough, they were finally erected by Hatton Equipment Limited at the International Combustion Plant at Derby. *Kolasin*, identified by its name on the lifebuoy up on the bridge front, was a Liberty ship built in 1943 by Bethlehem-Fairfield Shipyard, Baltimore, Yard No.2151. After several changes of name and ownership she was acquired by Prekookeanska Plovidba, Bar, Yugoslavia in 1965 and named *Kolasin*. The ship was wrecked after running aground in the Black Sea 35 miles south of Tuapse on 21 January 1970. The ten exported locomotives were all withdrawn from service by the mid 1990s but it is rumoured that some of them may still be around. [Ivor Innes Photographers, Hessle]

This historical image depicts the inauguration of North Sea Ferries' daily service to Rotterdam on 17 December 1965 with the mv *Norwave* (3540grt). The ship is berthed at the new ro/ro berth constructed in the south west arm of King George Dock. The Athel Line tanker to the right will have arrived with a cargo of molasses. [Ivor Innes Photographers, Hessle]

Norwind leaving King George Dock; it was the sister ship to *Norwave* and sports the original North Sea Ferries livery of black and orange. The Hull Container Terminal cranes with their booms raised can be seen above the stern of the ship which discharged and loaded through a bow door. [Patrick Hill]

The cost of the new dock, which is 2,800ft long and 500ft wide with a water area of 20 acres, was £6.75 million. It took two and a half years to construct and fulfilled the vision to extend King George Dock as mooted when that dock was opened by the Queen's grandfather King George V in 1914. The new facility is entered by the existing entrance lock; one mile of new quays provided an additional eight deep-water berths with two new transit sheds. When construction of Queen Elizabeth Dock commenced, Hull's imminent downturn in its fortunes was clearly not envisaged. It was a very brave venture, apparently built speculatively without any guaranteed customer! The eastern extremity of the south side of the new dock became the Hull Container Terminal which opened for business on 22 October 1971, following the installation of a 40 ton capacity container crane built by Clyde Crane and Booth Limited. The first vessel to use the container terminal was the mv *Nienhagen* operated by VEB Deutsche Seereederei to the East German port of Rostock. The twice-weekly Rostock container service had actually commenced temporarily in February 1971 in Albert Dock where on the north side the containers were discharged and loaded using an old hydraulic crane! The mv *Nienhagen* (299grt) and sister ship *Dierhagen* could only carry forty standard ISO 20ft containers but it was a start. They came

from the shipyard Elbewerft at Boizenburg which is on the River Elbe above Hamburg but just inside former East German border: *Dierhagen*, Yard No.273, was built in 1970 and *Nienhagen*, Yard No.300, was completed the following year.

Ro/Ro Revolution
The introduction of the roll-on/roll-off concept certainly revolutionised the carriage of freight by sea but it also heralded the demise of conventional general cargo ships and clearly did not warrant the manpower associated with the discharging and loading of conventional ships. In 1966 approval was given for the conversion of two conventional berths in Alexandra Dock on each side of 23 Jetty for stern loading ro/ro vessels at a cost of £332,000. They were provided with hinged shore bridges giving access to the ships' stern doors and became operational during the following year. These new facilities were used by the Argo Line operating between Hull, Hamburg and Bremen and the Holland Steamship Co with sailings to Amsterdam. In December 1970 Ellerman's Wilson Line inaugurated a new ro/ro service from Hull to the Norwegian ports of Oslo and Drammen using new facilities in King George Dock. Two new ships were used on the service: *Destro* (1571grt) and *Domino* which was completed in March 1972 to the same specification. They were designed to

carry containers which were loaded onto slave trailers for transit from the quayside to the ship. *Destro* and *Domino* were both ordered from the Norwegian Yard of Ankerlokken Verft Floro A/S, Yard Nos.87 and 92, but *Domino* was sub-contracted to Langvik Sarpsborg Mek. Versted, Sarpsborg, Yard No.45. They could carry a maximum of 185 x 20ft containers. Whereas Ellerman's Wilson was the sole owner of *Destro*, *Domino* was owned by Domino Container Ships Limited, a subsidiary of Ellerman Lines.

Ellerman's Wilson also ordered a third ro/ro vessel at this time for a service from Hull to Esbjerg in Denmark. A new specialised terminal was built at 10 Quay East in Queen Elizabeth Dock to accommodate the new vessel at a cost of £350,000. The terminal included the provision of a hydraulically operated two-level shore ramp, about 59ft long and 15ft wide designed to serve the new vessel's two decks simultaneously. A storage area of 4½ acres was allocated to the service with 30 refrigeration points for containers carrying bacon. The new service replaced a conventional one using a chartered ship that had operated from King George Dock since May 1971. The ship used on the service, which commenced early in 1973 was named *Hero* (3468grt) and was built by Robb Caledon Shipbuilders Ltd, Leith, Yard No.511. She was designed to carry 279 x 20ft containers on slave trailers in

Her Majesty the Queen opened the south east arm of King George Dock on 4 August 1969 and named it Queen Elizabeth Dock. This view taken later that year shows the newly built 15 Shed on the right with 16 Shed beyond. The ship alongside 16 Shed is the refrigerated mv *Northumberland* (10335grt) operated by the Federal Steam Navigation Co. Ltd, London which ran to New Zealand and Australia so she has probably discharged fruit. She was built in 1955 By John Brown & Co Ltd, Clydebank, Yard No.676. Following two changes of ownership and name she was broken up as *Golden City* at Hong Kong in 1978. The tug *Dockman* (68grt) was locally built by Henry Scarr Ltd of Hessle as *Stamford Brook*, Yard No.618 and completed in 1949, but for operation on the River Thames. She was first named *Dockman* in March 1963 when she was purchased by United Towing of Hull where she remained for ten years. Since that time she has been rebuilt at least twice and worked at a variety of east coast ports, including further stints at Hull. Since 2009 she has been owned by Thames Towage Ltd, Canvey Island. [Ivor Innes Photographers, Hessle]

a similar manner to the Norwegian service. The ship was jointly owned by Ellerman's Wilson and DFDS (UK) Ltd. Unfortunately she was destined to have a very short life being abandoned in the North Sea in heavy weather on 12 November 1977 and sinking the following day.

December 1972 brought about a dramatic change in the Ellerman organisation following a streamlining of its various operations to meet modern trading conditions. This impacted on the new Hull ro/ro services which became the responsibility of EWL (the transport division of Ellerman Lines Ltd), together with Ellerman Wilson's road haulage, ship agency and air freight businesses. So EWL was left with only three ships to manage: *Destro*, *Domino* and *Hero*. The 1970s were becoming increasingly difficult for British shipowners. As previously explained there was increasing industrial unrest at many British ports of which Hull was to the fore and there was a considerable excess of tonnage on the North Sea routes which depressed freight rates. In an attempt to compete, EWL ordered two larger ro/ro ships in May 1976 from the

Smith's Dock Company on Teeside; they were named *Cicero* (5108grt) and sister ship *Cavallo*, Yard Nos.1338 and 1339. In that same year EWL decided to withdraw from stevedoring and surrender its licence. As a result some 1,000 men were reallocated by the NDLB to Hull & Humber which gained some additional stevedoring revenue from working EWL vessels, but not nearly sufficient to cover the cost of such a large number of additional men who had to be paid, even though there was no work for most of them! When that situation arose it was known as the *Dint* – men legitimately going home on pay because there was no work for them. Not exactly a recipe for increased efficiency and while EWL gained some temporary relief from a deteriorating financial situation, the worst was yet to come. After only six months' service, *Cisero* was returned to the builders with EWL claiming that a number of serious defects had been discovered. This created a rumpus and EWL did not take delivery of *Cavallo*, the dispute being settled out of court. Competition on the North Sea routes intensified with the Swedish Government offering 30% grants to build

new ships with 100% loans on the balance of the building costs with no repayments required for three years. Moreover, new Swedish and other foreign ships operated with a crew of twelve whereas British manning regulations required crews of at least 20. This was too much for EWL who announced that as from 1 October 1978 all shipping operations from Hull would cease; the last sailing from Hull took place with *Destro* on 29 September; thus ended 150 years of continuous sailings out of Hull.

Compared to the misfortunes of EWL, North Sea Ferries enjoyed continuous and rapid expansion. New ships were introduced on the Rotterdam service in 1974 named *Norland* and *Norstar* built by AG Weser, Bremerhaven. These second generation ferries at 12988grt were at that time the largest ferries the world had ever seen. The pioneer vessels *Norwave* and *Norwind* were then used to operate a nightly passenger/freight service from Hull to Zeebrugge in Belgium which again has gone from strength to strength. The ships on both services engaged in the daily practice of locking in and out of King George Dock with the Zeebrugge sailing departing about 30 minutes before the Rotterdam sailing which is the time it took to lock out.

Hull & Humber Cargo Handling Co Ltd

In March 1977 I joined Hull and Humber as an Operations Manager. As previously mentioned the company was a wholly-owned subsidiary of the BTDB, formed in the aftermath of the Devlin Report. It was a major career change for me as the previous seven years had been spent at BTDB Headquarters in London in an administrative role. That gave me access to Board meetings to record the proceedings and so I was privy to a lot of policy making decisions – a stark contrast with daily life on the dockside! Geoffrey Cullington, MC, OBE (1920-1994) formerly of Hull & East Coast Stevedores Ltd was the managing director and his cousin Dennis Malcolm Cullington (1923-1991) was the commercial director. They were known as Mister Geoff and Mister Dennis. My key responsibilities were to look after the Finnish, Russian and (later) Mediterranean ro/ro services and vessels of the Ben Line which operated a conventional service to the Far East. It was very much a case of learning on the job and my mentors were master stevedore David Walter Parkinson (1937-2004) and his brother-in-law, Edmund Keith Lovewell (1940-1997).

The Finnish ro/ro service had been inaugurated on 23 January 1973 as a joint venture between the United Baltic Corporation of London (UBC) and the Finland Steamship Company of Helsinki. Both companies each provided two new vessels for use on the service – mv *Baltic Enterprise* (4668grt) and *Baltic Progress* of the same tonnage by UBC and mv *Sirius* (4469grt) and *Orion* of the same tonnage by the Finnish company. The joint venture was known as Finhumber Ferries and the agents were John Good & Sons Limited, whose business was founded in Hull in 1833 and still thrives today. The Finnish ports served were Helsinki, Kotka, Mantyluoto and Turku. This initiative proved very successful and strengthened the strong trading links between Hull and Finland which continue today. The vessels had stern ramps and were berthed at 15 Shed, 9 Quay, Queen Elizabeth Dock. The new terminal cost £280,000 and a special feature was the fixed shore ramp 60m long and 18m wide capable of accommodating four lanes of traffic. The foreman, Peter Lamping, stood on the ship's ramp in between the two lanes as in his words *it was the only position from where I could control what was going on*. The Russian ro/ro service to Leningrad (now St. Petersburg) also used 9 Quay with quarter ramp vessels *Inzhener Machulskiy* (4009grt) and *Inzhener Bashkirov* of the same tonnage and stern ramp vessels *Mekhanik Tarasov*

(4262grt) and *Mekhanik Evgrafov* of the same tonnage. I became very familiar with these ships and struck up a good working relationship with all involved in their operation. The main Finnish imports were forest products including timber, board materials and paper. The principal Russian imports were Lada cars – Hull being the sole UK port of entry for those vehicles. Exports for both services comprised containerised cargo, agricultural equipment and a mixed bag of general cargo all of which had to stowed and secured by Hull dockers on ships' trailers which were known as mafis after the German company, Mafi, which had pioneered their design.

I could not have been *in the thick of it* on the docks at a more interesting time. Deep sea general cargo ships with five to six hatches and upper and lower 'tween decks, contrasted most markedly with the modern methods of transportation. Loose bagged cargoes of castor seeds, cocoa beans, coconut shells, illipe nuts, palm kernels, shea nuts and plumbago, together with bales of coir fibre and tea in plywood chests, discharged in slings using ships' derricks overside to craft or by quayside cranes via quay to transit sheds, seemed most incongruous compared to driving cargo on and off modern ro/ro ships. The deep sea ships were in port for days or even weeks, whereas their modern equivalents were in and out in 24 hours.

This fascinating scenario was interrupted by negative daily encounters with shop stewards of the most militant kind who were hell bent on relentlessly preserving what used to be, against impossible odds. There were endless arguments, even rows, about manning scales, dirty cargos and the definition of dock work aimed at preserving jobs. Stoppages for one reason or another were rife. At times the situation was not helped by the shipowners who wanted their ships away at any cost. The shop stewards never showed any personal animosity towards me as I was deemed to be just doing my job but they displayed sheer obstinacy, even if offered a chance of new business.

The way to get things done was to engender a good rapport with the docker foremen. They were men of vast experience but they were also registered dock workers who were duty bound to acquiesce when it came to strikes and other forms of industrial action. The chief foreman was Jack Thomas Rumble (1925-2017) – a giant of a man, always known as Nick, who had seen action in the Royal Navy during World War Two. No one rubbed him up the wrong way, not even shop stewards who I think were rather afraid of his prowess and stature. Every morning around 9am, Betty Nicholson, Mister Geoff's secretary, would shout *Nick's On* after which all the Hull and Humber operations managers would gather to talk to Nick over a telephone intercom system with Mister Geoff taking the lead. The

progress of every ship in dock would be a subject of conversation and woe betide anyone who did not know what was going on. Poor output performances were legion when compared to the old days when piece work encouraged better outputs with higher rewards. The secret of success at these daily meetings was to spend an hour or so beforehand on the dock so that you knew exactly what was happening, thereby being one step ahead of the game. The worst malpractice at this particular time was the *Welt* – an unofficial practice whereby men went home when they should have been at work. It was a practice which stemmed from over-manning – two men were even allocated to each tractor unit (called tugmasters) used to pull trailers on and off ro/ro ships when there was only a seat for one man! I wonder what long distance lorry drivers thought of that. Discipline was ineffectual in such circumstances as it was handled not by the employer but by the Local Dock Labour Board who, surprise, surprise, had amongst its members the militant shop stewards!

Two particular events come to mind during my time with Hull & Humber which involved industrial action by non registered dock workers. One concerned a strike by the port authority's lockhead staff at King George Dock which prevented the movement of vessels into and out of that dock and the adjoining Queen Elizabeth Dock. This was overcome for ro/ro vessels by berthing in the bellmouth to the lock entrance, initially for the North Sea Ferries' daily services whose vessels berthed head east with their stern ramps lowered on the west knuckle but also with one of the Finnish vessels berthed head west with its stern ramp on the east knuckle near to the terminal at 15 and 17 Sheds. The angle of the stern ramp had to be constantly adjusted to cope with the rise and fall of the tide. I recall *Sirius* discharging on the morning tide and returning to load on the evening tide after the North Sea Ferries vessels had sailed. Everyone was primed to do a good job with a lucrative *twilight* (work up to 9.30pm) ordered for the dockers. All the cargo was successfully loaded including two races horses loaded in horse boxes carried on board by fork lift trucks. It just demonstrates what could be done in those difficult times. On another occasion Hull and Humber's maintenance staff went on strike and the nightly charging of the fork lift trucks became a problem. I became known as the *Phantom Charger* when, surprise, surprise the fork lift trucks kept running day after day after day!

Dockland had many peculiar titles for its workers, unknown outside the shipping community. The term tallymen – those who checked the cargo being discharged and loaded was pretty much universal to all docks but there were some terms peculiar to Hull. In Hull a runnerman was what elsewhere would

This 1978 scene in Queen Elizabeth Dock very much contrasts the old with the new. In the foreground, a conventional deep sea ship berthed at 16 Shed is discharging bags of shea nuts overside to craft in the time honoured way and will be in port for several days. The other three vessels are roll-on/roll-off vessels which will all discharge and load their cargos in the single day. North Sea Ferries *Norstar* (12988grt) is in the middle of the three on the Rotterdam service with a Zeebrugge service vessel to the right. The Finncarriers' vessel *Sirius* (4469grt) is berthed at 15 Shed and will shortly sail for the Finnish ports of Mantyluoto and Turku.

be called the banksman or signaller. The runnerman stood at the far side of each hatch and signalled to the crane driver telling him to lower or hoist, luff in or out or swing from side to side. Because of the configuration of the hatches and the stowage of the cargo, there were times when crane drivers could not actually see the load they were lifting or lowering. The creatively named dab eye was the man who stood by the hatch coamings when two ship's derricks were used in union purchase – a practice requiring much co-ordination by the two winch drivers. When coming back inboard, the empty running line with the hook on the end just trailed back over the ship's rail. At this point the dab eye gathered up the loose line and flicked the hook down below so that it landed at the feet of the gang. There could be several gangs in the hold making up slings of bagged cargo so at

times the hook would have to go to each gang in turn in each corner of the hatch – all clever stuff and quite skilled. There were still dockers designated as coopers but in my time barrels had disappeared and the coopers walked around with pockets full of 6 inch nails used to repair or strengthen damaged crates. In the fish docks, those handling the fish were called bobbers, unlike their counterparts at Grimsby who were called lumpers. I left Hull & Humber much the richer for my experience in November 1979 to become Assistant Docks Manager at the much smaller port of King's Lynn in Norfolk.

Demise of the BTDB
1982 was significant for two reasons. It was the last year of the BTDB's existence as, under the Transport Act 1982, it was abolished as a prelude to privatisation. Sadly at Hull, the year also witnessed

the closure of Alexandra Dock on 30 September. Hull's fortunes were still in the doldrums and its closure was part of yet another cost cutting exercise. Hull's trade was now concentrated on King George and Queen Elizabeth Docks with Albert and William Wright Docks being used primarily for the fish traffic.

Right. This is the deep sea ship that imported the shea nuts – Nigerian National Lines *Ahmadu Bello* (6127grt). She was actually boomed off the quay as craft are also positioned between the port side of the ship and the quayside. The quayside cranes are working to the craft between the vessel and the quay while the ship's gear is deployed to load the craft on the starboard side. The ship was Tyne built by Swan, Hunter & Wigham Richardson Ltd, Neptune Yard, Low Walker in 1963, Yard No.1996. Nigerian National sold her in 1981 after which she had three owners and was renamed twice. She was broken up at Gadani Beach as *Ionian Dream* in 1985.

Below. Queen Elizabeth and King George Docks on 12 May 1978 with almost every berth occupied – a port manager's dream – but it also illustrates a time of change and a significant problem. There are 18 commercial ships in port discharging and loading cargo but they include three container ships and six roll-on/roll-off ships which will be completed in the day and only required a fraction of the men allocated to the conventional ships. The Hull Container Terminal is in the foreground but notice the long queue of lorries waiting to offload their containers and that most of the boxes on the container park are only stacked one high as the registered dock workers had an issue about stacking boxes two-high. At the time the terminal did not have a good reputation for efficiency! For the record the ships in dock moving clockwise from the container terminal are: *Nieuwland* under the container crane; *Amazone* waiting to load containers; *Inzhener Machulskiy*, Russian ro/ro; *Donga* discharging shea nuts; *Baltic Progress*, Finnish ro/ro. The Royal Navy ship on 7 Quay at the west side of the lockpit is HMS *Kent* on a courtesy visit. Next are the North Sea Ferries' vessels *Norstar* – the larger vessel on the Rotterdam service and *Norwave* on the Zeebrugge service. An Egyptian ship *El Fayoum* is the only vessel on 3 Quay berthed at 6 Shed. On the north side of King George Dock starting at 1 Shed near the grain silo we have: *Ilse*, Medite Shipping Co; *Gembira*, Indonesian; *Protesilaus*, Ben Line; *Wladislaw Lokietek*, Polish East African; *Winchester Castle* discharging fruit; *Destro*, EWL Swedish ro/ro. The ships in the dry docks are British Rail's *Essex Ferry* (north) and *Miranda*, a fishery support vessel (south). The ships berthed on 10 Quay, Queen Elizabeth Dock moving from east to west (right to left) are: *Brage* with containers; *Lagos Palm*, discharging palm kernels and *Allemagne Express*, Adriatica Mediterranean ro/ro service. [Hull & Humber Cargo Handling Co Ltd]

Shortly after returning to Hull as Port Manager in 1987, I became involved in the arrangements for the opening of the new North Sea Ferries Passenger Terminal in King George Dock. Here Sir Keith Stuart, ABP Chairman is introducing me to Princess Margaret who performed the opening ceremony. My wife, Darral is to my right followed by the Port Engineer, Jack Wray and his wife, Muriel. The Company Secretary, R. Alastair Channing and his wife are behind Sir Keith. [ABP]

ABP and its predecessors had an extensive fleet of harbour craft in the form of dredgers, launches and buoy vessels. The *Humber Guardian* (618grt) was once a familiar sight on the Humber and was based at Hull. She was built in 1967 by Dunston's at Hessle, Yard No.850, as a buoy tender ordered by the Humber Conservancy Board, quickly passing into the ownership of the BTDB and then in 1983 to ABP. She had a rather splendid saloon which occasionally offered Board members/directors a superb venue for lunch following a board meeting and a river inspection. Local restaurateur Tony Cerruti has been known to serve a wonderful fish course while anchored off Spurn Point! The *Humber Guardian* was sold in 1991 and by 1993 had been converted to a cruise yacht named *Tropic Sun*. The conversion took place in the re-opened No.1 Drydock in Alexandra Dock. As far as is known the vessel is currently registered in Ecuador. [Patrick Hill]

9. Privatisation: 1983-2017

Associated British Ports

Associated British Ports (ABP), the first state-owned industry to be privatised under the Thatcher Government, came into being on 1 January 1983. All remaining 19 former BTDB ports were vested in ABP, a wholly-owned subsidiary of the newly created Associated British Holdings plc (ABPH) which was floated on the London stock exchange in February 1983. Moving clockwise around the coast the 19 ports were: Hull, Goole, Immingham, Grimsby, King's Lynn, Lowestoft, Southampton, Plymouth Millbay, Newport, Cardiff, Barry, Swansea, Port Talbot, Garston, Fleetwood, Barrow, Silloth, Ayr and Troon. The other ports originally acquired when the BTDB was formed had either been closed or passed to other port authorities under harbour reorganisation schemes. ABP also assumed the role as conservancy and pilotage authority for the Humber. The new organisation was headed by executive chairman Sir Keith Stuart who took over from Sir Humphrey Browne. Sir Keith had commenced his employment with the BTDB as the Board's secretary in 1972, becoming Managing Director in 1975 in succession

to Stanley Johnson. Hull's annual tonnage throughputs throughout the privatised era are shown in Appendix Two. After a troubled start the port has become a success story. I returned to Hull as Port Manager in April 1987 in succession to Stuart Bradley, having previously held the positions of Port Manager, King's Lynn and Assistant Port Manager at Goole. I recall at the time that Stuart had managed to significantly improve the port's finances through strict control of costs and reductions in manpower. However, the port had changed dramatically since my departure some eight years ago – the Alexandra Dock estate was derelict and rail traffic was almost non-existent apart from movements with rail tank traffic to and from the BP chemical factory at Salt End. An internal movement from King George Dock with bauxite traffic to Electro Furnace Products located to the east of that dock and served via a private siding had ceased during the previous year. Hull & Humber had been wound-up and the two remaining major employers of registered dock labour were ABP and North Sea Ferries. However, it was not all bad news. The grain silo had been converted to export

wheat and barley and was thriving, a new edible oil processing plant had been established in 1984 on the King George Dock estate attracting cargoes of vegetable oil and North Sea Ferries (NSF) were about to get a brand new terminal.

North Sea Ferries

One of the first of many official engagements was the opening of a new passenger terminal for NSF by Princess Margaret on 15 July 1987. There were several more royal occasions to follow. The year marked the arrival of two new ferries for the NSF Rotterdam service which represented a quantum leap in scale. The two new ships *Norsea* and *Norsun* turned the scales at 31,785gt with a length of 179m and a beam of 25.35m being built to the very limit of the parameters for vessels passing through King George lock. They came into service with a new corporate two-tone blue livery. Following the introduction of these ships the *Norland* and *Norstar* were literally cut in half and lengthened by some 20m with a major refit for the Zeebrugge service enabling the 1st generation ships *Norwind* and *Norwave* to be sold. *Norland* had earned fame

The new Rotterdam Terminal was opened by the author's wife Darral Fell on 1 May 2001. The Fell family is seen here outside the new terminal just prior to its opening with ABP's Chief Executive, Bo Lerenius and his wife Gunilla. Left to right are: Daniel Fell, Gunilla Lerenius, author, Darral Fell, Bo Lerenius and Matthew Fell. The brand new cruise ferry *Pride of Rotterdam* can be seen in the background. [Herbert Ballard/ABP]

The Saltend Chemicals Park looking north, obviously at low water! ABP's jetties are in the foreground; No.1 Jetty is to the left, No.3 is to the right. Hedon Haven can be seen wending its way above No.3 Jetty. The Kingston Terminal to the east of Queen Elizabeth Dock is to the extreme left, rather obviously also handling another bulk commodity in addition to coal. The Old Fleet Drain is to the right of the terminal and more or less opposite is a gas fired power station capable of producing 1,200MW. [Alamy stock image]

King George Dock on 22 April 2014, illustrating to good effect some of the more recent developments. The iconic grain silo at the west end of the north-west arm has gone. It was demolished in 2011. One of P&O's Rotterdam cruise ferries can be seen berthed on the River Humber with its connection to the passenger terminal opened by the author's wife. Other prominent features include the lockpit with the outer and middle gates in the closed position, the yellow roofed edible oil plant, the green roofed Finnish paper terminal and to the top right, the blackness of the 40 acre Kingston coal terminal. The biomass facility which became operational in March 2014 is in use but the Hull Container Terminal awaits its new cranes, the first of which arrived in 2016. [David Lee Photography Ltd/ABP]

Courtesy visits by ships of the Royal Navy were fairly common occurrences. HMS *Andromeda* (F57) a Leander Class frigate is entering King George Dock with the crew on their mettle. She was built in HM Dockyard, Portsmouth, launched on 24 May 1967 and commissioned on 2 December 1968. She took part in the Falklands War and was sold to India in 1995 for use as a training ship, renamed INS *Krishna*. She was finally decommissioned in May 2012. The storage tank to the right contains molasses. [Patrick Hill]

deep sea exploits, she arrived five hours late for the official welcome having been delayed by winds of up to 75mph whipping up the Humber estuary. After a major overhaul she returned to service on 20 April 1983.

HMS Sheffield

HMS *Sheffield*, a Type 22 frigate, was commissioned on 26 July 1988 at 3 Quay, King George Dock which was alongside the new NSF passenger terminal utilised for the reception. It was very unusual to commission a warship in a commercial port. She was originally intended to be named *Bruiser* but was named *Sheffield* in honour of the ship of the same name, a Type 42 Destroyer, sunk during the Falklands War. HMS *Sheffield* became an occasional caller at Hull on courtesy visits, the last such occasion being on 11 October 2002, shortly before her decommissioning on 4 November that year. Courtesy visits by Royal Navy warships were fairly frequent events. The commanding officer would visit me in full dress uniform and we would exchange gifts which usually took the form of a plaque depicting the ship's armorial device in return for the port plaque. He would then pay an official visit to the Lord Mayor in his/her capacity of Admiral of the Humber. In an evening, often accompanied by my wife, I enjoyed the privilege of being piped aboard following which there would be a cocktail party on deck with a display by the Band of the Royal

when she was chartered by the Ministry of Defence in 1982 for service in the South Atlantic as part of the Task Force sent to participate in the Falklands War, truly demonstrating the ship's ocean going capability. Her regular master, Captain Don Ellerby CBE (1931-2011) took command with Bob Lough as Chief Officer; all the crew were volunteers. When the ship joined the Task Force at Ascension Island, the crew

were told that she was to be used as a landing ship. *Norland* was one of the first vessels to enter San Carlos Water during the amphibious landings and she was nearby when HMS *Antelope* was sunk on 25 May 1982, having been bombed the previous day by Argentine Air Force A-4 Skyhawks. *Norland* returned home safely on 1 February 1983 with all of her crew to a rapturous welcome at King George Dock. Ironically, after her all

The North Sea Ferries vessel *Norland* (12988grt) also participated in the Falklands War, being chartered by the Ministry of Defence as part of the Task Force sent to the South Atlantic. This photograph shows her in San Carlos Water on 25 May 1982 witnessing the sinking of HMS *Antelope* which had been attacked by Argentine Air Force A4 Skyhawks on 23 May and sustained fatal damage the following day when attempts to make safe an unexploded bomb failed with disastrous results. The ship was abandoned and she later broke in two, sinking as seen here. After returning to Hull *Norland* was refurbished, acquiring an 'Antelope Lounge' in recognition of her wartime exploits. In 2002 the ship was sold to SNAV as *SNAV Sicilia* for service between Naples and Palermo. The ship was broken up in India during the summer of 2010. [Courtesy, Captain Robert Lough who was on board the vessel as Chief Officer at the time of the photograph]

One of the greatest gains for the port over the past 25 years or so has been the importation of coal and a substantial capital investment by Hull Bulk Handling (part of the Fernwood Group Limited) in equipment to handle it. The vast majority of the imported coal has left the port by rail as shown here. Class 56 Co-Co diesel electric No.56060 wearing EWS livery is leaving the Kingston Terminal to the east of Queen Elizabeth Dock with a rake of loaded HAA wagons bound for Ferrybridge power station, now closed. The terminal's conveyor system forms the backdrop with a substantial amount of coal on the stockpiles. [Tony Buckton]

Marines. A truly wonderful occasion enhanced by the spectacle of the sailing of the ferries to Zeebrugge and Rotterdam as they manoeuvred from their berths to the lock.

Hull Container Terminal

Although privatisation meant that ABP obtained total freedom to operate without Government intervention insofar as capital expenditure and the appointment of board members were concerned, it was still saddled with the regulation of the Dock Labour Scheme. A particular problem in Hull was the operation of the Hull Container Terminal which was grossly over-manned making it unprofitable. I decided to tackle the problem in 1988 but was met with the usual total obstinacy. In order to break the deadlock, I decided to close it which meant a substantial loss of earnings to the more skilled dockers and rather delicate negotiations with the customers, some of whom remained loyal to Hull using much slower Scotch derricks to handle the containers (as opposed to the container cranes) and others who moved to Immingham. All this meant that most of the revenue was protected with a substantial saving of costs. The 1988 pay negotiations were concluded

successfully apart from the Container Terminal issue so it was my turn to be obstinate. It remained closed.

Abolition of the National Dock Labour Scheme

In 1989 the Government announced its intention to abolish the National Dock Labour Scheme. A planned celebration of the 75th anniversary of the opening of King George Dock had to be called off in anticipation of a national dock strike even though souvenir brochures and ceramic plates had been produced in readiness. The Scheme was abolished and there was indeed a national docks strike. In Hull it lasted for just three weeks. The stranglehold held by the militant shop stewards disappeared overnight. As the legislation enacting the Scheme had been abolished before the strike commenced, it was no longer a criminal offence for management to undertake dock work. I recall asking my management staff – accountants, administrators, engineers, marine and operations staff – to walk through the picket line at King George Dock and drive off shipments of Lada cars from the Russian ro/ro vessels which they did with aplomb. Every Hull docker applied for the rather generous severance payment which was a maximum of

£35,000 and went away. I remember writing out the cheques. We could start again with a clean sheet. Some of the redundant dockers were lucky as they recommenced employment immediately with firms newly established to undertake the stevedoring. One such was Northern Cargo Services Limited managed by my old mentor David Parkinson and Andrew Brett, both mentioned earlier and Chris Hillan, another former ABP employee. Their co-operation enabled an almost seamless transition from the old out-dated practices to a new efficient way of working. The *Welt* disappeared overnight. The result was an immediate recommencement of stevedoring services and the reopening of the container terminal. Shortly afterwards an agreement was entered into with Humberside Sea & Land Services Limited (later part of PD Ports) for that company to work the terminal and maintain the three cranes. There was an immediate build up of container traffic as customers returned to find a very reliable service. Other new traffic was also being secured, for example, sea dredged aggregates using self-discharging vessels which hitherto could not have been entertained as the shop stewards would have demanded a gang

148

of men to *ghost* the operation making it totally uneconomic. They would have been paid to do nothing!

1990 – Another eventful year

1990 saw an increase in tonnage throughput of 1.6 million tonnes compared with the previous year, heralding that the port was once more on an upward trend following the abolition of the National Dock Labour Scheme. However, the year started off with a near disaster. On 26 February I received an early morning telephone call from Dock Master, Captain Malcolm T. W. Walker (1933-2015) telling me that there was a major problem at the King George lockhead. The conversation was cut short with the words: *'I've just lost the east inner gate!'* A sudden violent storm had blown up as the bulk carrier *Sealink* (18963grt) was approaching the lock in ballast under the control of two tugs, so the outer and middle gates were open to receive her. Suddenly the ship broke free from the tugs and landed on the river wall east of the lockpit. In the meantime the strong wave action from upstream ran along the lock chamber damaging the inner gates. The east inner gate came off its pintle and was floating upside down in the dock with the west inner also off its pintle but more or less still in its upright position. In spite of some damage to the outer gates the Dock Master managed to close them and the middle gates, so protecting the integrity of the enclosed dock by keeping back the head of water but it had been a near thing. Once the storm had subsided *Sealink*, owned by Sealink Shipping of Valletta, was re-floated on the next tide and the lock damage assessed by divers. The port remained operational but for two weeks we could only admit vessels across the high water periods using the middle gates to hold back the water in the dock once the tide had turned. The Engineering Department did a great job of putting us back together.

1990 also saw a major revival of the dock rail system following the importation of coal sent to Yorkshire power stations using HAA merry-go-round wagons in standard 36-wagon rakes and the export of British Steel products from Scunthorpe to India. Other rather unexpected rail movements also took place during the year. The Gulf War commenced on 2 August 1990 and Hull with its excellent but much under-utilised rail connection was chosen as an ideal port to export bombs and ammunition for the conflict using vessels of the United Arab Shipping Company. The Secretary of State for Defence waived the port's very restrictive explosives' licence so permitting the arrival of frequent ammunition trains from the Ministry of Defence depots at Chorley in Lancashire and Kineton in Warwickshire. Some movements even took place on Sundays which had not happened for many years. I recall noting that some of the rail vans had not turned a wheel for many a year! During this episode a very alert security guard noticed a protrusion from a railway embankment on the dock estate. It turned out to be an unexploded German bomb from the last War. Residents in nearby Hedon Road were evacuated while the Army's Bomb Disposal Unit defused the bomb and took it away to Holmpton beach on the east coast where it was dealt with by a controlled explosion. Phew! 1990 was quite a year.

Coal Imports

Ports can be very adaptable. I have already mentioned the alterations made to the King George Dock grain silo in order to switch it from importing to exporting grain, a clear illustration of adapting to changing markets. The same happened with coal. Who would have imagined that a port designed to cope with ever increasing tonnages of British coal exports would switch to importing foreign coal. As mentioned above the imported coal started arriving in 1990 using up to six quayside cranes to discharge a typical vessel carrying 25,000 tonnes. The cranes were of only of 10 and 7½ tons capacity so the operation was somewhat slow but such was the increasing demand that the firm responsible, Fernwood Fuels Limited of Nottingham, entered into a 40 year lease of a site to the east of Queen Elizabeth Dock and installed two 25 ton capacity cranes and an overhead conveyor system. The terminal is known as the Kingston Terminal and it became the key to reviving the King George Dock branch railway as the vast majority of the imported coal was moved by rail to coal fired power stations. Between 1990 and 2017 just over 23 million tonnes of coal has been imported through Hull with the majority of it leaving the port by rail, the peak year being 2006 when nearly 2.5 million tonnes was handled – see Appendix Two. But now it has suddenly gone, overtaken by a green energy policy designed not to burn coal. Port authorities have absolutely no control over that but have quickly to adapt to find alternative traffics like biomass in order to secure replacement revenues. The Kingston Terminal now has covered accommodation to handle bulk materials than cannot be stored in the open.

Alexandra Dock Re-opened

With the sudden resurgence of traffic it was time for Alexandra Dock to wake up from its slumber. I recommended to the ABPH Board that it should be re-opened and to my delight my proposal was approved. Here was a chance to bring the most profitable part of the Hull & Barnsley Railway back to life. The new business in sea dredged aggregates had already been established using the western approach jetty to the lock as a berth, but the plan was now to re-open the entire dock. It had been closed for almost a decade and was badly silted. A survey found depths of only 1.2m or less and this had to be dredged to a depth of 7.4m. The ABP grab dredger *Cave Sand* literally dug her way into the dock with the help of land based grabs. This enabled the trailing suction dredger *Humber Dolphin* to enter the dock where it was able to pump the dredged spoil via a pipeline into the Humber, thus negating the need to leave the dock. The whole operation took just over two months during which time a total of 575,400 tonnes of spoil was removed to achieve a guaranteed depth of 7.4m.

In the meantime the engineering staff lead by Port Engineer, Jack Wray, worked on renovating the middle pair of lockgates and converting them for operation with new top-mounted hydraulic rams. Initially the dock was worked with the middle gates only; they were opened across each high water period to make a level with the river. The inner and outer gates were renovated later. The opening, which cost a modest £1.3m, was marked by a ceremony which took place during the morning tide on 16 July 1991 – on the dock's 106th birthday. The proceedings commenced at the lock entrance at 8.00am where a champagne breakfast was served in a marquee. Sir Keith Stuart performed the ceremony with the Lord Mayor of Hull in attendance. In explaining the rationale for the reopening, Sir Keith said: *It will make substantial extra facilities available to meet growing demand; it is the largest single expansion of port capacity in the UK since the abolition of the National Dock Labour Scheme and the re-opening relives the commercial hopes of the people who built this dock and gathered for the original ceremony on the same day in 1885.* Everyone present at the ceremony and all members of the port's staff were presented with a bronze medallion, produced by the Birmingham Mint, which replicated the one issued in 1885.

At 9.25am the Russian timber carrier *Pioner Yakutii* (4814grt) with a cargo of 7,915 cubic metres of packaged timber from the Kara Sea port of Igarka, became the first commercial vessel to enter the dock for some 10 years. She was fully laden and had a maximum draught of 6.4m. The ship was followed by mv *Canford* (956grt) with a cargo of soya bean meal from Rotterdam and mv *Condor* (1395grt) with maritime pine and fibre board from Portugal and Spain. In 1993 Hull re-established itself as the UK's Top Timber Port handling over one million cubic metres during that year, a large proportion of which was handled at Alexandra Dock.

More Capital Investment

As business through the port rapidly gained momentum, ABP was able to invest in new infrastructure, not only as a reaction to customer demands but also to replace ailing assets. Within the

Alexandra Dock in 1989 after nine years of closure, virtually the only income being that derived from the storage of Hull built caravans. The derelict River Pier is in the foreground and the amount of siltation can be seen at its worst on the North Wall opposite the lockpit, river water being allowed to flow through the spiked outer lockgates. When Alexandra Dock was closed it was never envisaged that it would reopen. Some of the dock walls were thought to be unstable such that they would collapse if the lock gates were abandoned and the dock left to become a tidal basin. Conversely, if the outer lock gates were left permanently closed, the high tides would have subjected them to excessive pressure possibly leading to failure. The solution was to keep the gates closed but spike them at an average height to allow the pressures to equalise on either side of the gates, but as always when the water came in so did the silt. However the chosen solution did prevent the dock waters from becoming stagnant. The Alexandra Dock Extension seen to the right remained relatively silt free. A sign of great hope for the future is evidenced by the ABP grab dredger working alongside the western approach jetty. It is clearing a berth for self-discharging aggregate vessels operated by ARC Marine Limited. The provision of such a facility was not possible during the life of the National Dock Labour Scheme as the aggregate would have been classified as cargo requiring the allocation of dock labour, even though there was absolutely nothing for the men to do! [ABP]

latter category came the installation of four 15 tonnes capacity travelling cranes on the north side of King George Dock, the renewal of the western approach jetty to that dock and the reclamation of a large tract of foreshore to the east of Queen Elizabeth Dock. The reclamation retained the concrete sea going barge *Cretestreet* as part of the bund wall. The barge, built at Shoreham in 1918 as part of a World War One initiative to save steel, sank in King George Dock when loaded with coal on 10 February 1920. The coal was removed but the barge remained on the dock bottom near to the No.2 Coal Conveyor until 22 January 1925 when it was successfully raised. It was subsequently abandoned on the foreshore where it has remained ever since. Albert Dock also received attention with the renewal of the bullnose and the modernisation of the lock; the scheme was inaugurated by Hull's Lord Mayor, Councillor James Sidney (Jim) Mulgrove MBE on 6 June 1996.

Customer demand schemes included the conversion of No.2 Drydock in King George Dock as a berth to service a new chemical tank farm and the construction

of a series of sheds to accommodate Swedish timber carried by the Ahlmark Line. One of the most significant schemes was River Terminal 1, a project to construct a ro/ro terminal in the River Humber to the west of the King George Dock entrance for use by North Sea Ferries freight-only vessels. The new facility which cost £12m was inaugurated on 9 November 1993. On 2 October 1997 Sir Keith Stuart opened the Hull Steel Terminal which was built over No.1 Dry Dock in King George Dock so that ships discharging or loading steel could berth completely under cover with cargo being received or forwarded from road or rail also under cover. On 19 July 1994, in an attempt to boost rail traffic, I named Class 56 Co-Co diesel-electric locomotive 56 039 *ABP Port of Hull* on 3 Quay, King George Dock. It was hoped to use this locomotive as part of the opening day celebrations for the steel terminal but it was not available and so the nameplates were transferred to sister engine 56 087 which did the honours wearing EWS livery. Following a reduction in demand for imported steel, the terminal is now known as Hull All Weather Terminal, still handling steel

but also other weather sensitive cargos.

On 17 May 2000, His Excellency Pertti Salolainen, Ambassador of Finland opened the Finland Terminal at Queen Elizabeth Dock. The negotiations for this scheme were very protracted but were successfully concluded in Helsinki during the previous year based on a ten year agreement with guaranteed annual revenue. The deal was struck with the shipowner and three paper manufacturers. It involved repositioning the Hull Container Terminal and constructing a huge new transit shed to accommodate paper imports with over 30,000 tonnes of paper reels being accommodated at any one time.

The largest single investment during my time at Hull was the Rotterdam Terminal which was officially opened by my wife, Darral Fell, on 1 May 2001 at an inauguration ceremony hosted by Bo Lerenius, ABPH Group Chief Executive. At a cost of £14.3m, including associated river works, the new terminal was built on the back of a long-term agreement with P&O North Sea Ferries to accommodate the world's largest cruise ferries the *Pride of Rotterdam* (59925gt) and sister ship the *Pride of Hull* which

Standing opposite the Alexandra Dock bellmouth on 29 June 1990 are George Robinson, Deputy Port Manager on the left and the author, Port Manager on the right. In between is Veronica Storr, our very efficient secretary who would later marry local shipowner, John Robert Rix (1934-2017). Behind is the aggregate dredger *Arco Adur* discharging from a berth established on the Western approach jetty, a business secured by George. The ship was built in 1988 for ARC Marine Ltd by Appledore Ferguson Shipbuilders, Yard No.144, and registered at Southampton. She is currently owned by Hansen Aggregates Marine Ltd of which ARC formed a part. [Herbert Ballard/ABP]

1999 to inaugurate the installation of modified outer lock gates at King George Dock as part of a flood defence scheme. Her Majesty activated the opening of the gates and once opened, a Geest North Sea Line vessel waiting in the lockpit gave one long blast of the whistle indicating the she was about to leave the port, which I know very much impressed the Queen. The royal party them boarded the survey launch *Humber Ranger* for a short trip up river to Hull's Corporation Pier and I know that she was highly amused at sighting *Dead Bod*. This is a well known and now preserved piece of maritime graffiti featuring a dead bird which was daubed on the side of a derelict transit shed on the old Alexandra Dock River Pier. *Dead Bod* can now be seen in Humber Street Gallery, a major new development undertaken as part of Hull's status as UK City of Culture 2017.

ABPH De-listed

I retired as Port Director, Hull & Goole on 31 March 2003, so have not been privy to the detailed information on developments that I hitherto enjoyed over the previous 16 years. However, I have been made aware of significant projects through former colleagues and these are summarised below. There was a major organisational change in 2006 when a consortium led by Goldman Sachs made a successful bid of £2.9 billion for ABPH which was subsequently de-listed from the London stock exchange. There have been subsequent changes in the ownership of the business and as at the close of

berth at the former River Terminal 1. The ships were built by Fincantieri-Cantieri Navali Italiani S.p.A at the Marghera shipyard in Venice. They are 31.5m in beam with an overall length of 215.45m and a draught of 6.05m. Each vessel can carry 1,360 passengers with 3,255 lane metres available for cars and lorries. The terminal opened by Princess Margaret in 1987 is now used solely for the Zeebrugge sailings using the *Pride of Bruges* (formerly *Norsun*) and the *Pride of York* (formerly *Norsea*).

Royal Visits

HMY *Britannia* came to Hull on 19 May 1993 and berthed at 7 Quay, King George Dock. Earlier that day the Queen and Duke of Edinburgh had disembarked from the royal yacht at Grimsby to participate in various engagements on the south bank of the Humber, moving over to the north bank and Hull for similar engagements during the afternoon. That evening a reception was given on board the *Britannia* hosted by the Queen and the Duke. The Royal Marines Band played on the quayside and after the reception all the guests were invited to gather at the lockpit to see the royal yacht sail with the royal party on board. It was a wonderful evening and the weather was kind.

On 8 June 1992 I accompanied the Princess Royal on a tour of King George Dock on board the ABP buoy vessel *Humber Sentinel*. The princess was at that time Honorary President of the

Chartered Institute of Transport and had attended a meeting of the Institute's Humberside section earlier that day. The Queen accompanied by the Duke of Edinburgh returned to the port on 4 June

The Alexandra Dock welcoming party at the re-opening on 16 July 1991. Left to right are Captain Malcolm Walker, ABP Dock Master; the author, ABP Port Manager, Hull; C. Stuart Bradley CBE, ABP Managing Director; the Lady Mayoress of Hull; Sir Keith Stuart, ABP Chairman; Dennis Woods, Lord Mayor of Hull. The vessel forming the backdrop is ABP's bed leveller/buoy vessel *Humber Sentinel* dressed overall for the occasion. [Herbert Ballard/ABP]

The Russian *Pioner Yakutii* (4814grt) was the first commercial vessel to enter the reopened dock on 16 July 1991 with a cargo of timber from Igarka. *Lady Joan*, completed by Cochrane Shipbuilders Ltd of Selby in 1988, Yard No.137, acted as stern tug. The other vessel is the ABP grab dredger Cave Sand which was employed to dredge the dock prior to reopening. [Herbert Ballard/ABP]

2016 the company was owned by a consortium of the following investors: Borealis ABP Holdings BV and Borealis Ark Holdings BV, both owned by OMERS Administration Corporation; Canada Pension Plan Investment Board; Cheyne Walk Investment Pte Limited, owned by GIC (Ventures) Pte Limited; Kuwait Investment Authority and Anchorage Ports LLP (Note 94).

Dock Rail Traffic
On 3 November 2007 work began on a £14.5m investment project to boost the capacity on the dock rail branch from 10 to 22 trains in both directions daily. The project was spearheaded by ABP, Network Rail and the regional development agency. It was prompted by increasing rail movements, especially for imported coal. Nowadays the branch runs from Hessle Road Junction for approximately six miles to serve King George and Queen Elizabeth Docks, with branches to the Kingston Terminal

and the Saltend Chemicals Park (see below). The work involved installing a new double junction at Hessle (it was singled in 1984), a new track signalling system, doubling one mile of track, strengthening fifteen bridges, removing a redundant bridge, major track and other works on the swing bridge over the River Hull and smoothing and realigning track throughout the branch. The work was completed in June 2008 but the upgraded signalling arrangements did not come into operation until the following September. In 2013 two overbridges on the branch were replaced at a cost of £4.2m: one at Spring Bank West and the other at James Reckitt Avenue.

The very latest development insofar as rail traffic is concerned is the completion of a dedicated handling and storage facility for biomass which is being transported by rail to Drax power station from King George Dock in specially designed covered wagons built

to the extremes of the permitted loading gauge. This new facility, costing £16m became operational in March 2014. The biomass is stored in warehouses before being delivered by truck to the new facility and unloaded into feeders which take it to a 250m long conveyor carrying it to the top of a silo. The silo, capable of storing 1,800 tons of wood pellets, is filled by 60 truckloads of biomass over a three-hour period, twice a day, loading at the rate of 600 tonnes an hour. Sophisticated technology ensures an even load as the biomass is discharged into the rail wagons which pass slowly through the corridor at the base of the structure. The automated system is capable of loading up to 25 rail wagons with 1,600 tonnes of material in just 35 minutes. The facility was officially opened by the Lord Mayor of Hull, Councillor Mary Glew, on 4 December 2014. The new cargo flow will go some way to countering the loss of coal traffic.

Saltend Chemicals Park

Saltend Chemicals Park is the current title given to the land east of Queen Elizabeth Dock purchased by the NER in 1914 and served by Salt End Jetties. BP first had an involvement in the site in 1921 and in 1967 BP Chemicals Ltd entered into a long term lease of the site from the BTDB which continues under ABP. The main products produced on site are acetic acid, acetic anhydride and ammonia. The formation of the chemicals park took place in 2009 with BP Chemicals remaining in overall control but with other chemical companies occupying various parts of the site. Today eight companies operate on the site including Saltend Cogeneration Company Limited which owns a gas fired power station. The station, commissioned in 2000, provides electricity and steam for customers occupying the chemicals park, with the balance of the plant's output sold to the UK power market.

Other Significant Developments

The cranage available at the port has been modernised with the addition of several Liebherr mobile harbour cranes which can be moved from berth to berth as required, so reducing the reliance on the remaining quayside travelling cranes. In December 2010 work started on the demolition of the grain silo in King George Dock which was no longer needed due to shifting patterns in the movement of grain. The area formerly occupied by the grain silo was required for a new 10 acre terminal for TransAtlantic UK Ltd (formerly Pal Line) which hitherto had used ABP's Port of Goole with three scheduled sailings per week to Sweden. The cost was of the new terminal was £3.5m based on a ten year agreement. It is rail connected and includes a new 8,500sq m warehouse on the footprint of the old silo. As a result of the change of port, two Liebherr cranes were transferred from Aldam Dock, Goole to King George Dock, Hull by barge. At over 100 feet high and weighing at around 600 tons, the cranes drew quite a crowd as they travelled downstream under the Humber Bridge. The TransAtlantic terminal is currently operated by Thor Shipping & Transport AB with vessels calling at Amsterdam and Antwerp in addition to the Swedish ports.

On 1 May 2016 ABP took back direct control of the Hull Container Terminal following the expiry of the agreement with PD Ports. The transition was a smooth one with many of the former PD Ports employees joining the ABP workforce. On 16 May 2016 ABP announced that it had invested £15m in re-equipping the terminal including the provision of two new Liebherr gantry cranes and a fleet of 21 reach stackers. Two further gantry cranes will be operational by March 2018. Bearing in mind the terminal's chequered past, it is good to see so much new investment in its future. I have always believed that the key to a port's success is to deliver an efficient cargo handling operation at a competitive price. It is good to see ABP once again taking a direct involvement in stevedoring.

Green Port Hull

Styled *Green Port Hull*, Alexandra Dock is now undertaking another exciting role. A £310m project has just come to fruition which involved developing 130

The re-opened dock in 1992. Cranes, surplus to requirements in King George Dock, have been transferred for more productive use here. A, B and C Jetties are back in use for handling timber and an agri-bulk terminal has been established at the north west end of the Alexandra Dock Extension. The two drydocks await to be brought back into use by Rob Langton, Managing Director of MMS Ship Repair & Dry Dock Company Ltd, the current operators. [ABP]

Following the astonishing increase in cargo throughput, the 1990s saw an increase in rail traffic so much so that the operators of *Load Haul*, Trainload Freight North East, asked whether a Romanian built Class 56 Co-Co diesel electric locomotive could be named *ABP Port of Hull*. The locomotive selected was No.56039, the first locomotive to carry *Load Haul* orange and black livery. The author, who performed the naming ceremony, is on the right with Roger Pettit, Business Manager, Trainload Freight North East on the left. Not quite a royal occasion, but the ceremony did take place on the quay where King George V opened the dock on 26 June 1914 and gave it his name. [Herbert Ballard/ABP]

acres of the western end of the dock estate as a hub for off-shore wind turbine manufacturing, assembly and logistics, creating employment for up to 1,000 people. There has been a massive £310m investment injected into the project: £160m by Siemens AG and £150m by ABP. When the project was first confirmed in March 2014, it was proposed to install the manufacturing unit at Paull to the east of Queen Elizabeth Dock but it was subsequently decided to contain the whole development, including the wind turbine blade manufacturing facility, on the Alexandra Dock estate. The first turbine blade was manufactured in December 2016 – a remarkable achievement.

This enormous project has involved infilling one third of the dock at its west end with 780,000 tonnes of material and reclaiming 7.5 hectares of foreshore to create a new 620m quay wall that can accommodate up to three off-shore wind installation vessels at any one time. The work has involved the removal of the derelict HBR River Pier, dredging new berthing pockets in the river, the diversion of a footpath, removal of buildings no longer required, new

surfacing, building internal access roads and service networks and the construction of a new in-dock ro/ro ramp. ABP awarded the main contract to a joint venture between national construction, asset management and project investment firm GRAHAM and civil engineering and building contractors Lagan Construction Group.

The first vessel to arrive at the newly constructed river berths was the mv *Beltnes* (20312gt) which brought 30,000 tonnes of crushed stone from Jelsa in Norway on 11 August 2016. This vessel and mv *Bulknes* of similar tonnage, both owned by Stema Shipping, were used to ship 400,000 tonnes of crushed stone from Norway which was used to surface the Siemens' site. The stone was discharged at a rate of approximately 3,000 tonnes per hour via a ship on-board conveyor system and a boom which deposited the cargo directly onto the quayside. The first shipments of turbine components from the new installation took place on 5 January 2017 when the *Sea Challenger* (15934gt), a jack-up ship owned by A2SEA and specially designed for installing offshore wind turbines, sailed with a cargo of towers, blades and nacelles (Note 95) – the

components for four turbines for the Dudgeon offshore wind farm. This is located off the Norfolk coast, some 8-10 hours steaming time from the Humber Estuary. As the blades are stowed athwartships overhanging both the port and starboard sides of the ship thereby effectively increasing its beam, a special passage plan is required for all outward bound movements.

How good it is to be able to end on a high note. From the troubled times of the Hull & Barnsley Railway and a decade of dereliction, Alexandra Dock is now once more leading the way to an ever brighter future for the Port of Hull in a way that its original promoters could have never have imagined!

A Vision

Wouldn't it be great if Government in addition to its long standing quest of improving the movement of people and goods from north to south and vice versa with a focus on London also concentrated with equal fervour on improving an east to west axis. Whatever the outcome of *Brexit*, goods will still move from European countries, Scandinavia and the Baltic to the UK and vice versa. That is a fact. Why is there such an obsession with HS2 to the exclusion of other equally deserving initiatives? The Ports of Hull and Liverpool are receiving investment worth millions of pounds. Is it not beyond the wit of members of parliament to recognise the importance of this commitment? Motorways are a thing of the past, hopelessly outdated, congested, increasingly dangerous and environmentally unfriendly. Driving on them is *collective madness*. In the past there has been a total lack of vision when making decisions of strategic transport importance. How on earth was the decision to close the Woodhead railway route from Manchester to Sheffield allowed to come about? It suggests a total lack of vision from people who should know better. So Government of today, seize the opportunity to upgrade the railway between Hull and Liverpool both for passengers and freight. Take advantage on what is on offer and do not pussy foot about with bi-mode trains. The route needs full scale electrification and upgrading to ensure fast running throughout. Hull must be the only city in the country where its trains commence their journey with semaphore signalling under the absolute block system pioneered in the Victorian age. An efficient railway over or under the Pennines is the key to the future. Please act now, do not continue to pontificate! Turn the vision into reality.

The *ABP Port of Hull* nameplates were transferred from No.56039 to 56087 in August 1997 in readiness for the latter locomotive to participate in the inauguration of the Hull Steel terminal on King George Dock. The opening ceremony took place on 2 October 1997 and a resplendent 56087 wearing EWS livery is seen here entering the new terminal which was built over a former dry dock. All operations, including the berthing of the ships, take place under cover. The steel coils on the right can weigh up to 25 tonnes apiece. The terminal is now known as Hull's *All Weather Terminal*. [Herbert Ballard/ABP]

River Terminal 1 on 17 February 2001, a roll-on/roll-off facility for North Sea Ferries freight only vessels completed by ABP at a cost of £12m. It came into use in 1993. As shown here it is about to be modified to form part of the new Rotterdam Terminal seen under construction to the left of the freight-only ship *Norbank* (17464gt). *Norbank's* maiden voyage took place on 31 October 1993; she was built in the Netherlands by Van der Giessen de Noord NV, Yard No.961. The new western approach jetty to King George Dock can be seen ahead of *Norbank's* bow alongside the storage tanks. The two P&O vessels in dock are alongside the passenger terminal opened by Princess Margaret in 1987. Also prominent is the edible oil processing plant operated by Anglia Oils with its yellow cladding. [Herbert Ballard/ABP]

155

On 8 June 1992 the Princess Royal visited the port in her capacity as Honorary President of the Chartered Institute of Transport. She had visited the Institute's Humberside branch earlier that day. The author accompanied her on a short tour of King George and Queen Elizabeth Docks on board ABP's buoy vessel *Humber Sentinel*. [Herbert Ballard/ABP]

HMY *Britannia* on 19 May 1993 about to enter King George Dock assisted by two tugs, the head tug of which is appropriately named *Lady Elizabeth* (285grt). The tug was built by Cochrane Shipbuilders of Selby in 1981, Yard No.114. Earlier that morning the Queen and the Duke of Edinburgh had disembarked from the royal yacht at Grimsby but later in the day they joined the ship in Hull to host a reception on board. The structure seen in the river shows that work had begun to construct River Terminal 1. [Herbert Ballard/ABP]

The Queen paid another visit on 4 June 1999. She is seen here with the Duke of Edinburgh rather precariously perched to the right of the west outer lockgate, shielded by a canvas dodger erected to deflect the south westerly breeze! She is about to inaugurate the modified outer gates as part of a River Humber flood defence scheme funded by ABP and the Environment Agency. The author on the left is instructing Her Majesty on how to open the gates.

The occasion went perfectly and the Queen certainly enjoyed herself, especially when the *Geest Atlas* sounded one long blast on her whistle to coincide with the opening of the gates. Here the Queen and the author are walking alongside the ship as it sails. The Dock Master, Captain David Train is between the two of us also looking well pleased that all had gone well. [Herbert Ballard/ABP]

Prior to the commencement of the imported coal traffic, virtually the only rail movements on the dock branch comprised tank traffic from BP Chemicals at Salt End and the return of the empties. EWS Class 37 Co-Co diesel electric No.37503 comes off the dock branch at Hessle Road Junction on 27 May 1999 with the CV14 Salt End – Baglan Bay acetic acid tanks. The junction had been singled in 1984 but it was reinstated in 2008. [Tony Buckton]

Occasional imports of gypsum through Queen Elizabeth Dock began in 2002. Looking resplendent in the morning sunshine on 11 September 2002, GB Railfreight Class 66 Co-Co diesel electric No.66709 *Joseph Arnold Davis*, runs alongside the eastern access road shortly after departure from 10 Quay with the 4Z50, 07.40 to Kirkby Thore. [Tony Buckton]

On 20 March 2000 a train loaded with Stanton pipes snakes along the dock branch about to enter ABP property; the train ran as 6Z71, 09.33 Toton-Hull King George Dock. The locomotive is Class 37 Co-Co diesel electric No.37516 in Load Haul livery and what a variety of wagons! [Tony Buckton]

This train of loaded biomass hopper wagons is the 08.47 Hull Docks-Drax Power Station passing Hessle Road Junction on 17 May 2014. Note the double junction which was reinstated in 2008 as part of the scheme to increase capacity on the dock branch. The locomotive is Class 66 Co-Co diesel electric No.66218 operated by EWS. [Tony Buckton]

Royal engine Class 67 Bo-Bo diesel electric No.67005 *Queen's Messenger* is hardly undertaking regal duties on 17 February 2006, its train having discharged scrap metal for export at 10 Quay West, Queen Elizabeth Dock. The train ran as 6D51 Doncaster Belmont - Hull Dock Enterprise Service. The scrap operation is run by Sims Metal Management Limited. The P&O Zeebrugge ferry can be seen in the distance and the old grain silo is to the right. [Carl Locker]

The Finland Terminal in Queen Elizabeth Dock was formally opened on 17 May 2000 by His Excellency Pertti Salolainen, Ambassador of Finland. It marked the culmination of a protracted negotiation to secure additional Finnish traffic for the port and involved the construction of a huge shed for the storage of paper manufactured by UPM-Kymmene, Metsä-Serla and Myllykoski. ABP's investment was based on a ten year agreement. Thousands of tonnes of paper were stored in the new shed and it required meticulous handling by stevedores Northern Cargo Services to avoid damage. The reels of paper shown here are perfectly stacked using clamps attached to fork lift trucks. [Herbert Ballard/ABP]

In stark contrast to the *Queen's Messenger* seen opposite, this is a real royal occasion with the Band of the Royal Marines performing on 7 Quay, King George Dock alongside the Royal Yacht Britannia. The date was 19 May 1993 and the Queen and the Duke of Edinburgh were on Board.

The brand new factory freezer trawler *Kirkella* H7 (4290gt) enters King George Dock on 3 March 2015. She was completed earlier that year in the Tersan Shipyard at Tuzla in Turkey, Yard No.1061; the vessel is equipped with a sophisticated fish processing plant and operates in the north east Atlantic. The Danish registered oil/chemical tanker *Oraholm* (3709gt) on 7 Quay was also built in Turkey in 2006 at the Desan Shipyard, Tuzla. The P&O ferry is the *Pride of York* (31785gt), formerly *Norsea*. She was the last large passenger ship to be built in the UK, being completed by Govan Shipbuilders Ltd on the Clyde in 1987, Yard No.265. She was renamed in 2003. [Tony Ward, Topcolor Fotoworx, Hull via a drone]

This view from the King George Dock lockpit on 25 June 2014 looks north towards an area of quayside known as North Gap, which is the space between 8 and 9 Sheds. Two huge mobile hoppers can be seen at either side of the gap lettered ABP and the huge silo seen in the distance on the left with its covered conveyor, is part of the new biomass installation. It receives wood chip pellets discharged from ships in dock for storage, prior to their transportation to Drax power station by rail. The first two cranes from left to right are new Liebherr mobile harbour cranes, while the two on the right are two of the four Butterley 15 tonne capacity electric travelling cranes purchased in 1992. The pusher tug *Shovette* (157grt) is operated by Dean's Tugs & Workboats Ltd and was originally built as *Grey Lash* by London & Rochester Shipbuilders, Strood in 1974, Yard No.111. She is manoeuvring a barge which is about to receive a heavy lift for transport upriver to Goole. [Tony Ward, Topcolor Fotoworx, Hull]

BLADE STORAGE
BLADE STORAGE
NACELLES STORAGE
OFFSHORE WAREHOUSE
TOWER SETS
SERVICE
OFFICE & WELFARE
BLADE FACTORY

This image graphically displays what has happened to the west end of Alexandra Dock following the completion of the £310m project jointly funded by ABP and Siemens AG to provide a hub for off-shore wind turbine manufacturing, assembly and logistics. The new quay wall jutting out into the river, where the old HBR River Pier used to be, can accommodate up to three off-shore wind installation vessels at any one time. The yellow line indicates the diversion of a public right of way which used to follow the foreshore and cross the lockpit. How fortunate that the dock was re-opened in 1991. Like Victoria Dock, it might have become a housing estate! [ABP]

The jack-up ship *Sea Challenger* on 5 January 2017 off the new river berths at Alexandra Dock with the first shipment of turbine components from Hull's new Siemens factory. The view looks west. [Sean Spencer, Hull News & Pictures/Siemens Gamsea]

163

CHAPTER NOTES

1. Thomas Telford (1757-1834) was the Institution's first President.
2. 14 Geo III, Ch 56, Royal Assent, 20 May 1774
3. *The History of the Town and County of Kingston Upon Hull from its Foundation in the Reign of Edward the First to the Present Time* by Rev John Tickell, Thomas Lee & Co, Hull 1798.
4. *Leeds Intelligencier*, 29 September 1778.
5. *Hull Packet*, 14 November 1815.
6. 42 Geo III Ch 91, Royal Assent, 22 June 1802.
7. *Hull Packet*, 4 July 1809.
8. 45 Geo III Ch 42, Royal Assent, 5 June 1805.
9. *Hull 1700-1835* in *A History of the County of York East Riding Vol 1, the City of Kingston-upon-Hull* published by Victoria County History, London 1969, pages 174-214.
10. John Cowham Parker (1773-1841) was Mayor of Hull in 1835.
11. The Wilberforce Monument subsequently became a traffic hazard and was removed to the east end of Queen's Gardens (formerly Queen's Dock) in 1935. It was rededicated by Anna Barbara Reckitt (1879-1962), Wilberforce's great granddaughter.
12. 7 & 8 Vic Ch 103, Royal Assent, 6 August 1844.
13. The new bridge had a weight restriction of 12 tons on four wheels at 9ft centres.
14. Edward Welsh was Resident Engineer of the Hull Dock Company from 1846 to 1861. He then went into general engineering practice on his own account until August 1863 when he was appointed engineer for the River Witham Commissioners and based in Boston, Lincolnshire.
15. John Beadle was Chairman of the Hull Dock Company from 1841 to 1847.
16. The *Ariel* was purchased for £1,067 in 1844 from a Cowes ship builder called White and, like her predecessor, was also cutter-rigged. She became the buoy yacht until 1854 when she was exchanged for a vessel called *Dream*.
17. *Fairy* was decommissioned in 1863 and broken up in 1868.
18. *Hull Packet*, 30 July 1857. Batches of timber, discharged into the dock, were gathered together and floated as rafts.
19. *North Eastern & Scottish Magazine*, Vol. 15, No.172, April 1925.
20. 6 & 7 Wm IV Ch 80, Royal Assent, 21 June 1836.
21. Patent No.7745, 26 July 1838.
22. 8 & 9 Vic Ch 51, Royal Assent, 30 June 1845.
23. *North Eastern Railway Magazine* Vol. 10, No.109, January 1920.
24. Walter McDougall Malt was born in Bangalore, Madras, India on 22 April 1867.
25. An article entitled *Swing and other Opening Bridges on the North Eastern Railway* by E.M. Bywell (NER) gives all the credit for the design of the bridge to Bruff – see *The Railway Magazine*, Vol.

21, October 1907. He was born in Agra, India on 9 July 1873.
26. Renamed Rye Hill on 1 July 1881 but reverted to its original name on 23 September 1929.
27. Winestead closed to passengers on 1 July 1904.
28. Cemetery Gates station was renamed Botanic Gardens on 1 November 1881.
29. Several stations were renamed. Sutton became Sutton-on-Hull on 1 December 1874; Marton became Burton Constable on 1 August 1864 changing again to Ellerby on 1 January 1922; Hatfield became Sigglesthorne on 1 October 1874 and Hornsea was renamed Hornsea Town in 1950.
30. 29 & 30 Vic Ch 187, Royal Assent, 16 July 1866.
31. 24 & 25 Vic Ch 79.
32. *Hull Packet*, 6 October 1871.
33. 29 & 30 Vic Ch 77, Royal Assent, 10 August 1866.
34. 30 & 31 Vic Ch 25, Royal Assent, 31 May 1867.
35. The swing bridge over the lockpit was replaced by one which accommodated a double-tracked railway circa 1906.
36. The *Duke of Ebinburgh*, built by Humphreys & Pearson of Hull with an inverted compound steam engine, cost £4,650 and was handed over to Hull Trinity House in May 1874 to replace the *Dream*. The new vessel, Hull Trinity House's first steam ship, was rebuilt and lengthened in 1881. In that guise she served until 1892 when she was sold by auction for £1,010 and replaced by the steam yacht *Queen* built by Earle's of Hull.
37. John West Wilson (1816-1889) became the Wilson Line representative in Gothenburg, Sweden and another brother, Edward Brown Wilson (1818-1874) became renowned for his involvement with the Railway Foundry at Leeds.
38. Three stations were subsequently renamed. Howden became South Howden from 1 July 1922 and on the same day Eastrington became North Eastrington. In September 1921 Newport was renamed Newport (Yorks) and with effect from 1 July 1923 was renamed again as Wallingfen.
39. 5 Edw VII Ch 41, Royal Assent, 30 June 1905.
40. ICE Minutes of Proceedings Vol. 92, January 1888.
41. *The Life and Work of James Abernethy* by John S. Abernethy, T. Brettell & Co, 1897, page 190.
42. The spade and wheelbarrow used by Gerrard Smith to cut the first sod were once displayed in a small railway museum opened in 1933 at Paragon Station. However, they and many other exhibits were destroyed during a Second World War air raid.
43. *Turnbull's Dock and Port Charges for the United Kingdom* 1904, published by W.J. Potts, engineering, nautical and mining publishers, Atlas Works, North Shields.

44. *Orlando* (1581grt) was built by Earle's of Hull in 1869. The vessel was sold on 5 August 1909 to French owner Paul Castinie, registered at Oran on Algeria's Mediterranean coast and renamed *Algerie*. She was wrecked off Canea, Crete in 1924 under Turkish ownership as *Vellissarious*.
45. *Eastern Morning News*, 10 January 1884.
46. Some nine miles was over contractor's track, the remainder over the permanent way.
47. Renamed Ellerman's Wilson Line with effect from 1 February 1917, following the sale of the business to Hull born shipowner Sir John Ellerman (1862-1933) in November 1916.
48. *Free overside* was abolished by the British Transport Docks (Hull Docks) Act 1973 which received the Royal Assent on 25 July 1973.
49. 47 & 48 Vic Ch 71, Royal Assent, 14 August 1884.
50. 52 & 53 Vic Ch 154.
51. 55 & 56 Vic Ch 198, Royal Assent, 24 August 1893.
52. 62 & 63 Vic Ch 242, Royal Assent, 9 August 1899.
53. Built in 1891 by O.A. Brodin, Gefle, Sweden for Rederei A/B Nordstjernan, Stockholm – manager Axel Johnson. Sold to German owners in 1900 as *Breitzig*. Captured by HMS *Centaur* off the Dutch coast in 1917, became *Polalp* then *Rondo* under the UK flag. Sold to Italian owners 1921; renamed *Ascencione* and later *Nero*. Broken up at Newport, South Wales, July 1933.
54. 7 Edw VII Ch 67, Royal Assent, 26 July 1907.
55. Built 1899 by Strand Slipway Company, Sunderland for Fenwick, Stobart & Company, London; sold in 1901 to Wm. France, Fenwick & Company Limited, well known collier operators. Sold to Italian owners in 1931 and renamed *Leonardo Palomba*. Sunk by torpedo and gunfire from HM submarine *Unruffled* on 22 September 1942 while on passage from Polermo for Tripoli with gasoline.
56. The *Archangel* was built in 1910 by John Brown & Company of Clydebank (Yard No.397) for the Great Eastern Railway's Harwich service to the Hook of Holland. The ship was originally named *St. Petersburg* but was renamed in 1916; she was acquired by the LNER at Grouping but had a sad end on 17 May 1941 when she was bombed and sunk off the east coast of Scotland.
57. *North Eastern Railway Magazine* Vol. 9, No.98, February 1919.
58. Formerly the Wilson Line.
59. *North Eastern Railway Magazine*, Vol. 12, No.139, July 1922.
60. *Bradford Daily Telegraph*, 28 May 1906.
61. *Hull Daily Mail*, 9 May 1907.
62. *North Eastern Railway Magazine*, Vol. 10, No.114, June 1920.
63. *Hull Daily Mail*, 15 July 1908.
64. 62 & 63 Vic Ch 242, Royal Assent, 9 August 1899.
65. *The Railway Magazine*, Vol. 35,

No.206, August 1914.

66. His full name was Charles Basil Demetrius Hastings Dent (1864-1956)

67. This locomotive (NER Class Z1, later LNER Class C7) was built at Darlington in May 1914. It was renumbered 2970 in September 1946 and withdrawn by British Railways in December 1948 without further renumbering.

68. This vessel was built by Palmer's Ship Building & Iron Co Ltd, Jarrow (Yard No.639) and was completed in August 1890. She was sunk by a German mine on 9 November 1915 1½ miles ESE of the Tongue Light Vessel on a voyage from Harwich to London.

69. HMS *Skirmisher* was one of two *Sentinel* Class scout cruisers and was the only ship of the Royal Navy to bear that name. The vessel was built by Vickers Limited, Barrow and commissioned in July 1905. During World War One she was initially stationed on the Humber but also saw service in the Mediterranean and the Aegean, afterwards returning to Immingham. She was sold for scrap on 3 March 1920.

70. 3 & 4 Geo V, Ch 47, Royal Assent, 15 August 1913.

71. Both dredgers were built by Lobnitz & Company, Renfrew in 1905 and 1906, respectively, Yard Nos.582 and 613. The LNER sold *Lord Joicey* to the Workington Harbour and Dock Board in 1938 and the vessel then remained in that ownership until broken up at Barrow in 1952. *David Dale* was based in Hull for all its working life, passing through the ownership of the LNER, BTC and the BTDB and surviving until 1964 when the ship was broken up at Rotterdam.

72. *Hull Daily Mail*, 9 April 1907.

73. Bunches or stems of bananas contain several hands. Hands are what we see on the shelves of modern supermarkets; individual bananas are known in the trade as fingers and so we have bunches or stems, hands and fingers.

74. *North Eastern & Scottish Magazine*, Vol. 14, No.164, August 1924.

75. *London & North Eastern Railway Magazine*, Vol. 23, No.5, February 1933.

76. *London & North Eastern Railway Magazine*, Vol. 26, No.2, February 1936.

77. *Railway & Other Steamers* by C.L.D. Duckworth and G.E. Langmuir, Shipping Histories Ltd, 1948.

78. *London & North Eastern Railway Magazine*, Vol. 36, No.3, March 1946.

79. *London & North Eastern Railway Magazine*, Vol. 30, No.4, April 1940.

80. *London & North Eastern Railway Magazine*, Vol. 37, No.3, March 1947.

81. DIWE Minute 411, 5 January 1949.

82. DIWE Minutes 953, 31 January 1950 and 980, 21 February 1950.

83. DIWE Minute 1861, 31 July 1951.

84. The total of 348 included those acquired from the HBR.

85. *Saga* was built by Lindholmens Varv, Gothenburg, 1966, Yard No.1093.

86. *Commercial Motor*, 18 November 1966.

87. *Svea* was built by Lindholmens Varv, Gothenburg, 1966, Yard No.1096.

88. *Spero* was built by Cammell Laird & Co (Shipbuilders and Engineers) Ltd, Birkenhead, 1966, Yard No.1322.

89. Further renamings were *Santorini 3* in 2002 and *Santorini* in 2003. The ship was beached for breaking up at Alang Beach, India on 9 January 2004.

90. *Final Report of the Committee of Enquiry under the Rt. Hon. Lord Devlin into certain matters concerning the Port Transport Industry*, Cmnd. 2734, August 1965. Decasualisation was implemented by Statutory Instrument 1967 No.1252 – the Dock Workers (Regulation of Employment) (Amendment) Order 1967.

91. Stanley Johnson was born at Southport, Lancashire on 10 November 1912. While working for the Singapore Harbour Board as a Chartered Accountant he was forced to escape following the Japanese invasion of 1942. He became a Lieutenant in the Royal Navy Volunteer Reserve (1942-1945) and returned to Singapore after the Second War, becoming Chairman and General Manager of the Singapore Harbour Board. He was Managing Director of the BTDB from 1967 to 1975 and died at Vero Beach, Florida, USA on 23 December 2007 in his 96th year.

92. Statutory Instrument, 3 November 1967: Humber Harbour Reorganisation Scheme 1966 Confirmation Order 1967.

93. An *Austerity* 0-6-0 saddle tank built by Robert Stephenson and Hawthorns Ltd in 1945, Maker's No.7293; it was withdrawn from service in December 1968 but was not scrapped until February 1976.

94. Associated British Ports Holdings Limited Annual Report and Accounts 2016.

95. A nacelle is a cover housing all of the generating parts in a wind turbine, including the generator, gearbox, drive chain and brake assembly.

BIBLIOGRAPHY

ATKINSON, Graham and RIX, John
Rix Shipping, Ships in Focus Publications, 2014. ISBN 978-1-901703-59-7
BALDWIN, M.W.
The Engineering History of Hull's Earliest Docks – paper read at the Science Museum, London on 10 October 1973
BEAUMONT, Martin
Sir John Hawkshaw 1811-1891, Lancashire & Yorkshire Railway Society, 2015. ISBN 978-0-9559467-6-9
BURTT, Philip
Control on the Railways, George Allen & Unwin Ltd, 1926
BYWELL, E.M.
Swing and other Opening Bridges on the North Eastern Railway, The Railway Magazine, Vol. 21, October 1907
CREDLAND, Arthur G.
John Ward of Hull – Marine Painter 1798-1849, Ferens Art Gallery, Hull, 1981
Marine Painting in Hull through three Centuries, Hull City Museums and Hutton Press, 1993. ISBN 1 872167 45 4
The Wilson Line, Tempus, 2000. ISBN 0 7524 1728 2

CREDLAND, Arthur G. and THOMPSON, Michael
The Wilson Line of Hull 1831-1981, Hutton Press Ltd, 1994. ISBN 1 872167 58 6
D'ORLEY, Alun A.
The Humber Ferries, Nidd Valley Narrow Gauge Railways Ltd, 1968
DUCKWORTH, G.L.D and LANGMUIR, G.E.
Railway & Other Steamers, Shipping Histories Ltd, 1948
FRASER, John Foster
The Hull Joint Dock, Souvenir Brochure, 1914
FAWCETT, Bill
George Townsend Andrews of York 'The Railway Architect'
Yorkshire Architectural & York Archaeological Society and the North Eastern Railway Association, 2011. ISBN 978 1 873513 76 7
GAIRNS, J.F.
Notable Railway Stations and their Traffic – Hull, Paragon, LNER, The Railway Magazine, Vol. 67, July 1930
HARROWER, John
Wilson Line, World Ship Society, 1998. ISBN 0 905617 72 X
HAWKSHAW, John Clarke
The Construction of Albert Dock at Kingston-upon-Hull – Discussion Paper No.1,417 presented to the Institution of Civil Engineers on 23 March 1875
HINCHLIFFE, B.
The Hull & Barnsley Railway Volume 2, Turntable Publications, 1980. ISBN 902844 51 2
HOOLE, K.
A Regional History of the Railways of Great Britain, Volume 4, The North East, David & Charles, 1965. ISBN 0 7153 6439 1
The Hull & Barnsley Railway Volume 1, David & Charles, 1972. ISBN 0 7153 5723 9
An Illustrated History of NER Locomotives, Oxford Publishing Company, 1988. ISBN 0-86093-323-7
LAMBERT, C.A.
Organisation and Freight Traffic Working Arrangements at Hull, North Eastern Railway, 1913
LAWRENCE, H.S.
Railway Ports, Hull – North Eastern and Hull & Barnsley Railways, The Railway Magazine, Vol. 24, January and February 1909.
Twenty-four Hours at Hull (Paragon), The Railway Magazine, Vol. 27, August 1910
LEAMAN, William John and POSTLETHWAITE, Roger Kelsall
Oil Jetties at the Port of Hull, ICE Proceedings, Vol. 29, Paper No.6798, October 1964
LEWIS, Brian
The Cabry Family – Railway Engineers, Railway & Canal Historical Society, 1994. ISBN 0 901461 17 2
MACMAHON, K.A.
The Beginnings of the East Yorkshire Railways as revised by Baron F. Duckham, East Yorkshire Local History Society, 1974; originally published in 1953
MACTURK, G.G.
A History of the Hull Railways as revised by Ken Hoole, Nidd Valley Narrow

Gauge Railways Ltd, 1970; originally published by the *Hull Packet* in 1879. ISBN 9500295 7 2

MARTIN, Kirk
Ferries Across The Humber, Pen & Sword Transport, 2014. ISBN 978 1 78383 102 9

NICHOLSON, M and YEADON, W.B.
An Illustrated of Hull's Railways, Irwell Press 1993. ISBN 1-871608-44-9

NOLAN, Keith
Municipal Politics and Regional Monopoly: Railways and the Port of Hull, 1840-1922, University of York, 2006

RCTS
Locomotives of the LNER, Part 9B Tank Engines – Classes Q1 to Z5, Railway Correspondence and Travel Society, 1977. ISBN 0 901115 41 X

SEWELL, Michael
Joseph Armytage Wade 1817-1896 The King of Hornsea, Hornsea Museum 1996. ISBN 0-950 7956-3-1

SLINGSBY, Alexander
The Story of Hull Paragon Station: From 1848 to the Present, Private Publication, 2017. ISBN 13 9781527207547

SMITH, Anthony, D.C.
Horsley, Smith & Company 1871-1971, Horsley Smith & Jewson Ltd, 1971

STOREY, Arthur
Trinity House of Kingston upon Hull, Hull Trinity House, 1967

THOMPSON, Michael
Fish Dock – The Story of St. Andrews's Dock, Hull, Hutton Press Ltd, 1989. ISBN 0 907033 87 3

Hull Docklands – An Illustrated History of the Port of Hull, Hutton Press Ltd, 1990. ISBN 1 872167 08 X

TIMPERLEY, John
An Account of the Harbour and Docks at Kingston-upon-Hull – Transactions of the Institution of Civil Engineers, 1836

TOMLINSON, William Weaver
The North Eastern Railway Its Rise and Development, Longmans, Green & Company, 1914

WATSON, Nigel
Through the Tides and Time – The Story of John Good & Sons Ltd – 175 years of a family business, St. Matthew's Press, 2007. ISBN 0 9543782-2-9

John Good in 2013 – An Historical Update, St. Matthew's Press, 2013

WELLS, Jefffrey
The Hull & Holderness Railway 1852-1862, Back Track Vol. 28 No.2, February 2014

WRIGHT, William
The Hull Docks – Discussion Paper No.1,416 presented to the Institution of Civil Engineers on 23 March 1875

YEADON, W.B.
More Illustrated History of the Railways of Hull, Challenger Publications, 1995. ISBN 1 899624 03 1

APPENDIX ONE: NORTH EASTERN RAILWAY STEAMSHIPS

TUGS ACQUIRED FROM HULL DOCK COMPANY

SHIP	GRT	Built	Builder, Yard No.	History
ACTIVE	58	1875	C.S. Swan & Company, Wallsend (22)	Note 1
LIVELY		1879	William Allsup & Sons, Preston	Note 2
HERCULES	82	1893	Cook, Welton & Gemmell, Hull (99)	Note 3

TUGS ACQUIRED FROM HULL & BARNSLEY RAILWAY

SHIP	GRT	Built	Builder, Yard No.	History
ALEXANDRA	66	1885	Earle's Shipbuilding, Hull (289)	Note 4
BARNSLEY	51	1886	Head & Riley, Hull	Note 5
HULL	94	1898	J.P. Rennoldson & Sons, South Shields (187)	Note 6

WILSONS & NORTH EASTERN RAILWAY COMPANY LIMITED

SHIP	GRT	Built	Builder, Yard No.	History
DYNAMO	594	1884	Earle's Shipbuilding, Hull (269)	Note 7
BRUNO	841	1892	Earle's Shipbuilding, Hull (365)	Note 8
HERO	775	1895	Earle's Shipbuilding, Hull (394)	Note 9
OTTO	836	1898	Caledon Shipbuilding, Dundee (140)	Note 10
TRURO	836	1898	Caledon Shipbuilding, Dundee (141)	Note 11
CITO	819	1899	Earle's Shipbuilding, Hull (452)	Note 12
JUNO	905	1900	Earle's Shipbuilding, Hull (475)	Note 13
HULL	1132	1907	Caledon Shipbuilding, Dundee (191)	Note 14
YORK	1132	1907	Caledon Shipbuilding, Dundee (192)	Note 15
DARLINGTON	1076	1910	Earle's Shipbuilding, Hull (567)	Note 16
HARROGATE	1168	1911	Earle's Shipbuilding, Hull (578)	Note 17
SELBY	1039	1922	John Duthie Torry Shipbuilding, Aberdeen (460)	Note 18
HARROGATE	1029	1925	Ramage & Ferguson Ltd, Leith (260)	Note 19

HULL & NETHERLANDS STEAMSHIP COMPANY LIMITED

SHIP	GRT	Built	Builder, Yard No.	History
SEA GULL	817	1892	Murdoch & Murray, Port Glasgow (123)	Note 20
SWALLOW	1004	1899	Earle's Shipbuilding, Hull (459)	Note 21
SWAN	1106	1899	Earle's Shipbuilding, Hull (460)	Note 22
SWIFT/SELBY ABBEY	996	1902	Earle's Shipbuilding, Hull (478)	Note 23
WHITBY ABBEY	1188	1907	William Gray & Co, West Hartlepool (755)	Note 24
RIEVAULX ABBEY	1166	1907	Earle's Shipbuilding, Hull (451)	Note 25
KIRKHAM ABBEY	1166	1907	Earle's Shipbuilding, Hull (452)	Note 26
JERVAULX ABBET	1188	1907	William Gray & Co, West Hartlepool (756)	Note 27
MELROSE ABBEY	1908	1929	Earle's Shipbuilding, Hull (674)	Note 28

APPENDIX ONE NOTES

1. ACTIVE was first registered at Hull on 11 December 1875 by owners Hull Dock Company which was acquired by the NER in 1893. Transferred to the LNER in 1923; sold to Peter Foster & Company, Hull on 22 May 1943 and again in 1953 to John H. Whittaker (Tankers) Ltd, Hull. Removed from the Hull register on 19 December 1955.

2. LIVELY was delivered to the Hull Dock Company which was acquired by the NER in 1893. The vessel was sold in September 1911.

3. HERCULES was delivered to the Hull Dock Company and entered on the Hull register on 4 May 1893. The HDC was acquired by the NER later that year and the tug passed from the NER to the LNER on the grouping of the railways in 1923. The vessel was sold to the South Stockton Shipbreaking Co Ltd on 29 May 1936 but was resold for further use to Wm. Pace Robson of Newcastle-on-Tyne. The vessel was mined and sunk on 22 November 1940.

4. ALEXANDRA was built for the HBR and passed to the NER on acquisition of the former in 1922. She was acquired by the LNER on the grouping of the railways in 1923. In 1929 she was sold to William Robson, St. Anthony's, Newcastle-on-Tyne and sold again in 1937 to James A. A. White of North Queensferry where she was broken up in the 1960s. When berthed in Hull's Alexandra Dock on 11 March 1888 her boiler exploded and one life was lost.

5. BARNSLEY was built for the HBR and was similar to ALEXANDRA; she passed to the NER in 1922 and the LNER in the following year. In 1927 she was

sold to Peter Foster, Hull and renamed ACE TUT remaining in that ownership until 1961 when she passed to United Towing. She was broken up at Hendrik Ido Ambacht, Holland during the following year after arrival on 26 April 1962.

6. HULL was built for the HBR and passed to the NER in 1922 and to the LNER in 1923. In 1928 she was sold to James H. Lamey of Liverpool and again in 1938 to the South Caenarvonshire Yacht Co Ltd, Pwllheli. In April 1940 she was on Admiralty service and was withdrawn in 1946. Her ultimate fate is unknown.

7. DYNAMO was launched on 1 March 1884 for Thos Wilson, Sons & Co and sold in 1906 to Wilsons & NER Shipping Co Ltd. On 4 July 1912 the vessel was sold to Leonard Brown, South Shields, as agent for Societa Trasporti Internazionali Marittimi G. Randazzo, Palermo and renamed UNIONE. In 1924 she was sold to Boccara & Scalabrino, Tunis and was broken up in Italy during 1926.

8. BRUNO was launched on 29 August 1892 for Thos Wilson, Sons & Co Ltd and sold in 1906 to Wilsons & NER Shipping Co Ltd. On 18 December 1909 the vessel was sold to Richard D. Newman, Victoria, British Columbia and renamed PRINCE ALBERT. She then passed through seven owners with that name before being sold in 1935 to Badwater Towing Co Ltd, Vancouver, renamed J.R. MORGAN and adapted for towing. She was sold to her last owner, Tahsis Co Ltd, Vancouver on 13 March 1950 and used as a lumber barge. Two months later on 19 May 1950 she foundered off Perez Rocks, British

Columbia after springing a leak while under tow from Zeballos, Vancouver Island to Victoria, British Columbia.

9. HERO was launched on 1 April 1895 for Thos Wilson, Sons & Co Ltd and sold in 1906 to Wilsons & NER Shipping Co Ltd. On 25 March 1924 she was sold to Ellerman Lines Ltd, London and placed under the management of Westcott & Laurence Line Ltd. She was sold again on 27 October 1927 to the General Steam Navigation Co Ltd, London and her end came in 1933 when she was sold to Metal Industries Ltd for breaking up at Charlestown, Fife where she arrived on 23 December that year.

10. OTTO was launched on 14 May 1898 for Thos Wilson, Sons & Co Ltd and sold in 1906 to Wilsons & NER Shipping Co Ltd. In 1935 she was sold to Malcolm Brechin for demolition at Granton, Edinburgh where she arrived on 29 September that year.

11. TRURO was launched on 5 July 1898 for Thos Wilson, Sons & Co Ltd and sold in 1906 to Wilsons & NER Shipping Co Ltd. On 6 May 1915 she was captured and sunk by the German submarine U-39 85 miles east north east of St. Abb's Head while on passage from Christiania to Grimsby with a cargo of timber. There were no casualties.

12. CITO was launched on 27 July 1899 for Thos Wilson, Sons & Co Ltd and sold in 1906 to Wilsons & NER Shipping Co Ltd. On 17 May 1917 she was sunk by gunfire from German torpedo boat destroyers S 53 and V 73 twenty miles east of the Noord Hinder Light vessel while on passage from Hull to Rotterdam with general cargo. The master, George Watson Orme (1859-1917) and nine of his crew of twenty were killed. They are commemorated on the Tower Hill Memorial, London.

13. JUNO was launched on 26 April 1900 for Thos Wilson, Sons & Co Ltd and sold in 1906 to Wilsons & NER Shipping Co Ltd. On 18 August 1923 she was in collision in the River Humber with the Ellerman's Wilson Line steamer SERGEI which sank. All the crew were rescued by the JUNO which returned to Hull with stem damage. On 22 April 1926 she was sold to T.W. Ward Ltd for breaking up at Preston, Lancashire.

14. HULL was launched on 27 February 1907 and was the first ship to be built new for the Wilsons & NER Shipping Co Ltd. On 2 August 1914 she was seized by German authorities at Hamburg, prior to declaration of war and all her crew were interned in Germany until 26 December 1918. In February 1916 the vessel was commissioned in the Imperial German Navy as a buoy tender ELBE II and was not returned to the Hull fleet until 28

February 1919, being transferred to the management of Associated Humber Lines in 1935. In June 1937 she was sold to Société Algérienne de Navigation pour l'Afrique, Algiers and renamed VILLE DE DJIDJELLI. On 8 November 1942 she was attacked and damaged by Allied Forces at Algiers but survived until 1956 when she was sold to Société de Material Naval du Midi for breaking up at La Seyne.

15. YORK was launched on 18 March 1907 and formed part of the Wilsons & NER fleet until requisitioned by the Admiralty for use as an armed boarding ship from 3 January 1915 until 4 April 1919 when she was returned. She was transferred to the management of Associated Humber Lines in 1935 and in June 1937 was sold to the same foreign owners as HULL (see above) and renamed VILLE DE BOUGIE. She too was damaged in the same aid raid at Algiers on 8 November 1942 but also survived until sold for breaking up at La Seyne, where she arrived on 21 January 1956.

16. DARLINGTON was launched on 5 July 1910 to become part of the Wilsons & NER fleet. On 13 February 1926 she grounded in the River Scheldt after suffering severe damage in collision with the LNER steamer ANTWERP in thick fog. She was later refloated, repaired and returned to service. On 4 October 1935 she was purchased by Ellerman's Wilson Line Ltd and renamed CASTRO. She was sold again on 21 October 1937 to Stanhope Steamship Co Ltd and renamed STANROCK and between then and 1939 successively carried the names LYDIA, OCU and ILONA before being sold in 1939 to her final owner, Margit Steamship Co Inc, Colón, Panama and renamed yet again as SONA. In April 1941 she met her end when she was bombed and sunk by German aircraft in Adamos Bay, Milos during the German invasion of Greece.

17. HARROGATE had a very short existence. She was completed in September 1911 and entered the Wilsons & NER fleet. On 20 February 1918 she foundered 50 miles off the Norwegian coast while on passage from Hull to Bergen with a cargo of coke. There were three casualties.

18. SELBY was launched on 21 September 1922 and entered the Wilsons & NER fleet, transferring to the management of Associated Humber Lines in 1935. In 1958 she was sold to H.I. Hansen of Denmark for breaking up breaking up at Odense, where she arrived on 18 May that year.

19. HARROGATE was completed in January 1925 and entered the Wilsons & NER fleet, taking the name of the ship lost in 1918. She was transferred to the management of Associated Humber Lines in 1935. On 12

September 1941, while on passage from London to Dundee with general cargo, she was attacked by enemy aircraft off Southwold, Suffolk and sustained damage from a bomb explosion but survived. She was sold in 1958 to V.V. Vereenigde Utrechtsche Ijzerhandel for demolition at Rotterdam where she arrived on 31 May 1958.

20. SEA GULL was built for the Hull Steam Packet Company which was managed by W. & C. L. Ringrose. In 1894 she was acquired by The Hull & Netherlands Steamship Company which was taken over by the NER in 1908. The vessel was sold in 1911 to the Hilal Steam Navigation Company of Istanbul and renamed MILLET. On 5 May 1915 she was shelled and sunk by Russian destroyers DERZKIY and BESPOKOYNIY at Eregli, off Turkey.

21. SWALLOW was completed in 1899 for The Hull & Netherlands Steamship Company which was acquired by the NER in 1908. She was sold in 1910 to Sicilian interests and renamed ROMA. She changed hands amongst Italian owners and was renamed TOBRUK before being scrapped in 1934.

22. SWAN, a sister ship of SWALLOW, was also completed in 1899 for The Hull & Netherlands Steamship Company which was acquired by the NER in 1908. She was sold in 1910 to Stoomvaart Maatshappij Friesland of Amsterdam and renamed MINISTER TAK VAN POORVLIET. She was torpedoed and sunk by German submarine UB-10 while on passage from Hull to Harlingen in April 1917.

23. SWIFT/SELBY ABBEY was completed in 1902 for The Hull & Netherlands Steamship Company which was acquired by the NER in 1908. The ship was immediately renamed **SELBY ABBEY** to reflect the change in ownership of the company and match the new naming policy. She was sold in 1913 to Gerhard & Hay of Windau, Riga and renamed TRITON. The vessel was deliberately sunk as a block ship in August 1914 at Windau but was raised and rebuilt by Kaiser Werft in Danzig for supply work retaining the same name. She was further renamed TRITON 1 in 1923 and FALKE in 1927 when resold within Germany. She became ILSE VORMAUER in 1930 when trading in the Caribbean and YUNQUE in 1933 when she was sold to Cuban interests. She was finally named COLOMBIA as a Cuban naval transport and ended her career after being stranded on the Cuban coast in 1944.

24. WHITBY ABBEY was completed in 1907 for the Hull & Netherlands Steamship Company which was acquired in the following year by the NER. She was taken over by the

Admiralty in 1914 as an armed boarding steamer, spending part of her duty in this guise in the Mediterranean. She returned to her owners in 1920 and was transferred to Associated Humber Lines' management in 1935 but was immediately considered redundant on account of her age. The ship was broken up in 1936.

25. RIEVAULX ABBEY was also completed in 1907 for the Hull & Netherlands Steamship Company, acquired by the NER in 1908. She was taken over by the Admiralty in March 1915 as a stores carrier and later in the same year was converted to an ammunition carrier. The vessel sank after hitting a mine off Rosse Spit Buoy in the River Humber in September 1916.

26. KIRKHAM ABBEY was another ship completed in 1907 for the Hull & Netherlands Steamship Company, acquired by the NER in the following year. She remained in the fleet during throughout World War One, surviving two attacks before being sunk by a torpedo fired by German submarine UB-40 off Winterton, Norfolk while on passage from Rotterdam to Hull on 27 July 1918. There were eight casualties.

27. JERVAULX ABBEY was the last of the four ships completed in 1907 for the Hull & Netherlands Steamship Company, acquired by the NER in 1908. She continued in commercial service in 1914 but following the blockade of Holland became deployed as an armed boarding steamer. She was returned to her owners in 1920 and was transferred to the LNER in 1923, coming under the management of Associated Humber Lines in 1935. During the following year she was sold to Chinese interests and renamed HOULEE. The Japanese Government acquired the vessel in 1941 and renamed her KORI GO MARU. In this guise she was sunk by USAAF B-24s on 25 March 1945 in the Yangtze estuary near Shanghai.

28. MELROSE ABBEY completed in 1929 was the final ship built for the Hull & Netherlands Steamship Company when it was owned by the LNER. In 1935 Associated Humber Lines became responsible for its management. Following the fall of the Netherlands during World War Two she operated in coastal convoys until 1941 when she was converted to a convoy rescue ship. However after conversion and on her delivery voyage she grounded and was struck by a mine which caused severe damage such that she would have been scrapped had it not been wartime. She was re-floated and repaired at Aberdeen, finally taking up service in February 1942 and resuming employment on the Hull-Rotterdam service in March 1946. She was renamed MELROSE ABBEY II in April 1958 to release the name for a new build. She was laid up in 1959 but was subsequently sold to Typaldos Bros, a Greek cruising and ferry company, and renamed KRITTI. She served with that company until 1966 when the company went into liquidation. The ship was laid up in the Port of Piraeus for some 18 years until she was finally broken up there in 1984.

APPENDIX TWO

PORT OF HULL – ANNUAL THROUGHPUTS IN '000 TONNES

YEAR	TOTAL	COAL IMPORTS	YEAR	TOTAL	COAL IMPORTS
1952	8,810	Nil	1992	8,609	538
1953	9,289	Nil	1993	8,966	427
1954	9,024	Nil	1994	10,181	318
1955	8,381	Nil	1995	9,998	273
1962	8,536	Nil	1996	9,721	140
1963	9,476	Nil	1997	10,047	243
1965	9,440	Nil	1998	10,249	123
1970	7,125	Nil	1999	10,119	334
1975	4,543	Nil	2000	10,722	492
1976	4,499	Nil	2001	10,586	1,221
1977	4,252	Nil	2002	10,298	330
1978	3,856	Nil	2003	10,529	104
1979	3,565	Nil	2004	12,443	1,098
1980	3,768	Nil	2005	13,363	2,327
1981	3,943	Nil	2006	12,785	2,460
1982	4,018	Nil	2007	12,497	1,873
1983	3,572	Nil	2008	12,249	2,155
1984	4,035	Nil	2009	9,771	1,335
1985	4,524	Nil	2010	9,236	459
1986	5,305	Nil	2011	9,286	832
1987	5,650	Nil	2012	10,081	1,626
1988	5,122	Nil	2013	10,910	2,017
1989	5,277	Nil	2014	10,925	1,312
1990	6,829	220	2015	10,029	265
1991	7,494	506	2016	10,167	55

NB. FIGURES PRIOR TO 1965 ARE GIVEN IN IMPERIAL TONS (1 Imperial ton = 1.01605 metric tonne)
COAL IMPORTS ARE INCLUDED IN THE TOTAL ANNUAL THROUGHPUTS